The Hemmings Book of

PREWAR FORDS

ISBN 0-917808-76-2
Library of Congress Card Number: 2001092942

One of a series of Hemmings Motor News Collector-Car Books. Other books in the series include:
The Hemmings Book of Buicks; The Hemmings Motor News Book of Cadillacs; The Hemmings Motor News Book of Chrysler Performance Cars; The Hemmings Motor News Book of Corvettes; The Hemmings Motor News Book of Hudsons; The Hemmings Motor News Book of Mustangs; The Hemmings Book of Oldsmobiles; The Hemmings Motor News Book of Packards; The Hemmings Book of Postwar Chevrolets; The Hemmings Motor News Book of Postwar Fords; The Hemmings Motor News Book of Pontiacs; The Hemmings Motor News Book of Studebakers.

Hemmings Motor News
Collector Car Publications and Marketplaces
1-800-CAR-HERE (227-4373)
www.hemmings.com

The Hemmings Book of
PREWAR FORDS

Editor-In-Chief
Terry Ehrich

Editor
Richard A. Lentinello

Designer
Nancy Bianco

Cover photo by Marc Madow: 1932 Ford Convertible Sedan

This book compiles driveReports which have appeared in *Hemmings Motor News*'s *Special Interest Autos* magazine (SIA) over the past 30 years. The editors at *Hemmings Motor News* express their gratitude to the following writers, photographers, and artists who made this book possible through their many fine contributions to *Special Interest Autos* magazine:

Arch Brown
Jeff Godshall
Ken Gross
Bud Juneau
John F. Katz
Michael Lamm

Marc Madow
Vince Manocchi
David Newhardt
Darryl Norenberg
Roy Query
Don Spiro

Jim Tanji
Philip Van Doren Stern
Russ von Sauers
Josiah Work
Vince Wright

We are also grateful to David Brownell, Michael Lamm, and Rich Taylor, the editors under whose guidance these driveReports were written and published. We thank S.A. Andre Citroen, John A. Conde Collection, Ford Archives, Henry Ford Museum, Image International, and *Road & Track* magazine, who have graciously contributed photographs to *Special Interest Autos* magazine and this book.

CONTENTS

Special Interest Autos (SIA) magazine's back issues are referred to in this book by issue number. If in stock, copies may be purchased directly from Hemmings Motor News at 800-227-4373, ext. 550 or at www.hemmings.com/gifts.

MODEL T
The Car that Henry Made, and Vice-Versa

by Philip Van Doren Stern

*Everything they tell you about the Model T is absolutely true.
Here's how Henry came to build Lizzie—and how it feels today to drive one.*

The Model T's history can and does fill books. To pare it down to magazine size means leaving out a great deal. In researching this article, the editors felt that rather than rewriting or paraphrasing what's already been researched and written, why not simply find and reproduce the best, most complete account of the Model T's beginnings?

That account appeared in a book published in 1955 by Simon & Schuster called Tin Lizzie. *The author, Philip Van Doren Stern, had done his research at the Ford Archives, Henry Ford Museum, Dearborn, making use of the same oral reminiscences and documents available today. It is with great pleasure that we reproduce parts of* Tin Lizzie *here.*

THE EVOLUTION of the Model T can be traced in detail, because Henry Ford seldom threw anything away. He also went to a great deal of trouble to preserve specimens of his early work. When he had learned all he could from the first crude little 2-cylinder quadricycle he built in 1896, he sold the car to Charles Ainsley for $200. But as soon as he began to earn large sums of money, he wanted the car and bought it back. It still exists.

The rough sketch of Ford's famous little quadricycle was made years later by Charles Brady King, who built the first automobile that ran on the streets of Detroit and who helped Henry Ford with the design and construction of his first car.

The first three hand-built cars and early racers show Henry Ford groping toward a solution of the basic problem of making an automobile that would function properly. Then, with the introduction of the Model A in 1903 (the newly organized Ford Motor Co.'s first car), we can see his initial attempts to build a small, useful, fairly low-priced car that could be turned out in reasonably large quantities. The big cars—Models B and K—were diversions which Ford probably resented. They were wanted by other stockholders who believed that automobiles could be sold only to wealthy people. But with the introduction of the little 4 cylinder runabouts, Model N in 1906 and its later improved versions R and S, Henry Ford was on his way to his lifetime goal—building what he called "the universal car."

Originally published in Special Interest Autos #38, Jan.-Feb. 1977

THE SUCCESS of the 4-cylinder Model N, R, and S runabouts convinced Henry Ford that he was right in concentrating all his efforts on the production of a small and inexpensive car. Analyzing the market that then existed for automobiles, he said:

"The automobile of the past attained success in spite of its price because there were more than enough purchasers…to take the limited output of the then-new industry. Proportionately few could buy, but those few could keep all the manufacturers busy, and price, therefore, had no bearing on sales.

"The automobile of the present is making good because the price has been reduced just enough to add sufficient new purchasers to take care of the increased output. Supply and demand, not cost, has regulated the selling price of automobiles.

"…the car of the future—'the car for the people,' the car that any man can own who can afford a horse and carriage—is coming sooner than most people expect.…

"A limited number of factories can supply all the demand for high-priced cars, but the market for a low-priced car is unlimited. The car of the future will be light as well as low in price. This means the substitution of quality for quantity, even to the use of materials not yet discovered."

The Ford Motor Co.'s first car was the 2-cylinder Model A, as mentioned. Its first 4-cylinder car was the Model B. Model C was an improved Model A; the next car to be produced was Model F. Models D and E presumably never got beyond the experimental stage and so died aborning.

Other gaps in the alphabet might indicate that experimental models were made but never put into production. It is known, for instance, that another 6-cylinder car preceded the Model K and that a 5-cylinder radial vertical engine preceded the 4-cylinder engine that was used in the Model N.

By the time the Ford Motor Co. had gone down the alphabet through the letters R and S (both of which represented improved Model N's), the pattern was pretty well established for the coming Model T.

WORK ON THE NEW Model T probably began early in 1907. One of the men who helped develop it, C. J. Smith, recalls those days as follows [from his *Reminiscences* in the Ford Archives]:

"The experimental room was…about 12 by 15 feet—big enough to get a car in; also milling machines, drill presses, and lathes. In that room we did all the main parts buildup for the experimental engines. It was what you would call advanced design.

"Mr. Ford spent a lot of time in that department. He was in there every day. He brought the idea to us. First, he would think the thing up, then he would have them [probably Childe Harold Wills] draw it up, and then we would make it up.…

"Our job was to get the advanced designs—the ideas that Mr. Ford and others would bring in to us—and actually put them together and test them. We would machine them all up, even get the castings and everything, and take them and build them in a car, and take the car out and test it.

"When we were working on the planetary transmission, we had quite a bit of trouble with the steel in the gears.… Sometimes we would tear that engine down twice a day and change gears in it. The gears wouldn't stand up because the steel was too soft. That was a problem that Wandersee worked on—the development of steel that would stand up in those gears.…

"Mr. Ford at that time wanted to build a car that everybody could own—a low-priced automobile. That's why he developed the Model N, which was a light, 4-cylinder car.… Even then, he had the idea he was going to build a light car for everyone.

"The Model T plans were drawn up by Joseph Galamb. Our section helped develop the final Model T by doing all the test work on the R, N, and S. When we had a new part, we'd put it in the car and go out and test it. Mr. Ford would be in every day. He would want to know how the parts worked out and all about the tests. His office was right next to the experimental room, and he would spend all of his spare time working with us.

"In testing the Model T, we tried it out on the road. The main thing in the Model T was the transmission and the magneto. The transmission was the biggest development.… Ed Huff was the man who developed the magneto. He worked on the electrical part.…

"Mr. Ford tested the Model T himself. He went

What It's Like to Drive a 1914 Model T

IT's A FACT that as cars have become more complicated mechanically, they've also become ever easier to drive.

The Model T—simple as it is—takes great skill to drive well. This skill comes through practice. The 1914 T you see here belongs to Lee and Sandy Wise, both high-school math teachers in Stockton, California, and this particular car adds to the T's driving complexity by having an accessory Warford 3-speed auxiliary transmission. Since there's no conventional clutch to disengage the engine from the drivetrain, you have to "walk" the Warford

through its ranges—make engine speed synchronize with gearbox speed.

It's touchy, but even before that, you have to unlearn everything you've gotten used to in driving a manual-shift car. You have to re-educate yourself to the 3-pedal, single-hand-lever, 2-mule-ear system of the T.

Of the three pedals, the leftmost is trickiest. It's marked "C," for clutch. What it does is to loosen and tighten a band inside the T's 2-speed planetary transmission. Hard down is low range; all the way released engages a multiple-disc clutch for high range; halfway down to a soft spot gets neutral. Sometimes.

Meanwhile you're also rowing the floor lever with your left hand. In its upright position, it "picks up" the clutch pedal with a cam and holds it in neutral. This can be overridden by pushing the pedal into low. All the way back on the lever still holds neutral but also applies the T's tiny emergency brakes on the rear wheels. Lee's car has the accessory Rocky Mountain brakes, which are much better than stock.

The rightmost pedal, marked "B," operates the stock service brake, which is actually a band inside the transmission that stops rotation of the driveshaft. And the central pedal, marked "R," actuates a reverse band when pushed all the way down.

To go from low to high range, though, you not only activate "C" plus the hand lever; you also have to push up the throttle mule ear (right side of the steering column) to decrease engine rpm. If all goes well (and it never did for me), the shift is fairly smooth and unemotional.

I found it much easier to walk the Warford up and down, and I halfway mastered the planetary's neutral. Good T drivers also play with the spark lever (left mule ear). By the way, there's no accelerator pedal in early T's—just the mule ear.

The stock T, like all early Fords, underrates its horsepower, because acceleration feels a lot stronger than any 20 bhp could make it. The car does move out, and it holds 40-45 mph beautifully—a speed that feels plenty fast for the T's braking and handling capabilities, even with the

Rocky Mountains. Super-quick, sensitive, light steering also tends to "narrow up" the road at higher speeds. As for parking-space handling, the fantastically tight turn circle (28 feet) makes for surprising maneuverability. The front tires can be flapped from side to side with no problem at all.

The T has certain built-in sets of gear whines, groans, and rattles, but nothing you can't live with. High seating gives a view of the road that only bus and truck drivers normally enjoy. And there's no worry about watching gauges, because there aren't any.

All in all, this is a challenging car to drive, and therefore fun. The T has more personality than even the Model A, so I well understand why so many people are still in love with it. It's been said that no man has ever really mastered the T, but true to her nature she's a willing servant to those who give her care. Says owner Lee Wise: "The T emerges not as a machine but as a roguish personality that can never be operated in a logical nor scientific manner. She's ever-changing, unpredictable, and always feminine."

—Michael Lamm

out with us many a time. Mr. Ford wouldn't let anything go out of the shop unless he was satisfied that it was as nearly perfect as you could make it. He wanted it right....

"After the Model T came out, we continued our work in the same experimental room.... At that time, we had no test track program. We had to do all the testing on the roads.... When we'd get a part built, we'd put it in the car and go out and test it. Sometimes we'd grind out a gear—run it hard out on the sand—and probably have to change the gear twice a day."

A NOTHER MAN who worked with Henry Ford, George Brown, describes building the very first Model T's:

"After they got the Model T through the experimental stage and they started building the Model T at Piquette, I remember when they built the first one, which was practically a hand-made car.... After they got the first one built, they tore it all down. I guess it was Frank Kulick [Ford's official race driver and chief test driver] who took it out on the road and tested it.

"In those years, they didn't have many paved roads. You'd take it out on the rough roads and give it the works, and then they'd tear it down. They'd go over it and check over the wearing parts and the engine, and tear it right down to pieces. In the early stages, there were a lot of changes made.

"Anyhow, they got the car going. After they got the first one built, they started easy and got the #2 built. From then on they started placing orders for their stock. It was a slow proposition. These different manufacturers had to tool up, like the forging company, and there weren't two cars alike in those years....

"Finally, they got the Model T going. I remember Mr. Ford used to get out there and say, 'I wonder if we'll get up to #10.'

"He'd be out there in the factory, watching

Early Fords from A to T

	Model A	Model B	Model C	Model F	Model K	Model N	Model R	Model S	Model T
Year announced	1903	1904	1904	1904	1905	1906	1907	1907	1908
Whb/chassis wt.	72/1,250	92/1,700	78/1,300	84/1,300	120/2,000	84/1,050	84/1,050	84/1,100	100/1,200
Engine type	Op.2	IL 4	Op.2	Op.2	IL 6	IL 4	IL 4	IL 4	IL 4
Horsepower	8	24	10	12	40	15	15	15	20
Transmission	Pl'ry	Pl'ry	Pl'ry	Pl'ry	Pl'ry	Pl'ry	Pl'ry	Pl'ry	Pl'ry
Clutch type	Cone	Cone	Cone	Cone	Disc	Disc	Disc	Disc	Disc
Base price	$850	$2,000	$900	$1,000	$2,800	$600	$750	$700	$680

Source: *Ford Times*, Ford Motor Co.

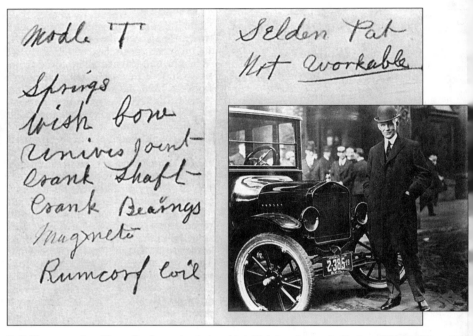

Left: Two pages from Henry Ford's notebook show his initial thoughts on the T, circa 1906-07. His spelling might have been off, but he surely knew carmaking. *Right:* Henry Ford poses with one of the early closed-bodied T's around 1920. By this time he'd become widely respected not only as the world's leading industrialist and carmaker but also as a folk hero.

Sectional View of Ford Model T Touring Car

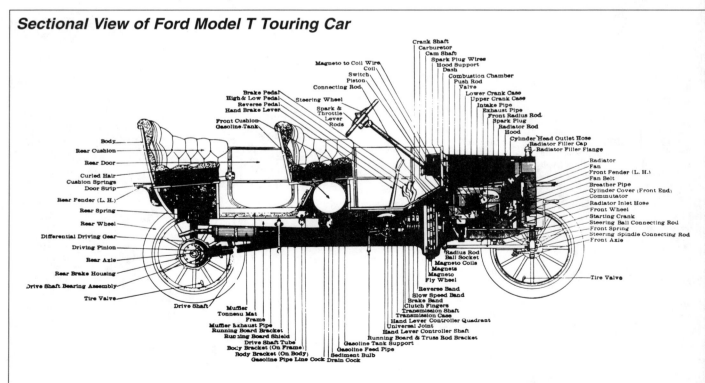

him and kidding them and telling stories. God! He could get anything out of the men, because he just talked and would tell them stories. He'd never say, 'I want this done!' He'd say, 'I wonder if we can do it. I wonder.'

"Well, the men would just break their necks to see if they could do it. They knew what he wanted. They figured it was a coming thing and did their best."

WHEN THE FORD branch managers arrived in Detroit on Sept. 14, 1908, they had come from all parts of the U.S. and Canada, and among them were also two European representatives. There were 15 men in all, and they had no reason to believe that the forthcoming sales conference would be much different from any other sales meeting that they and hundreds of other men in similar positions had been attending for years.

They had heard good things about the new Model T, and they had all seen and studied the advance catalogue. They expected the new car to do well, because on Sept. 5 the Ford Motor Co. had sent a letter to its dealers advising them that the demand was so great that they could send each dealer only one car for demonstration purposes and could not hope to fill stock orders used for booking customers' orders. But despite all this, no one had any reason to believe that the Model T would be anything more than a successful automobile which would hold the stage for a year or two and then be improved into a later model that might carry the letters U, V, or W.... No one—not even Henry Ford himself—could possibly foresee that this car was to be produced with only minor [mechanical] changes for 19 years.

Ford's First Assembly Line

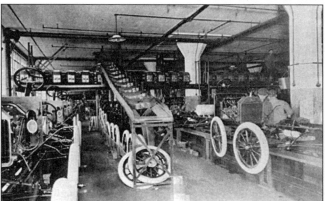

Above: Ford's assembly lines got going seriously late in 1913, the year this photo was taken in Highland Park. Wheels roll between two separate lines while radiators descend from overhead. **Below:** Flywheel magnetos were assembled mostly by hand, held 16 V-shaped magnets that produced alternating current at 16 cycles per revolution of engine, supplied electricity for ignition and later for lights and accessories.

BEFORE FORD began to use the moving assembly line, late in 1913, Model T's were produced by groups of men, as described in this oral reminiscence by William C. Klann:

"When we first moved to Highland Park, they assembled the chassis along Woodward Avenue, on the first floor of the A Building. They laid the frame on two horses and they assembled the front and the rear axle. Then they would tip it over and put on the four wheels. Then they would push it along on wheels to the next operation. You pushed it along by hand.... It wasn't a conveyor-type thing at all; you pushed it by hand. They had the stock in piles all along. That was another step in the evolution of the assembly line.

"They hadn't done this pushing process to any extent at Piquette. We had a pile of stock along the different stations. We wouldn't have the same men as teams; you would just help yourself to a part and put it on. They would have maybe 8-9 people on one car assembly....

"The motor was made over in the B Building at that time. We would bring the motors over on a truck, maybe 6-7 to a 4-wheeled truck. The motor was picked up by a hoist, and it would drop it in the chassis.... We put the motor in and then pushed it along to another spot, which was the dash and the steering gear section.... Then you drop your radiator in place. Then...put your tie rods on...steering gear post...put your starting crank on and it's done. Then you would drive it out of there right straight onto John R. Street, and Frank Hadas tested it out. Every one of those cars...were 100% tested. They put the body on after they tested it."

The earliest experimental assembly line reportedly used a rope to pull the chassis along. Eugene Farkas, later to become Ford's chief engineer, recalls in his *Reminiscences*:

"When I came in in 1913, the final assembly line was beginning to develop.... I remember Joe Galamb mentioning Clarence Avery [later to become board chairman of Murray Corp. of America] as being one of the inventors. This conveyor system included not only the chassis but the conveyor system all over the shop, and mainly the picking up of parts at the machine where it was finished, hanging it on a hook or chain or conveyor, which carried it to the place where it was assembled into the motor. (An engine assembly line predated a chassis line.]

"I don't recall what the first moving final assembly line was like. It's hearsay that it had ropes that hooked onto the axle. I just heard that that was the way they started to get it advanced far enough to put it in practical application. In other words, men going to the chassis to build it up would be in each other's way...so they separated the chassis and put in a moving line. They just moved it right up to the lap of each man who did the certain operation, and then it was moved up again."

Charles (Cast-Iron Charlie) Sorensen supposedly once remarked to Farkas, "Well, all we have to do if they tell us to make more cars is just speed up the line—just make the belt run faster."

The definitive account though, of the assembly line's birth is by Allan Nevins, in his first volume, *Ford: The Times, the Man, the Company* (Charles Scribner's Sons, 1954):

"Throughout the hot days [of 1913], men in two long lines toiled away, assembling 50 chassis at 50 different spots in each line; 100 cars in all. The Ford engineers timed them. They found that in August it took 250 assemblers and 80 parts-carriers, working nine hours a day for 26 days, to complete 6,182 chassis. Each chassis cost 12½ man-hours of labor. That was low average time for motor factories.

"The management—Ford, Martin, Avery, and Sorensen may all claim credit—installed a motor with a capstan and heavy rope and prepared to keep a line of chassis in continuous motion along the floor. Six assemblers kept pace with every chassis as it moved. From piles of parts brought up on trucks to the line, they picked out whatever was needed. At the point where the motor was to be installed, a heavy chain-fall with hooks was ready; it swung the motor directly over the frame, and the assembler lowered it into position. This, as Ford says, was a rough experiment; but the average number of man-hours needed to assemble a chassis fell [from 12½] to 5⅚.

"From that moment progress was brisk.... The assembly line was soon

lengthened to 300 feet, and on December 1, 1913, after careful motion-study, 177 assemblers finished more than 600 cbassis—an average of only two hours and 38 minutes of one man's time for a chassis...." Soon afterward, with further refinement, assembly time fell to one hour, 34 minutes.

Returning now to Philip Van Doren Stern in his book, *Tin Lizzie*: "These first experimental attempts at assembly-line production paid off quickly. Sales more than doubled when 168,304 cars were made during the fiscal year ending September 30,1913. They increased still further during the following year when 248,307 cars came oft the ever-expanding assembly lines. After that, as manufacturing techniques were improved (and also because the Model T itself was constantly being simplified and made even cheaper to produce), 730,041 cars were turned out in fiscal 1916-17. Sales fell off when production had to be cut during WW-I, but they reached astronomical figures in the early 1920s when the Model T was at the height of its popularity. It was at this time that its price was reduced to the all-time low of $290 for the touring car on December 2, 1924."

On Tuesday, September 15, the branch managers were taken through the old Piquette plant where the Model T was being built. They were also shown and were doubtless impressed by the new factory then under construction at Highland Park. When finished, it was to be the largest automobile plant in the world and the biggest single building in the state of Michigan.

At noon on September 16, the Model T was demonstrated to the branch managers, who liked the way it performed. The next day a luncheon was held at the Detroit Boat Club; afterwards everyone went for a sail on the Dodge Brothers' steamboat yacht *Hornet* [John and Horace Dodge manufactured parts and engines for the Model T; they were also Ford stockholders, selling out to Henry in 1919 for $25 million on a $20,000 investment]. The sales meeting wound up with a banquet at the Country Club, where the tables were arranged in a T shape, and the menus were printed as T-shaped booklets. The branch managers were told that 25,000 Model T's were to be built during the coming year, so they were assured of having plenty of stock, because no automobile company had ever scheduled so many cars for one year's production.

THE FIRST REGULAR factory-built car came through on September 24, and Henry Ford promptly took it on a hunting trip to northern Wisconsin. He left Detroit with Bert Scott and C. J. Smith, who were to do the actual driving.

Smith was distrustful of the new magneto, so he insisted on putting a storage battery in the back of the car to have it in reserve. Henry Ford scoffed at this, because he was sure the magneto would work. When they were halfway to Chicago they hit a bump, upset the storage battery, and spilled acid all over the floor. Henry Ford then told Smith to throw the battery away, which Smith promptly did.

They reached Chicago, 345 miles away, in 16½ hours, making an average speed of almost 21 mph. At Chicago, the local branch manager borrowed the car for a while to show it to a few selected people who had been told about it. The hunting party then went back to Milwaukee, where they saw the 24-hour automobile race being held there. Afterward they drove to northern Wisconsin, stopping in Iron Mountain on the way; *The Ford Times* for October 15, 1908, reported the details of the trip as follows:

"The car behaved admirably, requiring not even a single adjustment in the entire 10 days. A punctured tire sums up the difficulties encountered en route. The roads going were six inches deep in dust—returning after the rains, the roads were wet and muddy, and the car when it arrived in Detroit looked as if it had been taking a mud bath.

"A careful record of gasoline and oil consumption for the trip shows…an average for the tour of 20 miles per gallon of gasoline and 85 [mpg] of oil. It also shows a cost per mile per passenger of a little more than ⅓¢ or, adding depreciation, tire cost, etc., less than ⅔¢ per mile per passenger."

Henry Ford stayed on at Iron Mountain, while Scott and Smith drove the car back to Detroit. They had to go through a brush fire on the way and nearly got burned up as they tried to dash through it. Otherwise the return trip was uneventful. They arrived in Detroit on October 2, where the mud-stained car was photographed.

Model T Chronology of Changes

Years given are model years, not actual production dates. Emphasis is on appearance rather than mechanical changes. Information compiled by Philip Van Doren Stern in his book, *Tin Lizzie*.

1909—Initial 800 T's had two levers and two pedals, but this arrangement was quickly superseded by a 3-pedal, single-lever arrangement. Ford then offered a $15 kit by which earlier cars could be converted to 3-pedal control. Since the original parts had to be returned to the factory, the 2-lever T became so rare that in 1955 only one example was known to exist; now several are known. Also, the first 2,500 T's came with water pumps instead of thermosiphon cooling, wings on the embossed Ford radiator script (on some 1910 cars also), linoleum-covered wooden runningboards (later changed to steel), and 13-inch steering wheels.

1911—Metal runningboards were stamped with "Ford" in script. Most bodies were built of wood until this year (some were aluminum in 1909); touring car became sheet metal over wooden framing. Steering wheel to 15 inches.

1912—Separate front-door units were made available as extras on 1912 touring cars.

1913—Front doors introduced on touring cars, but "door" on driver's side was a dummy, embossed but not cut. Few color choices. Wooden dashboard coil boxes replaced by metal ones.

1914—Last year for acetylene lights, cherry-wood dashboard, straight-topped fenders. From 1914-26 inclusive, all Fords black.

1915—Curved-top rear fenders appear; bulb horn replaced by hand-operated Klaxon or magneto horn; electric lights draw power from mag; steel cowl replaces wooden dashboard.

Mid-1916—Year of big change: black steel radiator shell replaces brass; all fenders curved and crowned; smoother cowl; nickled hub and radiator caps; electric vibrator horn replaces hand Klaxon.

1919—Electric starter, demountable rims offered optionally on closed cars only. In June these became optional on all cars.

1920—Composition steering wheels replace wood; diameter now 16 inches.

1921—All bodies made lower.

Late 1922—Four-door sedan introduced.

1925—Balloon tires available, sized 4.40 x 21.

1926—Nickel-plated radiator shell replaces black steel one on closed cars and optional on open cars; gas tanks moved into cowl (except in 4-door sedans); coil box moves under hood; steering wheel now 17 inches; colors re-introduced; wire wheels optional.

1927—No changes. Production ends May 27. Final U.S. engine number 15,176,888. (This engine—a replacement—was built on August 4, 1936.) Production in England runs to December 1927 with #302,000. Final Australian T was #24,301.

PHOTOS BY MICHAEL LAMM

Above: Mule ears on steering column are for spark (left) and throttle (right). **Below:** *Runningboard toolbox holds stock wrenches and extra parts that commonly failed—coil, hoses, patch kit for tires.*

Above: Model T's gas tank rests under front seat, feeds carburetor by gravity. **Below:** *Accessory Rocky Mountain brakes greatly improve T's stopping ability, still leave a lot to be desired.*

Two-man front seat puts driver up high. Triple pedals grace floor. Ford went to metal coil box on firewall in 1914. Box contains four vibrators, each putting high-voltage electricity to the spark plugs.

Above: Back seat has plenty of room. Upholstery is leatherette over curled horsehair. Both rear doors work. *Below:* Twin spares block driver's "door," which isn't cut into metal but has outline pressed in.

Above: Owner Lee Wise demonstrates how his 1914 T's windshield folds back slightly. *Below:* Sandy Wise has just ducked to get under sidecurtains. Passenger's door is only one for front seat.

Vanadium Steel & Highland Park

DURING A RACE he [Henry Ford] attended at Palm Beach, Fla., in 1905, a French car was badly smashed up. From the wreckage Ford picked up a valve stem, which impressed him by its lightness and strength. He had it analyzed and found that it was made of vanadium steel. Since no one in America could then make such a steel, he sent to England for an experienced man to supervise its production and found a small steel company in Canton, Ohio, that was willing to run a trial heat. Vanadium steel proved to be extraordinarily successful for automobiles, since it was tough enough to hold a car together on the rough roads of the day. By September 1907, the Ford Motor Co. had become so big a user of vanadium steel that it ordered more than three million pounds for delivery during the following year. This was 12 months before the first Model T was produced.

The company was making handsome profits on its runabouts and by April 22, 1907, was ready to build a new and much larger factory in Highland Park, which was then on the northern outskirts of Detroit. The board of directors authorized the purchase of a former 57-acre race course for $81,225. By December 11, the company was doing so well that it raised Henry Ford's salary to $36,000 a year. On July 29, 1908, the board of directors appropriated $250,000 to construct a plant on the Highland Park property it had acquired.

The Model T, which began its career in the older plant at Beaubien and Piquette Streets, was announced for October 1, 1908, but production was slow getting started, and only eight cars were built during the first month. Yet on October 27, 1908, the board of directors was able to authorize payment of a monthly dividend of 5% and an increase in capital stock to $2 million. A few days later, on November 3, a stock dividend of $1.9 million was declared out of surplus. At the end of the year, a bonus of 5% of their annual salary was given to employees who had been with the company for more than a year, and a 7.5% bonus was paid to employees who had worked for two years or more.

— Philip Van Doren Stern, *Tin Lizzie*

THE FIRST official American appearance of the Model T was made at the New York Automobile Show at Grand Central Palace, which was held from December 31, 1908, to January 7, 1909. But long before this, the Model T had made a deep impression on the American public. The full-page ad that had run on October 3 in *The Saturday Evening Post* was so successful that *The Ford Times* for October 15, 1908, said of it: "The 'ad' appeared on Friday. Saturday's mail brought nearly 1,000 inquiries. Monday's response swamped our mail clerks, and by Tuesday night the office was well-nigh inundated."

Although the advertisement in *The Saturday Evening Post* mentions the Model T's $850 price, it says nothing about what the purchaser received for his money, and its illustration of the car shows headlights and a folding top, which were then sold as extras. For $850 the purchaser got only three oil lamps, a horn, and irons by which a folding top could be attached to the car. He got only four wheels with four tires on them, and no provision was made for carrying a spare at a time when an extra tire was sorely needed, for in 1908 the best tires could not last more than a few thousand miles.

Most people think of the early Model T only as a touring car, but other body styles were made available from the very beginning. The first of these was the landaulet, of which 17 were shipped from the factory during the last three months of 1908. In January 1909, two coupes and

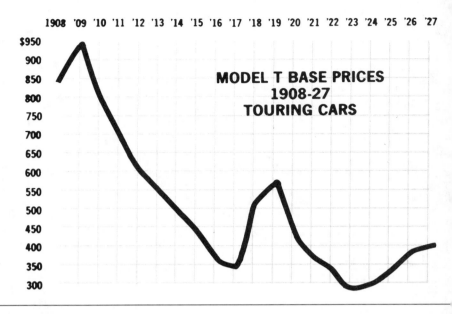

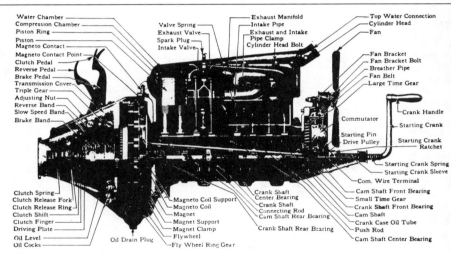

Left: The Model T owner had to be part mechanic, part lover, part sport. Keeping his car happy took great ingenuity. All parts, though, were easy to reach, ruggedly built, and inexpensive to fix or replace. *Above:* The Model T engine was radical for its time by being cast en bloc.

one towncar were also shipped. Three roadsters were delivered in February 1909, and after that a deluge of all kinds of body styles began, with the touring car predominating for many years.

Very few Model T's were produced from October 1 to December 31, 1908. The number has been given as 309, which might be true, but the branch auditing reports of the company show that only 126 Model T's were actually shipped out of the factory in 1908.

There is, of course, no such thing as a 1908 Model T. As is still customary. . .cars built during the last few months of 1908 were intended for the next year and were therefore called 1909 models. ᜒ

About the author: Philip Van Doren Stern is a noted American novelist and historian with a lifelong interest in automobiles. He lives in Sarasota, Florida.

specifications

Illustrations by Russ von Sauers. The Graphic Automobile Studio

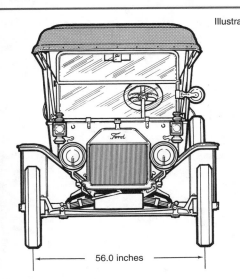
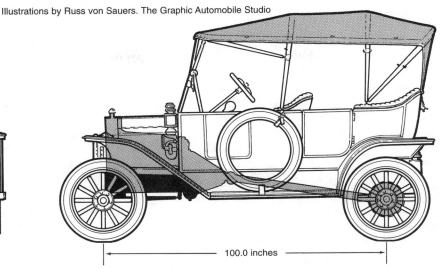

56.0 inches

100.0 inches

1914 Ford Model T touring car

Price when new	$490 fob. Highland Park (1914).
Accessories	Rocky Mountain brakes, Warford 3-speed gearbox, twin front wishbones, 6-volt battery.

ENGINE

Type	In-line, L-head 4, cast-iron block, 3 mains, splash & gravity lubrication.
Bore&stroke	3.75 04.00 in.
Displacement	176.7 cid.
Max. bhp @ rpm	20 @ 1,600.
Max. torque @ rpm	83 @ 900.
Compression ratio	4.5:1 approx.
Induction system	Updraft 1-bbl. carb, gravity fuel feed from underseat tank.
Exhaust system	Cast-iron manifold, single muffler.
Electrical system	5-30 volt depending on engine speed, flywheel magneto, coil box timer on front of engine.

CLUTCH

Type	Multiple disc, with 25 discs operating in oil.
Diameter	N.a.
Actuation	Mechanical, foot pedal.

TRANSMISSION

Type	2-speed planetary, band control via foot pedal & hood lever.
Ratios: 1st	2.75:1.
2nd	1.00:1.
Reverse	4.00:1.

DIFFERENTIAL

Type	Bevel gears.
Rate	3.63:1.
Drive axles	Full floating.

STEERING

Type	Planetary to shaft, worm & sector.
Turns lock to lock	2.0.
Ratio	4.0:1.
Turn circle	28.0 ft.

BRAKES

Type	Accessory 2-wheel external contracting, mechanical; foot pedal operates trans band.
Drum diameter	7.0 in. std., 12.0 in. accessory.

CHASSIS & BODY

Frame	U-section steel, ladder type.
Body construction	Steel over wood framing.
Body style	3-door touring car, 5-passenger, folding 2-man top.

SUSPENSION

Front	Transverse semi-elliptic leaf spring, I-beam axle located by wishbone.
Rear	Solid axle, transverse semi-elliptic leaf spring.
Tires	30 x 3 front, 30 x 3.5 rear, tube type.
Wheels	12-spoke wooden, clincher rims.

WEIGHTS & MEASURES

Wheelbase	100.0 in.
Overall length	123.5 in. without bumpers.
Overall height	74.6 in.
Overall width	67.5 in.
Front track	56.0 in.
Rear track	56.0 in.
Ground clearance	10.5 in.
Curb weight	1,510 lb.

CAPACITIES

Crankcase	4 qt
Cooling system	23.5 pt
Fuel tank	10.0 gal.

PERFORMANCE

Top speed (av.)	45 mph.

PHOTOS BY MICHAEL LAMM

Kerosene fires running lamps and taillamp; headlights burn carbide gas. Each lamp has to be lit individually.

Brass gleams here, but in the Brass T's heyday, owners tended to neglect brightwork.

Model T's sidecurtains look messy and complicated but make interior very snug in bad weather.

11

MODEL A
The Birth of Ford's Interim Car

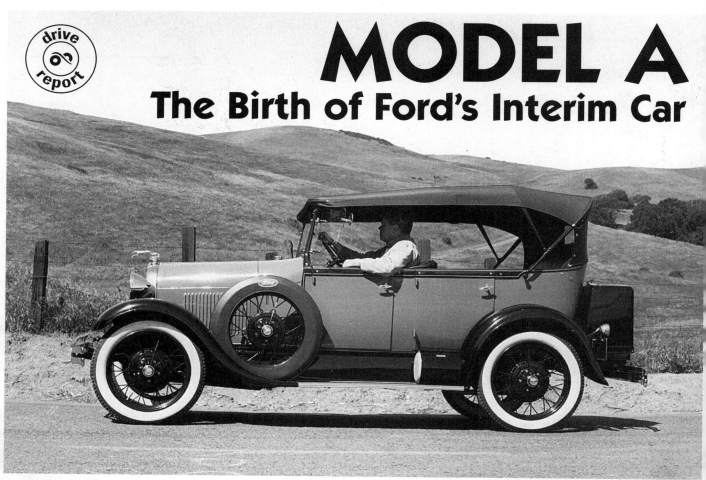

In all that Model A lore, very little has been said about the car's development. Until now.

by Michael Lamm, *Editor*

I WAS 16 WHEN I bought my first Model A—a red-and-black 1929 roadster. Paid $30. Fine car. I've owned five more Model A's since. The thing that impressed me over and over each time I got another one was the design's honesty. No waste, no excess, just logical, beautiful simplicity. Ford maximized everything.

It's always seemed to me that a tremendous amount of consideration went into the Model A. I've felt for a long time that the men who conceived the Model A must have had the sort of engineering integrity you simply don't find anymore. You couldn't design a Model A in 1973. There's an overwhelming straightforwardness about the A. Plus an overdoing. You don't see this overdoing at first glance, but you do if you own an A for a while. Everything's twice as strong as it needs to be.

Enough of that. In all that's been written about the Model A—the tons and tons of it—there's never been much said about the car's actual development. How and why did the A turn out the way it did? Who were those in-spired geniuses who conceived it? Were they geniuses? Inspired? What circumstances and company politics surrounded their frenetic day-to-day work? Was the car born as a whole or piece by piece?

It's a cloudy period in Ford history, probably because everyone in on the A project was too busy at the time to write down what happened. The evidence we do have today comes from oral reminiscenses—tape-recorded interviews gathered in the early 1950s by Owen Bombard, then a member of the Ford Archives Oral History staff and now public relations manager for Lincoln-Mercury. The Ford Archives Oral History staff went around to all the important living Ford ex-employees that could be found and taped their remembrances. These *Reminiscences* cover more than the A's birth, but they also cover that very thoroughly. Typed and bound in blue notebooks, these oral histories now fill about 45 square feet of stack space within the Ford Archives.

The Ford Archives has been kind enough to make this material available to SIA, and the story of the A's gestation is very clear now in my mind. Whether I can capsulize it and not squeeze out all the life remains to be seen.

No one knows exactly when work began on the Model A. It didn't start all at once anyway. People had been working on various components a year or more before Henry Ford decided there was to be a Model A.

One of the principal engineers, Eugene J. (Gene) Farkas, recalls in his *Reminiscences* that he had been reworking several Model T engines, trying to draw more power from them, for perhaps 1-1/2 years before Mr. Ford committed himself to the A. Farkas's main job wasn't to develop a 4-cylinder engine at all, though. Rather it

had to do with Mr. Ford's pet project, the X-8 engine. This was an 8-cylinder engine in a double-X configuration; very different and Henry's own idea. The X-8 never was successfully developed, but Mr. Ford nursed it along for years, both before and after the Model A. Prior to 1926, Mr. Ford had seriously looked forward to X-8 power for the Model T's successor.

There's an unsigned engineering memo in the Ford Archives, dated January 26, 1926, and probably written by Edsel Ford's brother-in-law, Ernest C. Kanzler, which says in effect: 1) Ford Motor Co. needs a replacement for the Model T—a more modern car. 2) Mr. Ford's X-8 car is nowhere near ready for practical consideration. 3) An in-line 6 seems much more reasonable than either a 4 or an 8. 4) An "interim car" should be designed immediately and put into production until a more radical X-8 car can be developed. This memo turned out to be very prophetic. The Model A became Ford's interim car, and the X-8 later ended up transformed into the 1932 V-8.

At the time of this memo, though, Mr. Ford wasn't at all ready to give up the T. He held onto it the way a child clings to a toy or a philosopher to a favorite idea. Despite pleading and reasonable arguments from those near him, principally his son Edsel and Ernest Kanzler, Henry wouldn't budge.

Laurence P. (Larry) Sheldrick, a young, green engineer who would soon begin laying out the 4-cylinder Model A engine, says in his

Reminiscences: 'The years before the Model A came out could be called the years of the Great Debate. Everyone but Mr. Ford wanted to change the Model T. He wanted to continue the Model T until he had his X-car, or a very radical car, ready for production. Openly, Edsel and Kanzler were against it. Rockelman was against it, not openly but quite frankly. Sorensen and Martin were against it, in a very veiled way. No one was really happy with continuing the Model T until this new X-car could be developed."

Edsel's good friend and ally was his brother-in-law, Ernest Kanzler. Kanzler, being young and perhaps too brash for his own good, pushed so hard for killing the T that he got himself canned several months before Mr. Ford came around to Kanzler's way of thinking. (Henry Ford II relied heavily on Kanzler's advice 15 years later.) Edsel, too, would sometimes get his father so furious with anti-T arguments that Mr. Ford would tell Charles E. (Cast-Iron Charlie) Sorensen, his production chief, to ship Edsel out to California just to get him off his back. Sorensen, who basically agreed with Edsel about dumping the T, used to wait two or three days before delivering such messages, by which time Henry had usually cooled off.

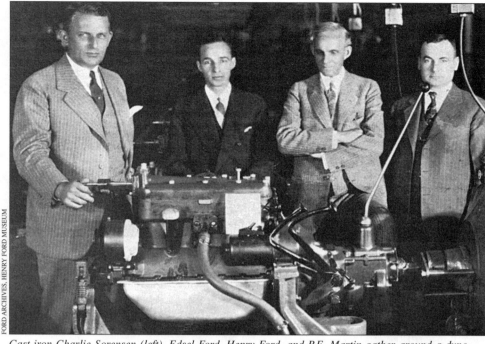

Cast-iron Charlie Sorensen (left), Edsel Ford, Henry Ford, and P.E. Martin gather around a dyno-mounted, pre-production Model A engine in October 1927. The huge Rouge plant was silent then.

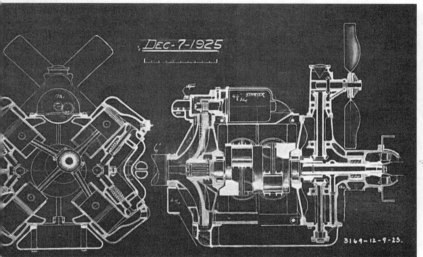

DEC-7-1925

3169-12-9-25.

Henry had hoped his radical X-8 would be ready when time came to replace Model T. After he realized the X-8 couldn't be done in time, Henry gave go-ahead on 4-cylinder "interim" car that became Model A. Drawing at left shows water-cooled version, but engine above was cooled by air.

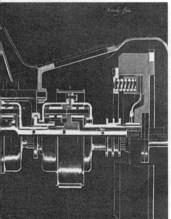

Henry opposed "crunch gear," couldn't shift one, reluctantly okayed it for A. "Armstrong" wipers embodied simplicity that Henry sought.

Ford's top engineers (l-r): Joe Galamb worked with Edsel on design; Sheldrick had responsibility for A's engine; Farkas did the chassis.

Familiar sight to most drivers over 30, Model A dash baffled no one. Henry added safety glass after Harold Hicks, designer of the A engine, flew through windshield in a crash during testing.

Sidecurtains take about 20 minutes to erect, give adequate protection.

Instrument panel mounts to cowl tank; thus gauge reads directly. With no knobs on dash, controls stand near wheel.

Model A Development Chronology

1925-26—Years of Great Debate. Edsel Ford, Ernest Kanzler, and others try to convince reluctant Henry Ford of need to replace the Model T. HF concentrates initial attention on X-8 experimental engine, hoping it might lead to T's replacement.

Jan. 26, 1926—Engineering memo states need to replace T, to forget X-8, to concentrate on 6-cylinder engine.

July 1926—Henry Ford decides privately to go ahead with A and to discontinue T. Settles on 4-cylinder engine.

Aug. 1926—HF informally tells his decision to top aides. On Aug. 7, he instructs Sheldrick to begin work on 4-cylinder engine in earnest.

Sept. 1926—Design for A begins seriously. Much groundwork had already been laid.

Dec. 1926—Farkas, Galamb, and Edsel create initial body layout for new A.

Jan. 17, 1927—Body and chassis "gotten together" in sketches for first time.

Mar. 26, 1927—HF's car runs off road, crashes.

In minor shock, he's put to bed. While in bed, first A chassis completed, running, and driven to Fair Lane.

May 26, 1927—Model T assembly ends at Highland Park, although production of parts continues. Move to Rouge plants and A's tooling begins.

July 7, 1927—Sapiro defamation suit ends out of court. HF apologizes for anti-Semitic remarks in Dearborn Independent.

Aug. 10, 1927—Edsel Ford announces that Model A is "an accomplished fact," but offers no details. Public curiosity grows.

Sept. 1927—Rouge assembly lines readied. Pilot line helps iron out initial production difficulties.

Oct. 21, 1927—First production A assembled. HF had stamped Engine No. 1 the day before.

Early Nov. 1927—About 20 A's a day begin coming off lines.

Nov. 28, 1927—Ford begins blitz advertising campaign to announce Model A. Full-page ads run five days in all U.S. dailies.

Dec. 2, 1927—Model A officially shown; meets tumultuous public acceptance.

B ut Henry knew deep down that Edsel, Kanzler, and the rest were right. He simply wasn't willing to admit it at first. Model T sales peaked in 1923 at 1.8 million and had been slipping since then. Chevrolet, meanwhile, came up from 262,000 in 1924 to nearly 600,000 in 1926. More and more, Mr. Ford heard people berate the Model T. Several states even threatened to outlaw the car because of its 2-wheel brakes. So did Germany. Ford dealers said people were tired of the T's antiquated looks and planetary transmission. Ford face-lifted the Lizzie for 1926 and again for '27, but sales kept dropping.

At first, Mr. Ford shrugged it off. He said he didn't care if he didn't sell so many cars—he had *enough* money in the bank. He didn't *need* to produce half the world's cars. The public was wrong and the product was right. So what if Chevrolet would soon introduce a 6 and Walter Chrysler would launch his new Plymouth?

But then sometime in July 1926, Henry Ford privately made up his mind to replace the T with a more modern car. He decided, too, to power it with another 4-cylinder engine. It wasn't a decision he liked, but he realized he had no choice. He would call the new car the Model A, probably because that's what he'd hoped to call his radically different X-car. Mr. Ford's reasoning was that for a car so new and revolutionary, he had to start his lettering system all over again. It marked the beginning of a new era. Yet in his mind, he might well have considered the 4-cylinder car an interim job between the T and the X-8. Several of Ford's engineers mention the A in their *Reminiscences* as an interim car, although Henry himself never did in so many words.

Larry Sheldrick, the young engineer who'd come over earlier from Lincoln to help Gene Farkas on the X-8, remembers, "... Edsel Ford and Mr. Kanzler were pressing for a new car, and there was a certain amount of conversation in favor of a 6-cylinder.... It didn't take hold at all. Shortly after this, on August 7, 1926, I was commissioned to start the designs of a new 4-cylinder engine of larger displacement for a new car to replace the Model T.... At that time, Mr. Ford and Mr. Sorensen, along with Mr. [P.E. "Pete"] Martin, had daily sessions with me to decide on what the general specifications should be on this engine. It was finally decided to make it 3-7/8 by 4-1/4. We made a number of very sketchy layouts before we settled down on that bore and stroke. I remember that it was 3-3/4 by 4-1/4 for quite a while. Finally, for good measure, an eighth of an inch was added to the bore...."

The average Ford worker didn't realize the Model A was coming until Model T production stopped. By that time, a good number found out via a pink slip. William C. (Bill) Klann, superintendent of Model T engine assembly at Highland Park, expresses the typical employee reaction in his *Reminiscences*:

"I became aware that there would be a changeover to the Model A in about September 1926. Mr. Ford came out to the motor assembly and said, 'You know, I passed a remark one day, Bill, that we would never change the magneto unless it was over my dead body. Well, we're going to change now. We're going to stop building this car next month and build something else.' This was the first I ever heard of it. I told [Clarence W.] Avery about it and he said, 'Yes, I know all about it. We heard about it at a meeting last week, Bill.' I said, 'You're going to stop building the Model T car?' 'Yes, we're going to stop building it.' I said, 'Why?' He said, 'Well, we're going to change it over to a brand-new car called the Model A.' I said, 'Well, what's the matter with this job here? It's going pretty good.' He said, 'It's not fast enough, Bill. We've got to sell more cars. We can't hardly make ends meet.' When they stopped just like that, I was pretty near stunned. Our cylinders [blocks] went on just the same. Our cylinders and other parts amounted to $1 million a day on service parts. We made more money on parts in those days than we did on the cars."

The last Model T left the assembly line on May 26, 1927, and it would be nearly seven months before the first A was sold. The A was about half engineered when T production ended. The effect of that 7-month fallow period is beyond the scope of this article: its impact on workers, dealers, the other car companies, and even the national economy. But rest assured, it was a critical time for everyone.

Larry Sheldrick became Mr. Ford's protege during the A's gestation. Sheldrick was young and eager to please, and Mr. Ford, who turned 64 in July 1927, took a sort of fatherly liking toward him. But Sheldrick soon found himself in trouble with the new 4-cylinder engine. He couldn't get enough horsepower out of it. Sheldrick soft-pedals that fact in his own memoirs, but Al Esper, a Ford mechanic and electrician, tells in his *Reminiscences*:

"I was working on aircraft engineering back in 1927.... They had been trying to develop this new Model A engine for possibly a year or year and a half [first under Farkas, then under Sheldrick]. They weren't able to get over 27 hp out of the revised engine.... When the Chrysler 52 came out...its performance was far superior to the new car they'd been working on. So at this point they had quite a meeting, which included Edsel Ford, Charlie Sorensen, P.E. Martin, and I believe Mr. Ford, Sr. The horsepower problem was discussed. Edsel Ford said he definitely would not accept this new engine of 27 hp, because it didn't have enough stuff to compete with the new Chrysler 52. It was quite a discussion, and Mr. Edsel Ford made the statement that, as they didn't have the engineers in the Ford Motor Co. who could produce something comparable [to Chrysler], he would go out and hire some new men and put them on the job.

"At this point, Mr. Sorensen suggested that they had a man in Aircraft by the name of Harold A. Hicks, who had done a lot of development on high-power boat engines.... Hicks was called in and asked how much power he could put into the Model T engine. With a couple of minutes of concentration, he [Hicks] came up with a figure of 40 hp."

Within 11 days, according to Esper, Harold Hicks had a reworked T engine putting out 42 bhp on the dyno. Hicks had designed a new cam, manifolds and carburetor, new ignition, and larger valves.

"We called in the boss, Mr. Henry Ford, to take a look at this job," Esper goes on. "He came over, and we ran up the engine.... About the only

 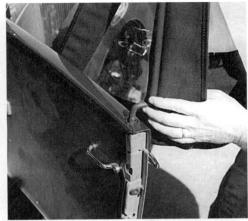

Phaeton sidecurtains stow in long compartment underneath the front seat and rear floor area.

Door curtains plant with rods that poke down into floors. Snap fasteners hold bottom edges.

Mal Staley, owner of Mal's A Sales in Martinez, California, demonstrates ease of lowering top. It's harder to put up than down. Bows rest on stops that screw into rear quarters (not visible).

As high-priced and prized as Model A phaetons are today, they were relatively inexpensive and looked-down-upon when new. Mal restored this one in 1963, passed 1,000 miles during driveReport.

thing Mr. Ford said was to shut it down before it flew apart..... I've always felt that this man Hicks was never given much credit for what he had done. In other words, they just said thank you... and he went back on the aircraft job."

Actually, Hicks had come up with the engineering breakthrough that made the Model A possible. Henry and Edsel were determined that the A should have a cruising speed of 55-60 mph and that it should out-accelerate nearly everything then on the road. Allan Nevins and Frank Hill, in their second volume, *Ford: Expansion and Challenge: 1915-33*, write, "Ford was so delighted with what Hicks had accomplished that he ordered him to go out on the roads and race everything in sight.... Hicks did just that. One day in late July 1927... he took a car out with the new engine, passed everything in sight, and finally headed home at 50 mph. As he attempted to go around another car, it suddenly turned left directly in front of him. A tremendous crash ensued.... Hicks was hurled through the windshield and landed in a ditch, his arm mangled. As a consequence of the collision, Henry and Edsel Ford at once took an additional step to give the new model distinction: They equipped the windshield with safety glass."

Henry Ford ran his company pretty much the way a dictator runs a small country. That's not unreasonable when you consider he built his empire personally and owned it outright. He directed every aspect, was largely responsible for creating the product as well as its unadvertised reputation, so his supreme power was amply justified.

Ford's basic idea was to take advantage of every possible opportunity and to simplify every part of the new car. The classic story about simplification involves the carburetor. Zenith and a rival company were both working with Ford to develop a very basic carburetor. After quite a bit of trial and error, Harold Hicks concluded that the Zenith carb gave more horsepower, but Henry Ford favored the rival carburetor. In typical fashion, Mr. Ford wasn't about to concede gracefully.

When Hicks brought him the prototypal Zenith, Ford looked at it, counted the number of bolts holding the float bowl onto the main body, and said, "Fourteen bolts—that's too many." Hicks took the carburetor back and returned in a week or so with another prototype, this one with only two bolts holding the float bowl to the carburetor body. Hicks handed it to Mr. Ford with a smile, confident that two bolts were the ultimate simplification. Mr. Ford scowled and handed the carburetor back again. "Too many," he repeated. Hicks looked at the carburetor and said, "But it only has two bolts in it now." Mr. Ford said, "I know—that's one too many." The production carburetor had one long bolt that went up between the bowl and the venturi.

Small groups of engineers worked separately at first on the various components of the Model A. One group was hardly aware of what the others were doing. Sheldrick had charge of the engine. Gene Farkas saw to the chassis, the cowl-mounted gas tank, axles, suspension, and brakes. Frank Johnson, who'd been chief engineer at Lincoln, developed the multi-disc clutch and transmission. Joseph (Joe) Galamb and Edsel

Ford designed the body. Lazlo Farkas (Gene's brother) and American Bosch worked together on the ignition system and generator. Clarence Avery, Charles Hartner, and John Findlater saw to the huge job of moving from the Highland Park Model T plant to the Rouge Model A plant and also to the equally huge job of retooling.

Ford actually had two staffs working on the Model A, one for development and one for testing. "Testing" simply meant putting each piece through the severest imaginable torture: twisting, bending, freezing, burning, hammering, etc. The testing staff had no engineering knowledge and wasn't expected to suggest improvements. Its job was merely to break what it could. Once the testers could no longer wreck a piece, it was considered good enough for production.

The Ford Motor Co. had no formal test track, so on-the-road testing was done on actual roads. Everyone would join in, especially on runs up to the Ford farms in upstate Michigan. Ray Dahlinger, manager of Ford's farms and a man with no engineering training whatsoever, had Mr. Ford's complete confidence and became the final judge of a test car's success or failure. The significant fact was that Dahlinger had only two reactions: "It is no goddam good," and "It is goddam good." There was never any in-between. Unless the car was goddam good, it was *no* goddam good. Henry Ford wanted only a car that was goddam good.

The man who coordinated and oversaw all this disparate activity during 1926 and 1927 was Henry Ford himself. He had good lieutenants in such men as Sorensen, Pete Mar-tin, A.M. Wibel, and Edsel Ford. Yet there were no star engineers on his staff—no one you'd call a genius or anything even near it. Most of Ford's engineers hadn't gone beyond high school. Henry Ford was the only real genius among them. As Charlie Sorensen said, "Mr. Ford did his work by intuition." Ford had to have his men accept that intuition, so he didn't really want any hotshot engineers on his staff. If they were practical, tractable, hard-working; if they would do things "right" ac-cording to Henry Ford, they were fine. Too bright or too original, they threatened Ford, and he got rid of them.

Mr. Ford purposefully didn't set up a formal corporate structure. This meant that he was everyone's boss, almost directly. People did answer to certain superiors during the A's development, but ultimately they all answered to Mr. Ford. His inner circle would have lunch with him in his private dining room. If any member of the inner circle displeased him, Mr. Ford would give him the "silent treatment"—would ignore him for a few days. Edsel often endured the silent treatment. After lunch during this period, Mr. Ford and some of his top aides would drop by Sheldrick's office, so eventually Sheldrick became, in effect, the Model A's chief engineer, although he was never called that.

Henry Ford realized that once he'd committed himself to the A, he had to come up with something pretty spectacular—an infinitely better car than the T. The world expected it, and so did he. His reputation and the future of the Ford Motor Co. rode on the new Model A.

William F. (Bill) Pioch, head of Ford's tool

design department, recounts in his *Reminiscences*, 'I know that on the first production of the Model A, Mr. Henry Ford was vitally interested in putting out a car that would stand up better than anything on the road. To accomplish that, he wouldn't allow any stampings in the chassis, like brackets and things of that sort. Everything had to be a forging. Of course, it was quite expensive. There were a lot of stampings on the [Model T] that were to be all forgings.... In other words, he wanted a car much better than our competitors' cars."

Almost everyone connected with the A's development mentions this insistence of Mr. Ford's on forgings. Sheldrick says they were a waste, and in the end Mr. Ford agreed. During tooling and even after production began, Ford changed at least 29 forgings to castings and stampings simply because forgings held no practical advantage. "My only analysis of the matter was that Mr. Ford felt he was being held up by the malleable iron foundries," says Sheldrick. "He felt they were gypping him on prices. It was also expressed a number of times that this was going to be the finest motorcar ever built, and I think the use of forgings was an indication of quality to him, regardless of whether it was in a place where a forging was required or not.... Mr. Ford always objected to stampings, right up to the last contact I had with him. He called them 'Hungarian stimpings.' Another expression he quite often used with reference to Joe Galamb [a Hungarian-American] was 'shit-iron Joe.' The reference was to *sheet* iron, but Joe, with his accent, would kill it. Quite often it was said that Joe would 'take a piss of shit-iron' and make thus or so from it. Anyway, Mr. Ford sure hated stampings."

Joe Galamb and Edsel Ford had primary responsibility for the Model A's body design. Technically, Galamb was Ford's engineering director and overall head of all en-gineering, even experimental. But as it worked out, Galamb contributed mostly to body design and also indirectly to chassis development.

Again, there's no way to date when work started on the A's body. Henry Ford, along with Edsel, Galamb, Sorensen, Farkas, and several others, settled on a 103.5-inch wheelbase, one inch longer than the contemporary Chevrolet's. Henry insisted on a cowl-mounted gas tank, which eliminated the need for a fuel pump and also the complication of an electrical gas gauge. Stewart-Warner and AC Div. of General Motors held most fuel-pump patents of that time, and Mr. Ford didn't want any dealings with either one. He tried for a while to develop his own fuel pump, based on non-patented principles, but he failed. So gravity feed from the cowl-mounted tank seemed the best alternative.

This cowl-mounted tank became the body's key factor. Everything else had to be built around it. It was actually Farkas who developed the A's tank, and a complicated thing it was, especially to manufacture. Farkas points out, "...the idea was to develop a method whereby you could use the skin of the tank for the skin of the body. We worked out a method with Riemenschneider in order to give it strength and the proper shape. He developed a seam welding. It was a stitch weld-

Kari-Keen trunk expands into open bin. This popular accessory came with bumper extensions shown. Mal's A also has set of Bear canisters.

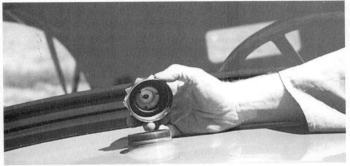

A's designers had to lay body out around gas tank. It doubled as the cowl and dash. Some states initially outlawed it as a fire hazard.

Farkas, Sheldrick, and Hicks patterned A engine on T but updated it. To get around fuel-pump patents, Ford stuck with gravity feed for gas.

Initial brakes put wheel/drum in one piece. Henry Ford wasn't anxious for 4-wheel brakes.

How about that reflection of Mal's shoes in the front seatback? All four doors are narrow and make getting in and out a chore, especially up front where sidemounts restrict doors' opening.

specifications

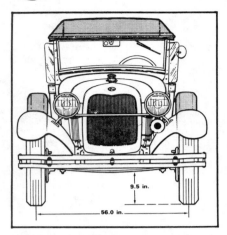

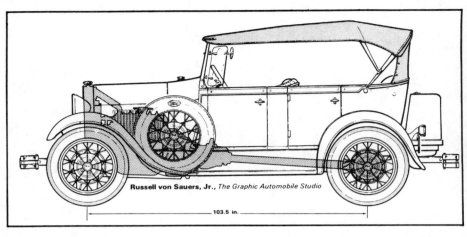

Russell von Sauers, Jr., *The Graphic Automobile Studio*

1929 Ford Model A 4-door phaeton

Price when new . . . . . $460 f.o.b. Dearborn, Mich. (1929).

Current valuation* . . . Xlnt. $5780; good $2890; fair $925.

Options . . . . Twin sidemounts, Kari-Keen trunk, Fuelmaiz, Airmaiz, Bear cannisters, windwings, greyhound.

ENGINE
Type . . . . In-line, L-head 4, water cooled, cast-iron block, 3 mains, splash & pump lubrication.
Bore & stroke . . . . . . 3.875 x 4.250 in.
Displacement . . . . . 200.5 cid.
Max. bhp @ rpm . . . 40 @ 2200.
Max. torque @ rpm . 128 @ 1000.
Compression ratio . . 4.2:1.
Induction system . . . . I-bbl. Zenith updraft carburetor, gravity feed.
Exhaust system . . . . . Cast-iron manifold, single muffler.
Electrical system . . . . 6-volt battery/coil.

CLUTCH
Type . . . . Single dry plate, molded asbestos lining.
Diameter . . . . 9.0 in.
Actuation . . . . Mechanical, foot pedal.

TRANSMISSION
Type . . . . 3-speed manual, floor lever.
Ratios: 1st . . . . 3.13:1.
       2nd . . . . . . 1.86:1.
       3rd . . . . . . 1.00:1.
       Reverse . . . . 3.71:1.

DIFFERENTIAL
Type . . . . Torque-tube drive, spiral bevel gears.
Ratio . . . . 3.70:1.
Drive axles . . . . ¾-floating.

STEERING
Type . . . . Irreversible worm & roller.
Turns lock to lock . . . 2.3.
Ratio . . . . 11.25:1.
Turn circle . . . . 34 ft.

BRAKES
Type . . . . 4-wheel mechanical drums, rod-operated, internal-expanding.
Drum diameter . . . . 11.0 in.
Total swept area . . . . 225.5 sq. in.

CHASSIS & BODY
Frame . . . . U-section steel, ladder type, 3 cross-members.
Body construction . . . Steel with some wood framing, folding canvas top.
Body style . . . . 4-dr., 5-pass. phaeton.

SUSPENSION
Front . . . . I-beam axle, single transverse semi-elliptic spring, Houdaille lever shock absorbers.
Rear . . . . Solid axle, semi-elliptic transverse spring, Houdaille lever shock absorbers.
Tires . . . . 4.50 x 21 tube type 4-ply whitewalls.
Wheels . . . . Welded spokes, drop-center rims, lug-bolted to brake drums.

WEIGHTS & MEASURES
Wheelbase . . . . 103.5 in.
Overall length . . . . . 155.16 in.
Overall height . . . . . 71.25 in.
Overall width . . . . . . 63.25 in.
Front tread . . . . 56.0 in.
Rear tread . . . . 56.0 in.
Ground clearance . . . 9.5 in.
Curb weight . . . . 2298 lb.

CAPACITIES
Crankcase . . . . 5 qt.
Cooling system . . . . . 12 qt.
Fuel tank . . . . 10 gal.

FUEL CONSUMPTION
Best . . . . 21 mpg.
Average . . . . 17 mpg.

PERFORMANCE (from **Motor Trend** test of 1931 Ford roadster, 8/62):
0-30 mph . . . . 7.9 sec.
0-45 mph . . . . 18.7 sec.
0-60 mph . . . . 30.1 sec.
Standing ¼ mile . . . 27.9 sec. & 52 mph.
Top speed (av.) . . . . 60.0 mph.

* Courtesy **Antique Automobile Appraisal,** Prof. Barry Hertz.

---

ing where you can take two pieces of metal, any shape... and run along a couple of electrodes, and just stitch it on. It was spot welding, really, but it was so close together it was continuous. The tank had to be made of terneplate in order to keep it rustproof. The only trouble [was that] the paint didn't seem to last as long on the tank as the rest of the body."

Sheldrick explains how Mr. Ford visualized all work on the A's components, including the body: "Mr. Ford had a great preference for seeing things full size, vertically, in front of him. He could see them at a distance; stand back and get an overall picture. It was a technique that Farkas had developed to a fine point. We speak of a blackboard, but it was really a blackboard *cloth*

stretched on a vertical drawingboard. After we finished one of these, we could roll it up and put it away."

Early bodies were drawn up full scale on black velvet, and they looked like slightly modified T bodies. Slowly, though, the A's lines began to emerge. Edsel had taken charge of styling, this being his area of greatest confidence. He had had

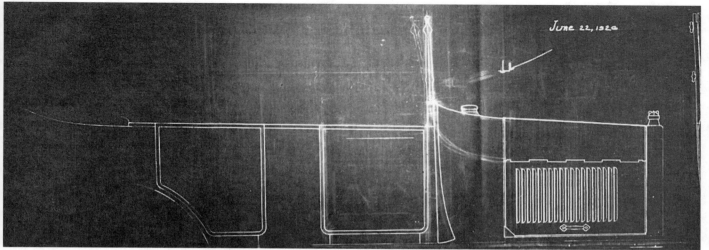

Edsel Ford, Joe Galamb, and Gene Farkas had primary responsibility for body design. This sketch from June 1926 shows A's lines emerging from T's.

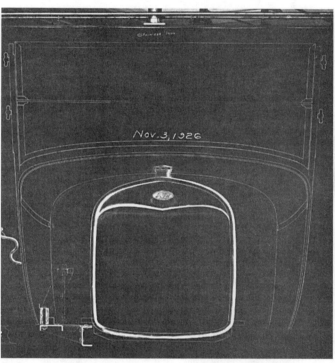

Farkas took credit for grille shell's widow's peak and slight bulging out on top. General lines (and greyhound) were taken from Lincoln.

By November 1926, A's shape was set, but Henry wanted higher roof than Edsel. When Henry saw taller body, however, he agreed to lower it.

a lot to do with custom Lincolns, and that might be why the Model A came out looking like a baby Lincoln. It wasn't a copy of the Lincoln exactly, but the general body shape, radiator shell, visor, and door handles were all scaled-down Lincoln, as was much of the running gear.

Joe Galamb was Edsel's mentor during the A's birth, just as Bob Gregorie became his mentor in V-8 days. Galamb would do sketches and clay models, and he and Edsel would discuss them. Galamb said later, "When we made the first sample [body], Edsel criticized the trimming and the material. He was very particular about the cushions we used. He was very particular about the riding qualities of the car. He knew what he wanted and insisted that he get it."

Gene Farkas takes credit for the radiator shell shape—the widow's peak and the slight puffing out of the front panel. Too, Farkas says that Edsel kept trying to get the body lower. Henry insisted

on enough room to wear a plug hat, plus three or four inches to tip the hat to ladies. This again led to arguments between Edsel and Henry. Farkas managed to get the frame three inches lower than the T's by tilting the engine rearward so the driveshaft stood lower.

Bill Klann got in on some of the body-height arguments when early sample bodies were being secretly built on the sixth floor of his Highland Park engine plant. The experimental bodies were always under lock and key. To fit the cushions, Edsel used himself and Pete Martin as typical *short* drivers and his father and Charlie Sorensen as typical *tall* drivers. Finally, after much argument about roof height, everyone finally agreed, so Klann made cardboard patterns showing cushion and roof height plus toeboard lengths.

Klann remembers: "We put that cardboard away in Mr. Avery's office. About a couple of weeks later, Mr. Ford came around and said,

'Bill, how about these cushions? How high are they going to be?' I said, 'Just the way they are now.' He sat in the car and he said, 'Well, this isn't what we had when I was in it three weeks ago.' I said, 'Yes it is.' 'No it is not,' he said. 'I want them a little higher.'"

So Klann called in Joe Galamb and told him what Mr. Ford had said. Galamb pointed out that everyone, including Mr. Ford, had okayed the less tall body, but after some soul searching, Joe decided to go ahead with raising the roof another 1½ inches; this despite the fact that body dies had already been started. Klann continues, "Joe had the panels made at the Rouge plant, and he sent them to Highland Park. I looked at it and said, 'My God, if that thing isn't top heavy! It's worse than the Lincoln car.' So Joe called Mr. Ford over and he said, 'Now here is that job 1½ inches higher.' Mr. Ford said, 'Who asked for that job?' Joe said, 'You wanted it 1½ inches

19

higher—there it is!' He said, 'Scrap that. It looks terrible.'"

The Model A's clutch and transmission were to be miniaturized versions of the Lincoln's, very literally. Frank Johnson, the Lincoln engineer, developed both, including the Model A's initial multiplate clutch. Lincoln used a multiplate clutch, as did the Fordson tractor, so the first A's did, too. Ford tried to invent a multiplate clutch that didn't release its torque load on the rear main engine bearing, but he was never able to work it out. Finally, after producing the A's multiplate clutch for a year, Ford changed to the cheaper, less com-plicated single dry disc in November 1928.

At the time of the Model A's development,

Henry Ford didn't know how to shift a standard 3-speed transmission. Nor had he ever mastered the conventional clutch. He called hand-shifted transmissions "crunch-gears." He was dead set against the crunch-gear at first and very reluctant to settle for it. What he really wanted and perhaps envisioned for his X-car was a planetary transmission that shifted itself hydraulically. In other words, he was hoping to develop something like the 1940 Hydra-Matic. When Ford finally did consent to the crunch-gear, he muttered to Sheldrick, "Well, if the public wants a sliding-gear transmission, let them have it. Let them find out what a contraption it is." He never did understand why the Model A's crunch-gear became such a resounding success.

Henry Ford told Frank Johnson (*Reminiscences*) that if there had to be a crunch-gear, the countershaft should stop turning in high. Ford felt that the continually rotating countershaft, which was commonly accepted in all sliding-gear transmissions of that day, was inefficient. It robbed power by turning the countershaft through heavy gearbox lubricant, and it also caused unnecessary wear and noise. Johnson did manage to make the countershaft stand still in high gear.

The Model T had used magneto ignition, which, with electric starting, had meant two electricity-producing units on the same car—mag and generator. In the early days of the T, when coil ignition was still unreliable, the magneto had made sense. But by the late 1920s, it was archaic and redundant. Ford realized this, but again he knew nothing about coil-ignition sys-

tems. Larry Sheldrick tells how Mr. Ford taught himself:

"In 1926, as I recall, Mr. Ford took a trip through the Caribbean on his yacht, *Sialia*. Before he started...he asked me to get together one each of all the various types of battery ignition systems...Remy Electric, Leece-Neville, DeJong, Bosch, and AutoLite. So I got together a collection for him. He said, 'Now get me a little set of tools together that I can use in taking these things apart. On the way down, when I'm bored with the trip, I want to take these things apart and study them.' When he came back, he handed me the box. Every one of them was in little bits and pieces. He had taken them all apart and obviously studied them. He had made up his mind what he wanted in certain respects from these distributors.

"One thing—he decided that he did not want a distributor [that] rotated in its entirety for timing adjustment. He wanted the distributor head to be stationary and the breaker plate only to be moved. He didn't want moving high-tension wires that would result from a moving head. So we devised the general idea of this distributor, so well known by every Model A driver, where the Bakelite cap has two arms...with little phosphor bronze springs acting as conductors...to the sparkplug terminals." Lazlo Farkas and a man named Martin from American Bosch worked out the A's ignition, and another man named Huff developed the early Model A's 6-pole generator.

The A's frame and suspension remained very much as they were on the T. Axles were lower, and welded-spoke wheels became standard (they'd been optional on the T). The major suspension change came when Henry Ford drove a prototypal Model A chassis out across a plowed field and decided it needed double-acting shock absorbers. He asked Farkas to name the best kind. Houdaille, said Farkas. Ford put Houdaille shocks on every Model A built, at a cost, according to Sheldrick, of $24 a set—very expensive.

Houdaille couldn't handle Ford's huge volume, so Ford prevailed on the Spicer Mfg. Co. to build a plant in Toledo. Ford had bought Houdaille's shop rights and gave them to Spicer. For a time, Ford wanted the Houdaille shocks welded shut, so there could be no leaks or tampering, but that proved impractical. Heat warpage and fluid boiling prevented welding. As it turned out, the adjustable feature on these expensive Houdailles was rarely used, and more often than not they froze up after a few seasons.

The last important new system to be engineered for the Model A was its brakes. Henry Ford had resisted 4-wheel brakes as long as he could, but Gene Farkas, in designing the front axle, trapped Ford into them. "I told Mr. Ford that instead of having a [front steering] yoke come out, which was a very difficult forging to make, have the axle come out straight and put the

yoke in the front-wheel spindle. I said, 'This change now would adapt the axle later for a 4-wheel brake design in case we wanted to go to it.' This was our opportunity. He said, 'Why don't you do it right away? You have a wire wheel here. Why don't you use the wire wheel housing—the hub—for the brake drum?'"

So the first experimental brakes had the drum integral with the wire wheel hub. It looked good on paper, because it eliminated a separate part for the brake drum; also the lug nuts and bolts. Bugatti had developed a similar one-piece wheel and drum earlier. But Sorensen, Martin, and others argued that different wear rates of the lining material plus the general difficulty of removing the wheel for a tire change made integral drums impractical. Mr. Ford finally agreed.

Bendix held most of the patents on 4-wheel brakes at that time. Ford didn't like the idea of working with Bendix or paying them royalties, because Bendix leaned too much toward General Motors (GM controlled Bendix soon afterward). So the integral drum idea was partly Ford's attempt to get around Bendix patents. When he found he couldn't, he developed his brakes along Bendix lines, then signed an agreement with Bendix.

Farkas had charge of the brakes and worked them out more or less as they finally went into production. His first design, though, had no equalizer. An equalizer, he felt, would leave the whole system inoperative if one brake rod or lever broke. Without the equalizer, you still had 3-wheel braking even if one wheel gave out.

Mr. Ford, however, wanted an equalizer, so when Farkas went down to Brownsville, Texas, on some legal business, Ford had Sheldrick rig one up. After about 1,500 cars were produced, equalizers were again eliminated, and a completely separate set of smaller rear-wheel drums were added for the emergency brakes to comply with certain state laws. It went against Farkas's ideas and also Ford's ideas of simplicity, but there was no other way to go—one of several compromises.

There were hundreds of little things still to do. Tests showed that the Zenith carburetor's float stuck occasionally and caused gas leaks, so Mr. Ford insisted on a shutoff valve under the dashboard. He also wanted a single control for the choke and carb idle adjustment. He got it. Sheldrick included one of those many small, considerate touches: the removable timing pin. And he also developed the quick-release rods for throttle and spark—those with the spring-loaded ends that slip over little balls. Anyone else would have used rivets with cotter pins. Sheldrick convinced Henry that in the volume they would build them, the spring-loaded rods would costs very little more than the cruder type.

It would strain any man of retirement age to work 18 hours a day, six days a week for the 17 months it took to birth the Model A. Henry Ford did it with exuberance, and so did all the men under him. Mr. Ford had not only the day-to-day responsibility, but at least two out-side events added to that strain.

On March 26, 1927, just a few days before the first prototypal Model A chassis was put on the road, Henry Ford had an auto accident. No one knows exactly how it happened, and it's not even certain it happened at all. Henry Ford might have fabricated it to keep himself out of court (see below). The only "witnesses" were two small boys whose testimony didn't hang together. At first the Ford family "suspected a kidnap plot," but that seems unlikely. Apparently, Mr. Ford had been driving home alone that Sunday, and as he approached the gate of his mansion, Fair Lane, he was either run off the road by another car or he simply veered off by himself. His car supposedly went down a 15-foot embankment and came to rest with one wheel against a tree. Ford was dazed, bleeding, and in partial shock. He dragged himself up the embankment on his hands and knees, made it to the Fair Lane gate-house, and was put to bed, where he stayed for several days. The first Model A prototype was taken to him during his recuperation, hut he could look at it only through the open door. His lieutenants visited him at Fair Lane, and for a short while he directed the A's development from his bedside.

Two weeks before his accident, one of several lawsuits brought against him—the Sapiro suit—came to trial. It centered on Ford's anti-Semitic remarks in his private newspaper, *The Dearborn Independent.* Mr. Ford was about to be put on the witness stand when, for technical reasons, the judge declared a mistrial, and Sapiro settled out of court.

Still another hurdle involved clearing the Model A legally so it would comply with various states' laws. Ford had run into problems with the T, especially because of its brakes, so he didn't want the same thing with the A. He sent Walter Fishleigh, an engineer, around to every state to clear the A's headlights, taillamps, brakes, and its cowl-mounted gas tank. The tank was particularly controversial—it had been even in the T. Connecticut turned the A's tank down flat and threatened to prohibit the sale of Fords in that state. New Jersey also balked, as did Massachusetts. Sheldrick said in his *Reminiscences,* "Mr. Crawford and I made several trips to those eastern states to confer with the enforcement agencies—try to placate them, give them a lot of reasons why the danger didn't exist, *although we knew in our hearts that it did* [italics ours]." Finally, by adding a strainer/flame arrester under the tank's filler, all states deemed the Model A safe and legal.

Designing the A was one thing; getting it into production was another. Just as no one can say when the Model A's development started, no one can say when it ended. Ford kept making running changes right through the gigantic retooling operation and even throughout the A's 4-year lifespan.

Converting the Ford plants (36 in the U.S and Canada, 12 overseas, plus countless suppliers) from T to A production meant the largest single changeover in industrial history up to that time. Again, it's beyond the purview of this article to mention all the details of this conversion, but it meant ripping out and replacing thousands of machines, rebuilding others, installing new power sources, making new tools and dies for the 5,580 separate parts involved in assembling the A, creating new departments (as for the clutch, water pump, coil ignition, etc.), refixturing entire plants, retraining men, and then making it all work. This actually became a much bigger job than designing the Model A.

After Ford shut down T assembly, the A began to create an enormous public appetite for itself. Everyone was dying to know what sort of car it would be. Henry said next to nothing, so by a process of natural fermentation, the public's curiosity got bigger and bigger. Finally, on December 2, 1927, Ford gave America its first official glimpse of the A. The millions who viewed it over the next few weeks agreed: It *had* been worth the wait.

The cost to Ford had been staggering—an estimated $250 million. The car itself, though, cost buyers no more on the average than the T

Left "mule ear" controls spark, right one is for gas. Light switch stands below the horn button.

had cost seven months earlier. As an automotive value, the Model A hasn't been beat since, but it took years for people to realize that.

The 1929 phaeton I borrowed for this driveReport belongs to Mal Staley, owner of Mal's A Sales, Martinez, California, one of the Bay Area's largest antique Ford stores. Mal bought the body for this car in 1960 and spent three years restoring it. He'd started collecting new-old-stock parts for it even before he got the body, and the phaeton now consists of more that 50% n.o.s. The rear doors, all four fenders, and 80% of the driveline were still in their original Ford boxes and wrappers before Mal installed them. Even today, 11 years after Mal put the car on the road, it's traveled just over 1,000 miles.

By today's standards, the A is a compli-cated car to drive. The starting ritual alone puts it beyond the ability of most teenagers. First you shove both mule ears up, then pop the ignition key, shove in the clutch with your left foot, reach over and pull out the choke, put your right heel on the round accelerator, your right toe on the starter button, then push down the starter. Once the engine catches, release the choke, release the toe starter, pull down the spark part way, then nurse the engine for about 30 seconds until it dies. Yes, it does die, because you forgot to flip open the fuel shutoff valve under the dash. Now do it all over again.

To launch the A, there's a delicate balance between letting out the clutch and pushing down the gas. The gas pedal is so touchy that you usually over- or underfeed, so you finally end up using the right mule ear to set engine rpm. Ah, much better, The phaeton moves away with just a little clutch chatter and a lovely moan in low.

And it takes off with surprising alacrity.

Shift to second (crunch), and she again moves out willingly. Up to 30 mph, the A really goes, but that's about the time you have to shift to high. At high rpm in second, the whole car shakes due to the un-counterweighted crank-shaft.

Steering feels quite stiff, but it's very fast, and the combination takes some getting used to. It's a front-heavy car, making the rear so light that it's easy to slide sideways on dirt and gravel. Understeer becomes noticeable even at 35 mph. The stiff suspension and skinny tires don't help cornering or traction on the wet or in snow. Yet there's not much lean in turns—surprisingly little considering that the frame attaches to the springs at the spring arches, and logically those two attachments (front and rear) make a perfect pivot axis.

The A tends to wander above 45 mph, and with its quick steering, I found myself having to keep a sharp eye on the center stripe. It's a matter of constant attention. Mal's brakes were well adjusted, but even so the pedal feels slightly mushy, and I never got really confident with them (funny—I was confident enough as a kid).

The front seat is strictly for two people. You *can* pull the gearshift lever up out of its socket if necessary for a small center rider, but it's not recommended. There's ample room for three in the rear. And there's floor space back there to build a convention center. No U.S. car made today has a floor that huge. Top up or down, though, it's very blowy in back; much more than up front.

Yes, the frame does flex, and if you park on uneven ground, the doors bind. But I was amazed by the body's tightness and the lack of odd noises. It's the heavy-gauge steel.

Mal's phaeton is one of 11 A's, T's, and early V-8s he owns. It's Bonnie Grey and Chelsea Blue, with Straw pinstriping and black wheels—a gorgeous sight from any view. I've always like the 1928-29 A's better than the 1930-31s. This car has won many first-in-class down through the years, including Silverado, Golden Gate Fields, Diablo Concours, and Northern California Model A Roundup. Mal asked me to mention that he recently expanded his store to include full on-the-premises restoration facilities, and if he restores other people's cars as well as his own, his new place ought to be jammed forever.

My own feeling about Model A's is this. I've never met one I didn't like. And if I were banished to a desert island and could take only one car to use for the rest of my life, it would have to be a Model A. ✍

Our thanks to Mal Staley. Mal's A Sales, 4968 S. Pacheco, Martinez, CA 94553; Henry E. Edmunds, Ford Archives, Henry Ford Museum, Dearborn, Michigan; Les Henry, Henry Ford Museum; David L. Lewis, Ann Arbor, Michigan; George De Angelis, Model A Restorers Club, Box 1930A, Dearborn, MI 48121; Jim Ryner, Model A Ford Club of America, Inc., Box 2564, Pomona, CA 91766; Michael W.R. Davis, Ford Motor Co., Dearborn; FORD LIFE Magazine, Box 393, St. Helena, CA 94574; and Charles Scribner's Sons, 597 Fifth Ave., New York, NY 10017, publishers of Ford: Expansion and Challenge; 1915-33, *by Allan Nevins and Frank Ernest Hill.*

1931 Chevrolet, Ford and Plymouth

by Arch Brown
photos by Vince Manocchi

GIVEN the increasing difficulty of distinguishing one make of automobile from another these days, it's refreshing to recall the time when there were real differences among cars, when each manufacturer left a unique stamp upon his product, when every marque had a "persoaality" of its own.

That's exactly what we encountered when we went driving in the "low-priced three" of 1931.

There are similarities, of course. Our Chevrolet, Ford and Plymouth are all rather light and relatively small—when compared, say, with 1931 cars of the Buick class. Somewhat Sparan they are, too, apart from the options with which some of the owners have adorned them.

More significantly, these three cars represent a startling advance over the state of the art just a few years earlier. Flip the calendar back to 1924, just seven short years. Chevrolet in those days coupled a competent, 170.9-cubic-inch four-banger to a notoriously fragile rear axle, linking the two by means of a jumpy, leather-faced cone clutch. Formula for disaster! Ford was still building the familiar Model T, sturdy but crude with its 20-horsepower engine and two-speed, pedal-operated planetary transmission. And Chrysler was billing the Plymouth's direct ancestor as "The Good Maxwell," which tells you all you need to know about the earlier cars from that source. For that matter, the Maxwell wasn't even a low-priced car. Its price put it in competition with the Dodge, not yet a part of Walter Chrysler's growing empire.

Customers for 1931's low-priced three had a wide choice of engine types, styling approaches, and standard features to select from. There were two fours and a six; refined design versus virtually unchanged design; all three offered terrific value for money.

All three of the "predecessor" cars back in 1924 were fitted with two-wheel brakes. Ford's were hardly even that, for the service brake was a single drum located in the transmission. All three vehicles rode on high-pressure tires. In a word, they were still rather primitive. And they looked it. Styling, in the mid-twenties, received almost no consideration at all. Not, at least, from the manufacturers of cheap cars.

But by 1931 all that had changed. Think back seven years from right now, and make a mental list of the major advances in automotive design that we've seen in that time. Pretty short list, isn't it? Now, contrast that inventory with the progress represented by our comparisonReport cars. By 1931:

• Closed cars—sedans and coupes—

had replaced the drafty open models as the dominant body styles.

• Power output had virtually doubled.

• Four-wheel brakes were *de rigueur*, with hydraulics beginning to appear.

• Balloon tires were standard equipment, even on the least expensive cars.

• The handsome, Hispano-Suiza school of styling (long hood; tall, narrow radiator) had come to dominate the industry, extending even to some of the low-priced cars.

And when it came to sheer dollar-value, these automobiles were simply impossible to beat! Two-door sedans, known as "coaches" in those days, were by far the best-sellers among inexpensive cars, and their prices ranged from a modest $490 for the Ford to a high of $575 for the Plymouth. In the case of the Model A, that calculates out to less than 21 cents a pound.

Of course, the market was a tough one in 1931. It was a miserable year for those millions of Americans who didn't have jobs and couldn't find them, for the disillusioned investors who had lost their shirts in the Wall Street debacle a couple of years earlier, for the frugal souls who had seen their life's savings wiped out in one or another of the 2,300 bank failures that had devastated the country.

Nineteen-thirty-one had its bright side, to be sure, even if one had to wear rose-colored glasses to find it, Technical progress, for instance, was evident on a number of fronts, in the automobile industry and elsewhere:

• Henry Ford turned out his twenty-millionth automobile, a Model A town sedan.

• Captain (later Sir) Malcolm Campbell set a new world's record, driving his 1,450-horsepower "Bluebird" 245.733 miles an hour over a one-mile course.

• Wiley Post set a record, too, circling the globe in the monoplane *Winnie Mae*. His time: 8 days, 15 hours, 51 minutes.

• The Columbia Broadcasting System established an experimental television station, maintaining a regular broadcast schedule.

• Radio-telephone service was established between the Pacific Coast and the Far East.

There were events of some considerable consequence in political-governmental circles, as well:

• President Hoover proposed a one-year moratorium on the payment of intergovernmental debts and war reparations. Since virtually none of the nations that were in debt to the United States could have come up with the money anyway, Congress gulped and endorsed the idea.

• For $25 million the United States bought the Danish West Indies, re-naming them the Virgin Islands.

• Congress declared "The Star-Spangled Banner" to be the National Anthem, over the opposition of those who preferred "America the Beautiful."

• And on the other side of the globe, in an event whose ominous significance was largely unrecognized at the time, Japan invaded Manchuria. Nobody knew it, but World War II had begun.

Nineteen-thirty-one was a good, if not quite a "vintage" year at the movies. The "talkies" were still a novelty, and if they were technically unsophisticated, many of the plays were good, and the public loved them. Movie-house pianists joined the swelling ranks of the unemployed, and the public watched—and listened—entranced:

• *Cimarron*, starring Irene Dunne and Richard Dix, took the Oscar as the year's best flick, while

• Wallace Beery copped the Best Actor award for his portrayal of *The Champ*.

• Fans were captivated by a glamorous new actress from Germany, as Marlene Dietrich made her American debut in *Dishonored*.

• And Charlie Chaplin starred in the last of the great silent films, *City Lights*.

It was a fine year for music, as well. Many of the pop tunes of 1931 are frequently heard, even today. From Broadway came Arthur Schwartz's "Dancing in the Dark" and Ray Noble's "Good-night Sweetheart." From the Cotton Club, up in Harlem, came Duke Ellington's "Mood Indigo." And out in Hollywood a newcomer called Bing Crosby was making quite a name for himself, crooning the likes of Johnny Green's "Out of Nowhere" and his own "Where the Blue of the Night Meets the Gold of the Day"—later to become his theme song.

In Detroit, meanwhile, the scramble was on for what few car buyers could be found. The Chevrolet six (see *SIA* #34), introduced a couple of years earlier as General Motors' response to Henry Ford's sensationally popular Model A (see sidebar, page 24), passed its rival in the sales race—despite the Ford's substantial price advantage—and except for two or three years has maintained its dominant position ever since. And a newcomer had entered the field in mid-1928. By 1931 it had elbowed Buick aside to take over third place in the industry. This was Walter Chrysler's low-priced entry, the Plymouth.

And when the final tallies were made for the year—though Ford's share of the

*Right: With its standard stone guard, Chevy took on an "expensive car" look, while Plymouth's front, **far right,** offered a tentative excursion into streamlining with its curved radiator shell. Ford, **below,** had front identical to 1930 edition except for painted area at top of radiator shell.*

market had fallen to less than 28 percent, compared with 40 percent the year before—among them the "low-priced three" had accounted for 63.25 percent of American automobile sales. Not only were dollars hard to come by in those difficult times, but the differences between the inexpensive cars and their medium-priced competitors had become much less significant than had been the case just a few years earlier.

For this report, photographer Vince Manocchi brought together three fine examples, representing the three marques that had among them cap-

tured nearly two-thirds of the market, back in 1931. The photo session took place at the historic Pio Pico mansion in Whittier, California (see sidebar, page 29). It is noteworthy, by the way, that all three of these cars are "drivers," frequently used for club tours and family outings. The Plymouth even sees occasional duty as a delivery car for its owner's printing business.

The Chevrolet is, of course, the only six-cylinder car in the group—though surprisingly, its engine has the smallest displacement of the three. Making much of the fact that it was "America's lowest-priced six" (though both Essex and Willys offered attractive alternatives priced only a few dollars higher), Chevrolet advertised "a six at the price of a four." Obviously, the ploy appealed to the public.

The Chevy is the heaviest car of the three (though the difference would have been greater had our comparisonReport car not been a cabriolet), and by far the smoothest of line. No fewer than 12 body styles were offered, ranging from a bare-bones roadster priced at $475 to a sophisticated, fully convertible two-door phaeton that fetched $650. (Ford, of course, offered an even broader range of choice—17 models altogether.)

Our Chevrolet, like the other two cars in this comparisonReport, was acquired by its owner as a basket case. Its restoration was no easy task, according to owner Tom Schay, for the car had no engine or transmission when he purchased it, and in general the body was in rather ratty shape. Tom stripped it to the frame and spent more than three years restoring it to pristine condition, cannibalizing four other Chevrolets for the necessary parts. A rebored and fully balanced engine was acquired, and the upholstery was done by a specialist; otherwise the entire project was the work of Tom Schay, assisted by his father.

Schay's car still looks good, despite the fact that its restoration was completed nearly a dozen years ago. It has been equipped with an impressive array of authentic Chevrolet accessories including twin sidemounted spares, trunk rack and trunk, spotlight, heater, dual

The Coming of the "Low-Priced Three"

Ford had reached a crisis point back in the mid-twenties when it finally dawned upon old Henry Ford that his beloved—and ubiquitous—Model T had become obsolete. The message was to be found on the sales charts, for while Ford was still selling far more cars than anyone else, Chevrolet—headed by Henry Ford's former production chief, "Big Bill" Knudsen—was rapidly gaining on him.

Accordingly, in the spring of 1927 Ford shut down, and for four full months there were no Ford cars coming off the line. During the interim, operations were transferred from the company's Highland Park plant to River Rouge, and the factory was re-tooled for the first really new Ford in 19 years: the Model A.

Henry Ford was, of course, something of a folk hero, and the excitement and anticipation with which the American public awaited the "new" Ford went far beyond that accorded any other car, before or since. There was even a popular song entitled "Henry's Made a Lady Out of Lizzie"!

Knudsen, meanwhile, was not one to sit on his hands. Taking full advantage of Ford's extended shutdown, as well as the glitches that resulted in an unexpectedly slow start in the production of the Model A, he expanded Chevrolet's output as rapidly as he could, and for two consecutive years—1927 and 1928—the production and sale of Chevrolet cars exceeded, for the first time in history, those of Ford. And by a country mile!

Knudsen knew, however, that sooner or later his former employer would get his act together, and there were plenty of people waiting for a chance to buy Henry's attractive new automobile. He was right, by 1929 new Fords were rolling out of the Rouge in record numbers. People were snapping them up as fast as they could be built, and Chevrolet was

back in second place.

Even so, Chevy stirred up a little excitement of its own with the 1929 introduction of "the world's lowest-priced six." Emerging as it did from Harley Earl's Art and Color design studio at General Motors, it was a beauty, and there is no question that it was smoother and more refined than its rival from Dearborn. It was also more expensive, significantly so by the standards of the time, but then, Chevrolets had always cost more than Fords.

Across town, Walter P. Chrysler had ambitions of his own, one of which was to crack the low-priced field. He did it with the Plymouth, introduced in July 1928. In reality, it was a crisply restyled version of the Chrysler 52, which in turn was a direct descendent of the Maxwell. Actually, the Plymouth wasn't quite price-competitive as yet with Chevrolet—much less with Ford. That would come a few years later. But the Plymouth, alone in its field, boasted hydraulic brakes, and in both styling and size it was impressive. Measurements were, in fact, identical to the six-cylinder De Soto, introduced a month later than the Plymouth (see *SIA* #59) and priced $155 higher. Chrysler advertised its new four-banger, not altogether inaccurately, as "America's lowest-priced full-sized car."

The new car caught on fast. In January 1929 a new Chrysler-designed engine replaced the Plymouth's Maxwell-derived mill, and sales were limited only by the factory's production capacity.

The three-way race was on. By 1934, the "low-priced three" would own three-quarters of the American automobile market, and throughout the decade all three produced automobiles that even today are prized by collectors and used as "drivers" as well as show cars.

Ford owners might have opted for moto-meter so they could monitor engine temperature, while Chevy buyers might have gone for the handsome accessory Eagle mascot. Plymouth, meanwhile, came standard with their new-for-'31 flying lady.

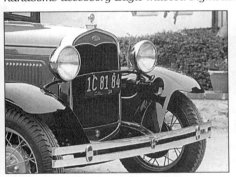

horns, windwings, dashboard clock, and a handsome eagle radiator mascot. Authentic in terms of the car's period, but not on the Chevrolet-approved list of "extras" are the Trippe driving lights and the radio. Tom has even fitted it with a hitch, and on long tours the car is used to pull a small box trailer.

The Chevy is a pleasant car to drive at moderate highway speeds. The composite wood-and-steel construction of its body provides better sound insulation than its all-steel competitors, and the numerically low axle ratio helps to keep engine noise from becoming intrusive.

The seat is comfortable, providing an adjustment that gives adequate leg room, even for a tall driver. The ride, for a car of this age and class, is good. Clutch action is smooth, and shifts are easy. Double-clutching is helpful, but clash-free shifts can be managed without that technique if the driver has a good sense of timing.

On the other hand, the Chevrolet's brakes, while effective enough, require a great deal of pedal pressure. And this car's acceleration, although adequate, is no match for that of either of its competitors. No wonder. Here's the heaviest car of the group. powered by the smallest engine and driven through the tallest gears.

Driving Dennis Griffen's Model A was an experience in *déjà vu*, for during our college days we owned a 1931 Ford. Ours was a bottom-of-the-line, standard business coupe for which we paid $75 in

After driving all three cars, we found the choice as difficult as before. They all offered terrific transportation value, and plenty of collector satisfaction today.

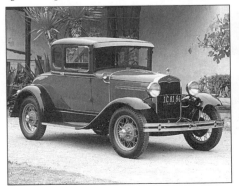

*All three used split stop/taillamps. Chevy, **above left**, included bow-tie emblem. Ford, **center**, used red and amber lenses, while Plymouth, **right**, offered two red lenses. Dashes were distinctly different, too. Ford, **below left**, grouped minimal instruments in center cluster. Chevrolet, **center**, had classy damascened instrument panel, and Plymouth, **right**, used symmetrical instrument layout and gobs of woodgrain.*

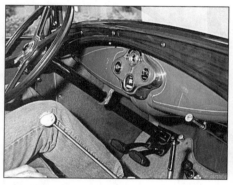
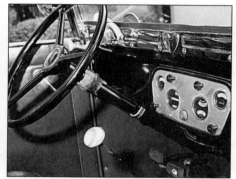

1939. Needless to say, it was in no sense a match for Dennis's immaculately restored deluxe model. But the ride and handling characteristics are just as we remembered them. The clutch is a little chattery, the ride a bit choppy. Shifting is easy, but double-clutching is almost a must. This car is not as comfortable as the Chevrolet, to be sure, but it is peppier and more fun to drive. Dennis's brakes work much better than ours ever did, thanks to his many hours of labor in bringing them back to—and perhaps beyond—factory standards. The pedal feels a little soft, but the binders get the job done.

Truthfully, we must say that the Model A—in its last year of production by 1931—is a bit primitive in some respects, compared with its rivals. For instance, it's the only one of the three which requires that the fuel mixture be adjusted by the driver. It's the only one without an automatic spark retard (and the operator had jolly well better remember what that left-side lever is there for!) And it's the only one without a full complement of dashboard instruments, neither a temperature gauge nor an oil pressure indicator being provided. Its low-compression engine extracts substantially less power per cubic inch of displacement than the more efficient

powerplants of the Chevrolet and Plymouth. Yet, thanks to the car's light weight, performance fairly sparkles.

The Ford's steering is very quick, contributing to the joy of driving this machine. It's the lightest and the shortest of the three cars covered in this report, and it turns in the tightest circle of the group. Leg room, surprisingly, is the best of the three, and an ample adjustment is provided. Best of all, as a new car the Ford sold at a substantially lower price than its competitors.

Dennis Griffin brought the Model A home in three truckloads, and spent eight months on a "frame-up" restoration. He regards it as a "driver" and has put well over a thousand miles on it since completing the refurbishing, yet just a month before we drove it, the car took Best of Show honors at the Southern California Regional Model A show.

Dressing up Griffin's Ford are a number of factory-authorized accessories: A Boyce Moto-Meter bearing the Ford script rides atop the radiator cap; there are windwings, and a spare tire guard stretching between the rear bumperettes. An extra stop-taillamp is mounted on the right rear fender, and set into the rearview mirror is a neat little clock. Altogether it's a smartly handsome little automobile!

The Plymouth had been part of the automotive scene for nearly three years when the PA series, represented here by Harley Pebley's fine coupe, was introduced in mid-1931. But it was the PA, rather than the earlier series, that was responsible for boosting Plymouth sales into third place. Small wonder, for it is a beautifully engineered car, ahead of its time in a number of respects.

• Its length—greater than that of either of its competitors—is accentuated by the fact that it is the lowest of the three in overall height.

• The engine's 56 horsepower—up from 48 in the previous Plymouth model—gives the Plymouth a distinct edge in that department.

• "Free-wheeling," a dangerous device but a highly popular one 50 years ago, was unique to the Plymouth in the low-priced field in 1931 (though Chevrolet would offer it the following year). Along with its hazardous coasting feature, free-wheeling permits the convenience of clutchless shifting, once the car is under way.

• Most important, the PA featured "floating power." There was nothing new about rubber engine mountings; Nash had pioneered that idea nearly a decade earlier. But Chrysler had suspended the engine on two points rather than three

or four, the forward mounting being high, the rear one low. An imaginary line drawn between the two points would pass through the center of the engine's mass. Were it not fixed in place, the engine would spin freely and smoothly on this axis.

At idle. the Plymouth's four-cylinder engine, thus suspended, shakes like a bowl of jello. But under way, the "floating power" gives the car a smoothness that rivals, perhaps even surpasses, conventional sixes.

We found the leg room in Harley Pebley's Plymouth coupe to be a little cramped for our six-foot-two frame. Oddly enough, though an adjustment is provided in the PA sedans, there is none in the coupe. Doubtless we would have found the four-door model more comfortable.

Performance is another matter entirely! The Plymouth's acceleration is even quicker than that of the Ford.

Good-looking wire wheel came as standard equipment on all three cars.

Comparative Specifications: 1931 Chevrolet, Ford, and Plymouth

	Chevrolet	Ford	Plymouth
Price* (2-door sedan	$545	$490	$575
Price* (model tested)	$615	$525	$610
Engine			
Type	ohv 6	L-head 4	L-head 4
Bore & stroke	3.3125 x 3~75	3.875 x 4.25	3.625 x 4.75
Displacement	194.0 cubic inches	200.5 cubic inches	196.1 cubic inches
Compression ratio	5.02:1	4.22:1	4.90:1
bhp @ rpm	50 @ 2,600	40 @ 2,200	56 @ 2,800
Hp per cubic inch	.258	.200	.281
Full pressure lubrication?	No	No	Yes
Fuel feed	Mechanical pump	Gravity	Mechanical pump
Clutch			
Type	Single dry plate	Single dry plate	Single dry plate
Diameter	9 inches	9 inches	8.875 inches
Transmission			
Type	3-speed selective	3-speed selective	3-speed selective
Ratios: (low, 2nd, reverse)	3.32/1.77/4.20	3.12/1.85/3.75	2.76/1.51/3.45
Rear axle			
Type	Semi-floating	3/4 floating	Semi-floating
Final drive	Spiral bevel	Spiral bevel	Spiral bevel
Ratio	4.1:1	4.64:1	4.33:1
Brakes			
Type	4-wheel mechanical	4-wheel mechanical	4-wheel hydraulic
Drum diameter	11.5 inches	11 inches	11 inches
Lining area	172.875 square inches	178 square inches	121.375 square inches
Steering			
Type	Worm and sector	Worm and sector	Worm and sector
Turns, lock to lock	3	2.5	3
Turning circle (right)	34' 11"	31' 9"	38' 3"
Body construction	Wood/steel	All-steel	All-steel
Capacities			
Crankcase	5 quarts	5 quarts	6 quarts
Cooling system	11.5 quarts	12 quarts	14.5 quarts
Fuel tank	11 gallons	10 gallons	12 gallons
Weights and measures			
Shipping weight (2-dr sedan)	2,610 pounds	2,375 pounds	2,495 pounds
Shipping weight, model tested	2,520 pounds	2,283 pounds	2,510 pounds
Wheelbase	109 inches	103.5 inches	109.375 inches
Overall length	166 inches	155 inches	169.1875 inches
Overall height	67.5 inches	68.5 inches	66.75 inches
Overall width	68 inches	68 inches	66.1875 inches
Tire size	4.75 x 19	4.75 x 19	4.75 x 19
Other statistics			
Ratio, lbs. per cubic inch	13.5:1	11.8:1	12.7:1
Ratio, lbs. per bhp	52.2:1	59.4:1	44.6:1
Calendar year production	627,104	541,615	106,259

*f.o.b. factory, with standard equipment

In the performance department, the Plymouth felt like the quickest car through the gears. All three offer comfortable cruising in the 40-50 mph range.

enjoy our Model A, back in those days before our world lost its innocence!)

• For maneuverability, the Ford takes it again. Its short wheelbase, quick steering, and tight turning radius can be a real convenience.

• Good brakes happen to be a high-priority feature with us. Here, the choice is clear: Plymouth, hands down.

• And for a combination of brisk performance together with smoothness and a comfortable ride, again the Plymouth leads the pack.

Three different cars, representing three distinct concepts of what a low-priced autombbile should be—and do. All three were, and are, fine machines

Clutch action is smooth and easy, and shifting—even with free-wheeling locked out—is a breeze. The ride seems marginally smoother than that of the Chevrolet. Somehow, this car feels heavier than it really is, yet it preserves the agility of a lighter vehicle. And the hydraulic brakes are clearly superior to the binders on either of the Plymouth's competitors.

So, let's imagine ourselves back in 1931 and in the market for a low-priced car. Which to choose? It's all a matter of one's priorities.

• For styling, we'd have to give the nod to the handsome Chevrolet, with Ford in

second place. Plymouth, though presenting the longest, lowest profile of the three, lacks some of the panache of its two rivals.

• For insulation against road and engine noises, again the nod goes to Chevrolet. Call it finesse; the Chevy's got it.

• In terms of a comfortable driving position—and bear in mind, this is from the perspective of a tall person—the Ford is clearly the first choice, with Chevrolet in second place.

• And for the sheer fun of driving, again it's the Ford, with the Plymouth next in line. (There maybe an element of nostalgia here, of course. We really *did*

that have stood very well the test of time. The public opted overwhelmingly for the Chevrolet, of course, despite a significant price advantage on the part of Ford. Yet that's no reason to believe that the Chevy was the ideal car for every buyer.

And after all, wasn't it the buyers' great good fortune to have had such a wide range of choice? ❧

Acknowledgments and Bibliography

Automobile Trade Journal, *various issues;* Automotive Industries, *various issues;* Don Butler, The Plymouth and De Soto Story; *George H. Dammann,* Illustrated History of Ford; *Beverly Rae Kimes,* "Chevy Goes Six," *Automobile Quarterly XIX-1;* Beverly Rae Kimes, The Cars That Henry Ford Built; *Julius Mattfield,* Variety Music Cavalcade; *Jerry Heasley,* The Production Figure Book for US Cars; *Paul R Woudenberg,* Ford in the Thirties; *"Ford, Chevrolet, Plymouth,"* Fortune, *October 1931; factory sales literature.*

Our thanks to Jim Benjaminson, Cavalier, North Dakota; Dwight Cervin, Granada Hills, California; Pete Gomez, Ranger, and the staff of Pio Pico State Park, Pico Rivera, California; Franca Manocchi, Azusa, California; Elmer Ryan and Duane Steele of the Vintage Chevrolet Club of America; Orange County Chevrolet Club; WPC Club, Walter Kahlenberg, President, North Hollywood, California; Telford and Ada Work, Pacific Palisades, California; Ralph Dunwoodie, Sun Valley, Nevada. Special thanks to Dennis Griffin, Garden Grove, California; Harley and Myrtle Pebley, Pico Rivera, California; Tom Schay, Brea, California.

1931's Big Three Body Style and Price Table

Body Style	Chevrolet	Ford	Plymouth
Roadster (2-passenger)	$475	$430	$535
Sport roadster (2-4 passenger)	$510	$435	n/a
Deluxe roadster (2-4 passenger)	n/a	$475	$595
Phaeton	$510	$435	n/a
Deluxe phaeton	n/a	$580	$595
Convertible cabriolet	$615	$595	$645
Convertible phaeton (conv. sedan)	$650	$640	n/a
Coupe, 3-window, 2-passenger	$535	n/a	$565
Coupe, 5-window, 2-passenger	$545	$490	n/a
Deluxe coupe	n/a	$525	n/a
Sport coupe, 2-4 passenger	$575	$500	$610
Coach (2-door sedan)	$545	$490	$575
Five-passenger (Victoria) coupe	$595	$580	n/a
Sedan, 4-door	$635	$590	$635
Special (Deluxe) sedan	$650	$630	n/a
Town sedan	n/a	$630	n/a
Station wagon	n/a	$695	n/a
Town car	n/a	$1,200	n/a

Prices f.o.b. factory, with standard equipment

Source: *Automobile Trade Journal,* August 1931; George H. Dammann, *Illustrated History of Ford;* Paul Woudenberg, *Ford in the Thirties*

About the Setting

As the locale for this comparison Report, photographer Vince Manocchi chose the historic Pio Pico mansion, in Whittier, California, near Los Angeles. A word of introduction is in order. In a very real sense, Pio Pico (1801-1894) represented the bridge between Mexican and American California. Governor of California in 1845-46, his term was cut short by the American invasion. Pico went to Mexico to seek support for his fight against the American Army. His quest was to no avail, however, and by he time he returned home in 1848, California was securely in American hands. Pragmatic by nature, Pico—a revolutionary in his youth—became a staunch supporter of law and order.

Investing both time and money in the development of education, banking and town sites, he served as a Los Angeles city councilman and helped to finance California's first oil venture.

Pio Pico's mansion was erected on a portion of the 9,000-acre ranch that he purchased (for about half a dollar an acre!) in 1850. Completed in 1852, the house served as his residence until the year before his death. Given to the State of California in 1917, it was completely restored in 1946.

Known officially as California State Historical Monument #127, the 13-room mansion is a historic link with that exciting period when two cultures met and merged to create modern California.

Below left: Chevy's "stovebolt" six was in its third year of production in '31. The same fundamental design would continue to power millions of cars for decades. *Below left and center:* 1931 would mark the final year for the simple, strong, reliable Model A four-banger. *Below:* Plymouth's four had its last full year production run in 1931; was superseded by the model PB six in April 1932. *Bottom left:* Model A interior is like rest of car, functional, straightforward, and attractive. *Bottom center.* Woodgraining helped Plymouth interior have a deluxe aura. *Bottom right:* Chevy had flashiest interior of all three.

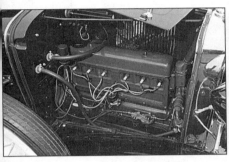

1932 MODEL B FORD

drive report

SON OF MODEL A

by Arch Brown
photos by Roy Query

SURELY no automobile in history has ever been more eagerly awaited, or more enthusiastically received than the Model A Ford. It is said that despite the nasty winter weather, within 36 hours of its public introduction on December 2, 1927, more than ten million people had waited in line to see it. Showrooms were so crowded that the display models — generally no more than one per dealer — often had to be cordoned off, lest they be pushed all over the floor. Orders were taken, usually with a small deposit, as fast as the salesmen could fill out the necessary papers; and the better part of two years would pass before the supply of these sturdy and unexpectedly stylish little cars caught up with the demand.

But in spite of its stout construction and its Lincoln-inspired good looks, the Model A was not a particularly advanced automobile — except, of course, in comparison to its antiquated predecessor the Model T; and by 1931 its popularity was fading rapidly. In 1929 the Ford had outsold Chevrolet's new Six by a margin of better than three to two, but two years later their positions were reversed, and the Ford Motor Company lost some $37 million.

The Depression had wreaked havoc

with all of the nation's automakers by that time, but Chevy had taken a far less severe beating than Ford, and now enjoyed a 16 percent advantage over its rival. Meanwhile, upstart Plymouth, which had not yet come on the market when the Model A made its debut, had leapfrogged its way into third place, posing yet another threat to Ford's position in the scheme of things.

Henry Ford, despite his conservative nature and his stubborn disposition, was nevertheless aware that the time had come for his company to build a more sophisticated automobile. As 1929 drew to a close, the old man — spurred on, no doubt, by the introduction of Chevrolet's new Six — ordered his staff to proceed with the development of a new engine. And in keeping with Ford's sense of the dramatic, it would be a V-8. Nobody had ever attempted anything of the sort in a low-priced car. Many observers, in fact, were sure that it couldn't be done. After all, V-8 engines

in those days were customarily made up of three castings — one for each cylinder block, one for the crankcase — which of course added up to an expensive manufacturing process.

As a matter of fact, Ford engineers had already been experimenting with some new engines, the most intriguing of which was an X-8 (see *SIA* #19) whose development got under way in 1923. Both air- and water-cooled prototypes were built, but by 1926 Ford had concluded that however novel the X-8 might be, it simply wasn't practical. Somewhat later, at Henry Ford's insistence, there were experiments with a prototype five-cylinder engine, but its inherent imbalance made it unacceptable, and the project was eventually shelved.

Logic might have suggested a Six; for in-line six-cylinder engines, noted for their smoothness of operation, were highly popular in those days. But Henry Ford would have none of it. In the first place, for him to have introduced such an engine, right on the heels of the new Chevrolet Six, would have cast the Ford Motor Company in the role of follower rather than leader. And besides, Ford's only six-cylinder car — the 1906 Model K — had been, arguably, the worst sales

Driving Impressions

Counting standard and deluxe models separately, Ford offered no fewer than 14 body styles for 1932. Twenty-eight, if the Model B's and the V-8s are tallied independently. And that total doesn't include the station wagon, which was listed as a commercial vehicle rather than a passenger car. All are highly collectible today, but the convertible sedan, the cabriolet, the phaetons, and the roadsters are considered especially desirable.

And so, when the late Bill Harrah undertook to add a Model B to his fabulous automobile collection, he wanted one of the open styles. This proved to be easier said than done, according to Ralph Dunwoodie, former manager of the collection. "We found plenty of V-8s," Dunwoodie recalls. "But the four-cylinder cars were something else."

A suitable car was finally located in 1965, in the San Francisco area, but the owner, an elderly gentleman named G.B. McClelland, was reluctant to part with it. He had purchased the roadster new, and although he was no longer able to drive, he felt a strong attachment to it.

Finally, Norm Griswold, who was handling the transaction for Bill Harrah, promised the old man, "If you'll let us have it, we'll restore it immediately and bring it back for you to see it, ride in it, have your picture taken in it." At that point, Mr. McClelland consented, and the roadster was on its way to Reno. The figure agreed upon was $1,000, exactly double the factory list price—a fabulous bargain by today's standards, but a fairly stiff figure for those days.

Ralph Dunwoodie recalls that the Model B wasn't beat up, but after 33 years of use it was a well-worn automobile when it arrived at the Harrah shops. Honoring their promise to G.B. McClelland, the Harrah staff went immediately to work on it, and in a relatively short time the roadster, handsomely refinished in its original Black and Apple Green wheels and pinstriping, was transported to San Francisco for a brief reunion with its former owner. There is an appreciative note from Mr. McClelland in the files at the National Automobile Museum, successor to the Harrah Automobile Collection, in which McClelland confesses that he shed a few tears upon seeing his old car once more, restored this time to new condition.

As one might expect, the Model B drives very much like its predecessor. Yet it is really a much better automobile.

• For starts, based on its actual brake horsepower of 52, rather than the advertised figure of 50, it is 30 percent more powerful than the Model A. Thus it can cruise smoothly at speeds that would create some strain in the earlier car.

• The new transmission, with its taller gears, "silent second," and synchronized second and third speeds, is a vast improvement over the previous unit. It must be confessed, however, that as wear took its toll of this gearbox, it typically developed an annoying habit of jumping out of second gear.

• The automatic spark advance, replacing the Model A's manual control, is a welcome improvement.

• The longer wheelbase, together with an even longer springbase, results in a somewhat improved ride—though the Model B is still no limousine.

• With ten percent more lining area, only partially offset by a three and a half percent increase in weight, as compared to the Model A, the Model B definitely has more braking power. Which is not to suggest, by the way, that these binders are any match for the Plymouth's hydraulics.

Familiar to veteran Model A drivers are several Model B characteristics: the slightly chattery clutch; the steering—still relatively heavy, despite the slight increase in ratio; the heavy pedal pressure required in order to stop the car; and the paucity of instrumentation. In addition to the speedometer, an ammeter and a fuel gauge are provided, but there is no clue to the oil pressure and engine temperature figures. And on open models such as this roadster, no provision is made for adjusting the position of the seat. At six-feet-two, we found leg room to be adequate, if less than generous—which suggests that the short driver might be well advised to bring along a pillow.

We can recall wondering, when these cars were new, why anyone would buy the Model B, instead of the hot new V-8. But we like the four-banger, and in retrospect, particularly in view of the excessive oil consumption experienced by owners of the early V-8s, the four-cylinder car may well have been the better choice.

shield was given a ten-degree slant, an[d] the exterior visor was eliminated. Ribbe[d] single-bar bumpers replaced the prev[i]ous double-bar design, and the overa[ll] lines were more sweeping than ever b[e]fore. The net result was an automobi[le] that is still, 60 years later, noted for i[ts] smart good looks.

Chassis improvements included [a] longer wheelbase (106 vs. 103.5 inches[)], though that measurement was sti[ll] three inches shorter than the Chevrol[et] and six inches shy of Plymouth's ne[w] PB series. Ford's already archaic trans[-]verse springs were retained, but the re[ar] unit was relocated aft of the axle. Th[is] not only increased the springbase, co[n]tributing to a slightly better ride, but [it] also helped to reduce the car's overa[ll] height. Larger (12-inch vs. 11-inc[h]) brake drums were employed, while the[re] was a ten percent increase in the bra[k]ing area. And the steering ratio wa[s] increased from 11.5:1 to 13.0:1, resul[t]ing in reduced effort on the driver's pa[rt].

Rubber mountings were employed f[or] both the four- and eight-cylinder en[-]gines; though the Ford setup lacked th[e] balance that made Plymouth's "Floatin[g] Power" engine mountings especially e[f]fective. A new transmission feature[d] taller first and second gear ratios, [a] "silent second," and synchronized sec[-]ond and third speeds. The high-spee[d] second gear, with its 1.60 ratio (reduce[d] from 1.86 in the Model A) was particu[-]larly useful in mountain driving. An[d] the gas tank, previously located in th[e] cowl, where it had been criticized — per[-]haps unjustly — as a fire hazard, wa[s] moved to the rear of the car. At the sam[e] time, a mechanical fuel pump replace[d] the Model A's gravity feed.

All of these modifications were share[d] by both the eight-cylinder Model 18 an[d] its four-cylinder counterpart. Mean[-]while, Ford engineers had undertake[n] to update the Model A engine for use i[n] the new Model B. A number of signif[i]cant improvements were made, the mos[t] important of which was a new crank[-]

1932 Ford Table of Prices, Weights, and Production

Body Style	Price, B/V-8	Weight, B/V-8	Production, B/V-8
Roadster	$410/$460	2,095/2,203	948/520
Deluxe Roadster	$450/$500	2,102/2,308	3,719/6,893
Phaeton	$445/$495	2,238/2,369	593/483
Deluxe Phaeton	$495/$545	2,268/2,375	281/923
Coupe	$440/$490	2,261/2,398	20,342/28,904
Sport Coupe	$485/$535	2,286/2,405	739/1,982
Deluxe Coupe	$525/$575	2,364/2,493	968/20,506
Tudor Sedan	$450/$500	2,378/2,508	36,553/57,930
Deluxe Tudor Sedan	$500/$550	2,398/2,518	4,077/18,836
Fordor Sedan	$540/$590	2,413/2,538	4,116/9,310
Deluxe Fordor Sedan	$595/$645	2,432/2,568	2,620/18,880
Cabriolet	$560/$610	2,295/2,398	427/5,499
Victoria	$550/$600	2,344/2,483	521/7,241
Convertible Sedan	$600/$650	2,349/2,480	41/842

Note: During 1932, station wagons were considered a part of the Ford truck line. Production for the model year totalled 334, including both four-cylinder and V-8 units.

fiasco in the company's history.

So work was undertaken on the new V-8. Henry Ford mandated a monobloc casting, believing — correctly, as matters developed — that it would keep his manufacturing costs within acceptable limits.

But there was a cautious side to Henry Ford's nature. As sensational as he expected the V-8 to be, some potential buyers would inevitably regard it with suspicion. At best, it would be a new, untried powerplant. And to the economy-minded motorist, eight cylinders might suggest excessive fuel consumption. There wasn't much validity to that perception, as it happens, but the V-8, Ford realized, would have to prove itself before some cautious members of the public would accept it.

Hence the Model B, a four-cylinder car that represented a refined and substantially improved version of the Model A. It was planned that the V-8, officially known as the Model 18, would share virtually all of its chassis components as well as its styling with the Model B. Indeed, only the V-8 logo on the tie-bar and the hubcaps distinguished the

eight-cylinder car, visually, from its less powerful companion. Styling — the work of Joe Galamb, with an assist from Edsel Ford — featured a slightly vee'd radiator grille (a first for Ford) and smaller (18-inch) wheels with fatter (5.25-inch) tires and lug nuts hidden beneath the large hubcaps. The wind-

Above left: Cowl lamps are miniature version of B's headlamps. *Above center:* Taillamp closely resembles earlier Model A units. *Above right:* B rode on lower, 18-inch steel wire wheels.

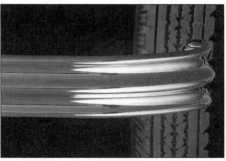

shaft, ten pounds heavier and very much stronger than the previous unit. The lubrication system was revised for greater effectiveness, and an improved water pump was fitted.

In response to complaints of bearing failures in the Model A, crank and rod journals were enlarged. Main bearings were increased in size from one and five eighths to two inches, which made it easible to boost the compression ratio from 4.22:1 to 4.60:1. This, in combination with a larger Zenith carburetor, raised the Model B's advertised horsepower to 50, a 25 percent increase over the Model A engine. (Evidently Ford's marketing people were enamored of round numbers, for in point of fact the reworked engine developed 52, rather than 50 horsepower.)

Fifty horsepower in a low-priced car would have been an impressive figure a few years earlier, but by 1932 the Chevrolet was rated at 60 bhp, Plymouth at 65. And for an extra $50 the Ford buyer could opt for that sensational V-8, also rated — conservatively, in this instance — at 65 horsepower.

Predictably, a multitude of problems were involved in developing the V-8 engine and putting it into production. Casting problems plagued the factory, with the rejection rate approaching 50 percent during the early weeks. As a result, the new Fords were not introduced to the public until April 2, 1932, some four or five months behind the competition. (Picture, if you will, the plight of the poor dealers, who had nothing to sell during that long winter except a few leftover 1931 Model A's. Times were tough enough in those days, without having to cope with such a handicap as that.)

As a matter of fact, the Model B was on line as early as November 1931, with stockpiles of the new engine on hand. But Henry Ford wisely refused to dilute the impact of the new V-8 with the premature introduction of the nearly identical four-cylinder car. Thus, production of the Model B was actually delayed until after that of the V-8 got under way.

At first, V-8 production — though lim-

Above left: Sleek, simple radiator cap crowned redesigned shell and grille. *Above right:* Pretty bumpers are unique to 1932 model year. *Below left:* Instrument panel is bare-bones but attractively presented. *Below right:* Door handles would look right on a 1992 car.

Low-Priced 1932 Roadsters: A Comparison Table

	Ford B; V-8	Chevrolet BA	Plymouth PB
Price, dlx roadster	$450/$500	$485	$595
Weight (lb.)	2,102; 2,308	2,500	2,600
Wheelbase	106 inches	109 inches	112 inches
Overall length	165.5 inches	167.1875 inches	175.03125 inches
Cylinders	4; 8	6	4
Engine c.i.d.	200.5; 221.0	194.0	196.1
Compression ratio	4.5:1; 5.5:1	5.2:1	4.9:1
Hp/rpm	50/2,800; 65/3,400	60/3,000	65/3,200
Valve configuration	L-head	ohv	L-head
Brakes	Mechanical	Mechanical	Hydraulic
Braking area	186 sq. in.	216.75 sq. in.	121.3125 sq. in.
Axle ratio (:1)	3.77; 4.33	4.10	4.33
Tire size	5.25/18	5.25/18	5.25/18
Hp/c.i.d.	.249; .294	.309	.331
Lb./hp	42.0; 35.5	41.7	40.0
Lb./c.i.d.	10.5; 10.4	12.9	13.3
Production*	3,719; 6,893	8,552	2,163

*Deluxe (or Sport) Roadster only

Note: The Plymouth production figure shown here covers the PB series only. This series was announced on April 3, 1932, superseding the 1931/32 PA series. 2,680 Sport Roadsters had been produced in the PA series, an undetermined number of which would be regarded as 1932 cars.

*Above left: Sturdy little four-banger engine was outsold by better than 125 percent by Ford's sensational new V-8. **Above right:** Headlamp control was incorporated in B's steering wheel boss. **Below:** From the back, the B could still be mistaken for a Model A by the casual observer. **Bottom:** Transverse springs help give B good cornering capabilities.*

Interest in the 1932 Fords ran high, initially; five and a half million people are said to have visited the Ford showrooms on introduction day, March 31st. But the hapless dealers had nothing to sell. Indeed, at that point just over 1,100 1932 Fords had been produced, and most of the dealers had yet to receive so much as a single car for display purposes. And in any case, with the nation's economy at its all-time low point, few Americans could afford to buy a new car. Not even one that sold, like the Model B, for as little as $410. Ford's output for the calendar year came to just 232,125 cars, the lowest figure since 1913. ∂

ited — far exceeded that of the Model B. Then by May 1932, with the four-cylinder car in full production while problems continued to plague the V-8, that situation was reversed. At that point the four-cylinder cars out-numbered the eights by three to two, but thereafter it was the V-8s all the way. By the end of the model year the box score was 178,749 V-8s to 75,945 Model B's, a difference of 135 percent. Ford deliberately de-emphasized the Model B, in fact, to such an extent that certain body styles — victoria, convertible sedan, deluxe coupe and cabriolet — could be purchased with four-cylinder power only on special order.

By 1933 the ratio was 40 to one in favor of the eight-cylinder line. The four-banger, which was provided with a counterbalanced crankshaft commencing in early December 1933, remained in production until March 1934, but it failed to garner a significant share of the market.

Acknowledgments and Bibliography

Automobile Trade Journal, *August 1932; Ford factory literature; Kimes Beverly Rae and Henry Austin Clark, Jr. Standard Catalog of American Cars 1805-1942; Lewis, David L., Mik McCarville, and Lorin Sorensen, Ford 1903 to 1984; Naul, G. Marshall, Th Specification Book for US Cars, 1930 1969; Woudenberg, Paul R., Ford In Th Thirties.*

Our thanks to Dave Brown, Durham California; John Cavagnaro, Stockton California; Ralph Dunwoodie, Sun Valley, Nevada; Marshall Lewis, Empire California. Special thanks to the staff o the National Automobile Museum, Renc Nevada, especially Charles C. "Chuck Hilton, Executive Director; Bob MacMil lan, Master Technician; Rod Lungstrom Automotive Technician; Janet Ross Librarian.

illustrations by Russell von Sauers, The Graphic Automobile Studio
© copyright 1992, Special Interest Autos

specifications

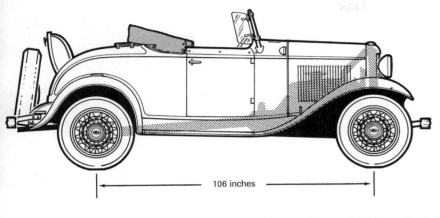

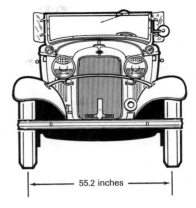

106 inches

55.2 inches

1932 Ford Model B

Original price	$450 f.o.b. factory with standard equipment
Standard equipment	Safety glass windshield and windwings; rumble seat; leather upholstery, front seat
Options on dR car	None

ENGINE

Type	4-cylinder, in-line, L-head
Bore x stroke	3.875 inches x 4.25 inches
Displacement	200.5 cubic inches
Compression ratio	4.6:1
Horsepower @ rpm	50 @ 2,800
Torque @ rpm	127 @ 2,800
Main bearings	3
Fuel system	Zenith 1.125-inch updraft carburetor, mechanical pump
Lubrication system	Pressure and splash
Cooling system	Centrifugal pump
Electrical system	6-volt battery/coil

CLUTCH

Type	Single dry plate
Diameter	9 inches
Actuation	Mechanical, foot pedal

TRANSMISSION

Type	3-speed selective with silent second speed; synchronized 2nd and 3rd gears; floor-mounted lever

Ratios:	1st	2.82:1
	2nd	1.60:1
	3rd	1.00:1
	Reverse	3.83:1

DIFFERENTIAL

Type	Spiral bevel
Ratio	3.77:1
Drive axles	3/4 floating
Torque medium	Torque tube

STEERING

Type	Gemmer worm and segment
Ratio	13:1
Turning diameter	39 feet
Turns, lock-to-lock	3

BRAKES

Type	4-wheel internal mechanical
Drum diameter	12 inches
Lining area	186 square inches

CONSTRUCTION

Type	Body-on-frame
Frame	Double-drop, ladder type, U-section steel; 5 crossmembers
Body construction	All steel
Body style	Deluxe roadster
Body builder	Ford

SUSPENSION

Front	I-beam axle, transverse leaf spring
Rear	Rigid axle, transverse leaf spring
Shock absorbers	Double-acting hydraulic, lever type
Wheels	Welded steel wire
Tires	5.25/18 4-ply, tube type

WEIGHTS AND MEASURES

Wheelbase	106 inches
Overall length	165.5 inches
Overall width	67 inches
Overall height	68 inches
Front track	55.2 inches
Rear track	56.7 inches
Min. road clearance	8.25 inches
Weight	2,102 pounds

CAPACITIES

Crankcase	5 quarts
Cooling system	12 quarts
Fuel tank	14 gallons
Transmission	2.5 pounds
Differential	2.25 pounds

CALCULATED DATA

Hp per c.i.d.	.2494
Weight per h.p.	42.04 pounds
Weight per c.i.d.	10.48 pounds
Weight per sq. in.	11.30 pounds (brakes)

There's plenty of padding for rumble-seat passengers.

by Michael Lamm, *Editor*

Henry Ford's Last Mechanical Triumph

In secrecy, single-mindedly, Henry Ford brought forth his monobloc V-8 engine, a job that took him 4 years. His Model 18 became and remains one of the world's most influential automobiles.

In SIA #18, you'll remember, we chronicled the development of the Model A Ford—The Birth of Ford's Interim Car. By using the actual words of the engineers and workmen who helped Henry Ford bring the Model A to life, we feel we were able to recreate not just the history but the mood and feeling of the times—those hectic days of 1926-27-28.

We want to use that same technique now for the first Ford V-8's development. The words of the men closest to Henry Ford tell the story best. These Reminiscences *were tape-recorded in the early 1950s by the Ford Archives Oral History staff. Ford Archives interviewers traveled around the country to talk to scores of longtime Ford employees and ex-employees. The taped*

Reminiscences *were later transcribed. Certain transcriptions have very generously been made available to SIA by Henry Edmunds, director of the Ford Archives, Henry Ford Museum. Dearborn, Mich.*

"MR. FORD was developing this V-8 in secret for a while," recalls William F. (Bill) Pioch, head of production engineering. "He had a fellow by the name of Carl Schultz who laid out the first V-8 engine the way he [Ford] wanted it made. It was called the Model 24. They did this work in Greenfield Village in a secret room. I was one of the few people who was allowed to enter the secret place. Mr. Ford didn't tell me not to tell anybody; he

just took it for granted. It was a hard place to g[et] into and then keep your mouth shut. I used to g[o] in with Sorensen [Charles E.] and Martin [P. E.] over there and discuss some of the producti[on] problems with them. . . . Mr. Zoerlein was wo[rk]ing on the ignition. . . . Mr. Sheldrick came [in] after the engine was laid out. It was unusual f[or] the chief engineer not to come in before that. b[ut] that again was Mr. Ford's idea. He worked [on] that thing every day.

"Mr. Ford was interested in developing an [X] engine during this period. That was an 8-cylind[er] engine. . . like an airplane engine [X-8]. I thi[nk] they built one engine and put it on a chassis a[nd] tried it out. The next engine they worked on w[as] the V-8."

Ford experimental engineer Fred Thoms recalled that. . . "The reason that Mr. Ford was led to the V-8 away from the X-style 8 was this: The day Chevrolet went from a 4 to a 6, Mr. Ford came in and said, 'We're going to go from a 4 to an 8, because Chevrolet is going to a 6.' Then he went on to tell me, 'Now you try to get all the old 8-cylinder engines [V-8s] that you can.'

"I guess we picked up nine in scrap yards. We washed them up and laid them all out to get some kind of idea, because an 8-cylinder was a much more expensive car than Mr. Ford was going to [build]. He was going to put an 8 into a $550 car, and that was never done before. . . . They were all expensive cars.

"Those 8-cylinder engines were all in two or three pieces. The cylinder block was bolted to the crankcase [including Ford's own Lincoln V-8]. One of them was in two halves [the 1917-18 Chevrolet V-8]. They were very costly, and you couldn't make them cheap. . . . That's why we went to the idea of making a V-8 cylinder block in one piece—for cheapness. . . . Everybody said it couldn't be done.

"The first V-8 was laid out in the spring of 1930—May [actually the first V-8 in this series came earlier—1928—but Thoms is referring to the one made by Arnold Soth under Henry Ford's direction]. That one kept burning out because they didn't have the proper oil feed. It couldn't be made on account of the angle of the banks [60°]. The next one was drawn up in November 1930, and Carl Schultz was put on that one.

"There were no drawings at first on the V-8. We just had sketches but no drawings. The patterns were made from the sketches. I went to work there on a Friday and worked all day Friday, worked all Friday night and all day Saturday. Carl Schultz and I would take turns sleeping for a couple of hours on the floor. We would go home for half a day on Sunday and sleep and go back again. That's how we worked when we were designing that V-8.

"Mr. Ford was not impatient because he knew the terrific load [we were] carrying. . . . He wouldn't talk much about anything while he was down there watching us. He was very serious and wouldn't joke or laugh. . . . He just came in there and looked over things and was very quiet and slow-moving. He was thorough and wanted everything to be done. . .exactly right. He suggested all the things that he wanted done. We would try it out on a test or in a car, and if it didn't work out, we would go to something else.

"Mr. Ford wouldn't let Carl Schultz determine how he wanted to lay out the engine. He came there and told us just what he wanted—such as, I want the fuel pump here. distributor here, and so on. After all his suggestions, Schultz would detail it up. You could tell by the way the engine was constructed that it was his [Ford's] idea. We had to do just what he said. I imagine that is why Carl Schultz and I got along with Mr. Ford so well. . . . Mr. Ford was really doing the engineering, and Carl Schultz and I were drawing up his ideas."

Henry Ford once made this statement: "We do nothing at all in what is sometimes ambitiously called research, except as it relates to our single object, which is making motors and putting them on wheels. In our engineering laboratory we are equipped to do almost anything we care to do, but our method is the Edison method of trial and error. . . ."

Mr. Ford was his own chief engineer. He had no "star" engineers the way Chrysler Corp. and General Motors did—no Breers, no Seaholms, no Olleys, no McCuens. Ford's men had little enough formal training. They were competent, capable people, but like Henry Ford himself, they engineered by intuition. And they didn't talk back. Ford chose them not for their brilliance nor bursting creativity but because they did what he told them. They knew the limits of suggesting. When Eugene I. (Gene) Farkas, chassis engineer, developed a simple oil pump for one of the prototypal V-8s—and he did this on his own—Henry Ford snapped, 'When I want an oil pump, I know a man who can do it for me." That hit Farkas hard. He said later in his *Reminiscences*, "Of course, I couldn't make any more suggestions. I just went ahead and did the best I could. I wasn't in a very happy frame of mind doing it.'

What Fred Thoms mentioned about the Chevy 6 goading Mr. Ford to jump from the 4 to an 8 is only partly true. The Chevy 6 influenced Ford's decision to bring out the Model A much more than it prompted the V-8. Ford knew long before 1929 that Chevy would bring out a 6. A great number of other pressures came into the V-8 decision. One of the strongest was Walter Chrysler's new Plymouth, with Floating Power engine mountings. Floating Power was ballyhooed out of all proportion to its true merit (although it was an important refinement). When Walter Chrysler left a brand-new 1931 Plymouth PA on Ford's doorstep with a note on the windshield about "if you like it, keep it," Henry Ford got mad.

He'd been kicking around different 8-cylinder engine ideas for years—since 1921, at least. The configuration Ford liked best was the X-8 (*see* Experimental Ford Engines, SIA #19). The X-8 had been Mr. Ford's dream during the decline of the Model T. He and his engineers designed numerous versions, both air- and water-cooled, but they couldn't work out all the bugs.

Mr. Ford was never happy about having to abandon the T in favor of another 4-cylinder car. He would have much preferred to go from the T directly to a radical X-8-powered car instead of bringing out the Model A. Henry Ford thought of the A as an interim car—a stopgap between the T and his X-8-engined dream.

It turned out, of course, that the A was an interim car. It stayed in production a bare 4-1/2 years, whereas the T had lasted 19 years and the V-8 would go on for 21.

So, knowing that the Model A's days were numbered, Mr. Ford kept a concerted research program pointed toward its replacement. Call it trial-and-error in the Edison vein, it was amazingly broad and diverse. Ford's experiments during the Model A's lifetime included much more than just the search for another engine. He had groups working on automatic transmissions, 2- and 4-wheel independent suspension systems, front-wheel drives, rear engine placements, hydraulic brakes, and hydrostatic drive systems. Some of this research went on for years, and all

of it started in the Model A's heyday.

Deep down, Henry Ford wanted the Model A's successor to have an 8-cylinder engine. His son Edsel and Charles Sorensen and other higher-ups in the company kept campaigning for a 6, so 6s were grudgingly a part of Ford's research program. At least a dozen 6s were designed, built, and tested, some of them with overhead cams, all of them with seven main bearings (common practice at the time), and none very successful. Ford placed so many restrictions on the 6s that they couldn't possibly succeed, nor did he want them to.

Ford's engineering staff was small even by 1930 standards. For the largest automaker in the world, it was downright tiny—some 200 men in all, including draftsmen. Today, Ford Motor Co. employs 12,000 engineers in its Research and Development Center. But in 1930, 200 men could and did handle the engineering and production preparation of an entire automobile.

Then, too, Henry Ford wasn't in the habit of assigning titles. At General Motors or Chrysler, Laurence P. (Larry) Sheldrick would have been called chief engineer. Gene Farkas would have been chief chassis engineer and Joseph (Joe) Galamb chief body engineer. But Mr. Ford didn't hand out formal titles. His idea was to keep a loose chain of command, so everyone answered to him instead of to an intermediary.

By not assigning titles, Mr. Ford could have a number of engineers working on the same problem at the same time and on the same level. That's how he arranged research on the V-8. He had at least four small groups working on V-8 development, starting with C.J. (Jimmy) Smith's in 1928. To quote Smith's *Reminiscences*, "It was around 1928 when I first started working on the V-8 engine instead of the X. This V-8 engine was Mr. Ford's idea. He wanted an engine that wouldn't have any pumps on it. We tried the same thing as on the Model T, but we couldn't make it work because there was too much heat in there. There was no water pump—just thermosiphon. It just wouldn't work—it would get too hot." Smith, who had worked on various experimental projects since Model T days, also confided, "If Mr. Ford brought in a new idea, none of the workmen dared to tell him it wouldn't work."

The second V-8 development group was Arnold Soth's, beginning in May 1930. Henry Ford set Soth up in a room with a draftsman and then directed Soth's work personally. Under Mr. Ford's eyes, Soth designed the mi-begotten 60 V-8, 3-5/8 by 3-5/8 square, 299 cubic inches, again without an oil pump. Several such engines were built, and they all burned up on the dyno. It was for this engine that Gene Farkas took it upon himself to design his ill-fated oil pump.

The third group was Carl Schultz's, which began work in November 1930. Ford would eventually choose Schultz's engine for production. Schultz, of course, became Henry Ford's hands. Harold Hicks, who five years earlier had engineered the successful Model A engine and who had employed Schultz at that time, said later in his *Reminiscences*, ". . . . I can truthfully say that Carl Schultz knew practically nothing about engines when he came to work for me. He did the layout and detail work under my direction,

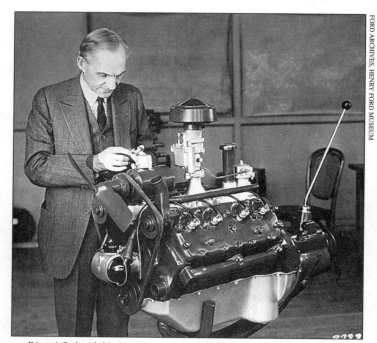

Dissatisfied with his "interim car," Henry Ford masterminded the V-8. He was 66 when it bowed. The engine outlived Mr. Ford by six years.

Rudy Martinez's 1932 convertible sedan originally belonged to F.D.R.'s war secretary, Henry Stimson. Car remains unrestored at 61,000 miles.

because I didn't have time to do it myself. That way he learned a lot."

During the V-8's design period, Mr. Ford stood over Schultz day after day and dictated the engine's layout. Fred Thoms and a draftsman were in this group. They at first occupied the Engineering Laboratory in Dearborn and then later moved into the reconstructed Edison Laboratory at Greenfield Village. This was Thomas Edison's old lab, which Ford had bought in 1925 and moved to Dearborn from Ft. Myers, Florida. Edison, who was a 'very good friend of Henry Ford's, had used this laboratory for some 40 years.

Fred Thoms continues his *Reminiscences*: "I will take a typical engine and follow through on it. I was working with Carl Schultz then, and he would draw up an engine and give me the blueprints. The first thing I would have to do [was] get my motor mountings. . . . The next thing would be to work on the tools. The tools had to come along just about the same time as the cylinder block did—pistons, rods, and everything. [Blocks came down from the foundry, each cast by hand, of course.] I didn't order the casting myself from the Rouge—Carl Schultz usually did that. The casting would be machined right in the Engineering Lab machine shop. When the block was all machined and the other parts machined, I had to put it together. We tested these blocks for leaks over in the tin shop and repaired them there. Any little leaks. . .can all be fixed. They would probably throw them out nowadays, but those cylinder blocks cost. . .as much as $20,000. . . ."

More often than not, these engines would burn out. With dippers, one bank got the oil while the other bank starved. Several different sorts of simple oil pumps were tried—an Archimedes screw, more dippers here and there—but finally Ford okayed a conventional gear pump as on the Model A, and that solved at least one major problem.

There was a fourth independent group working on V-8s, this one headed by Ray Laird. Laird

The Autocar's test of 1932 V-8 raved about its performance, listed Ford's top speed at 78.3 mph.

Because Ford rushed into production without much testing, owners soon found serious flaws. Engines cracked, burned oil, needed new pistons, overheated, and fuel pumps froze in cold weather.

The 1932 Ford's design history isn't clear. Most experts agree that Edsel Ford and Joe Galamb had overall charge. Some say the B was a scaled-down Lincoln mated to Model A panels. Others claim Briggs laid down the lines but originally intended them for Plymouth. This scale model shows shovelnose grille, odd parking lamps, and brackets on fenders that possibly held headlights.

worked with Schultz down in the Edison Lab and went on later to design a smaller V-8 that became the 60-bhp job introduced in the U.S. in 1937. It was actually ready for production in 1933 and might have been conceived as a replacement for that year's outgoing 4-cylinder engine.

Several additional groups and individuals were working on 6s concurrently with the V-8s, among them Schultz, Laird, Farkas, and Zoerlein. At the time, none of these groups knew what the others were doing. It came down to a sort of competition.

Strict secrecy surrounded these experiments, as explained by Ford's tough security boss Harry Bennett, in his book *We Never Called Him Henry* (Fawcett Publications, 1951): "While Mr. Ford was developing the V-8 and the six, he was extremely sensitive about it. He heard a rumor that [Fred L.] Rockelman [Ford's sales manager and later president of Plymouth] had discussed the engines with Walter Chrysler and threatened to fire Rockelman if the rumor were true. He had almost everyone in the plant afraid for his job, and got everyone so tense over the whole thing that he [Ford] achieved the opposite result. . . . Employees were discussing the engine much more than they would have under more relaxed circumstances.

"Mr. Ford had me working my head off to find out if there were any leaks. Things came to such a pass that I actually refused to look at the engines myself. A dozen times he tried to get me to look at them, and I said. 'No, I don't want to go in there. I don't want to know anything about the things.'

"Then one day [president] Alfred Sloan of General Motors and another GM executive came out to the plant to pay a visit to Mr. Ford. After a short chat, Mr. Ford led Sloan and his companion out into the plant and, to the everlasting confusion of every man in the Ford plant, calmly showed them the two engines. Why Mr. Ford did things like that I don't know. He just did them."

The V-8 evolved quickly enough once there was an oil pump, but there were still many details

to clean up. Since Henry Ford traditionally spent the months of February and March at his winter home in Richmond Hill, Georgia, much of the V-8's road testing took place on highways and roads between Dearborn and Georgia.

Larry Sheldrick, Ford's untitled chief engineer, remembered it this way in his *Reminisences*: "There again, a great deal of test work was done on trips between Dearborn and. . .Georgia. . . . Jerry Wolfe, Ray Dahlinger, and George Burns would usually make these trips. They would give us test reports, but not the kind. . .I'm accustomed to nowadays. Their reports amounted to *Damn Good* or *Damn Poor* and how much gasoline [the car] consumed. . .and how much oil. As far as getting any intelligible mileage figures at different speeds, we couldn't. . . .

Working inside Edison's old lab in Greenfield Village were not only Carl Schultz and Fred Thoms but eventually Ray Laird, Lew Walters,

Jimmy Smith, Bob Heine, and Emil Zoerlein. They set up an air dynamometer in the lab, plus some machine tools. Fabrication of blocks, pistons, cranks, heads, and so forth still went on at the Rouge, though.

About the construction of the engine itself, Mr. Sheldrick said, "Mr. Ford placed some controlling factors on the design of the ignition system. It had to be driven off the front of the camshaft. The coil must be a unit with the distributor. Again, the distributor could not be rotated, which was the same limitation put on the Model A. The breaker plate itself was rotated, not the body. The ignition system on the front of the engine was a bad one. It cost the public untold millions in maintenance."

Emil Zoerlein, the man who actually designed the Ford V-8's ignition system, said in his *Reminiscences*, "Mr. Ford wanted high-tension wires from the distributor to the spark plugs all molded in plastics, with just the ends of the spark plugs attached. As a matter of fact, he just wanted the terminals coming out of the side of the molded harness and then use spring clips. . . . We tried that and had some of these molded. Of course, they would break down dielectrically. The current would jump from one conductor to the other [and] cause misfiring. At that time, there just weren't any high dielectric materials. . . . There was an awful lot of time and energy and cost went into that. It was finally decided that it wouldn't work, and we would use Bakelite tubes. We would put regular ignition wires and threaded them through these tubes. That was better.

"The first engine was run over at the Ft. Myers [Edison] lab. . . . After the first one ran, Mr. Ford decided to build up an old garage in back of the Ft. Myers laboratory and test it in there. We installed engines in revamped Model A's and took them out on the road and drove them. [The engine] didn't develop as much power then as it does now. Later on, in June of 1931, it was decided to send an engine over here and I would mount it on the dynamometer. Sorensen was in it by that time. He came in at the time the cylinder blocks were supposed to be cast down at the Rouge—the

Confusion still reigns over 1932 Ford designations. V-8s are called Model 18s, while Model B applies only to 4s. New top snaps snugly to fixed window frames but produces big blind spots.

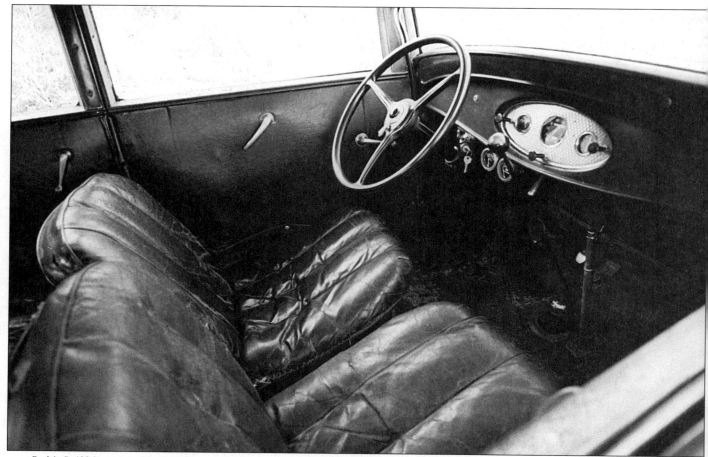

Rudy's B-400 has original leather, carpets, and rugs. Damascened instrument board borrows from Lincoln. Oil and temp gauges are recent additions.

MARC MADOW PHOTOS

mono-piece cylinder blocks. He and Herman Reinhold did an awful lot to accomplish the casting of the mono-piece cylinder blocks.

"The engine ran rough in 1931. It was a combination of carburetion, manifolding, and timing—valve timing particularly, and ignition timing, too. In the design of a new engine, you have to have, first, a manually adjusted distributor to adjust the spark advance. . . . From that you calibrate an automatic curve. . . . Schultz did some work on the camshaft, the valve timing, and Detroit Lubricator came into it then to do work on the carburetor. They changed the mixture ratio on it. That was a single [-barrel] carburetor for eight cylinders. The manifold at that time was not the type that we have now [the over-and-under, 2-plane type]. We tried various camshafts and carburetor adjustments, and we finally smoothed the engine out. As I recall, the first reading we got was 65 bhp maximum."

Rumors about the V-8 went ricocheting. Henry Ford mass-produced the final American Model A on November 1, 1931, but didn't finish shipping A's until April 1, 1932. The B had been designed in early 1932, but supplier orders were cancelled when some 50,000 of them were already "in float." ". . . his old smile didn't come back," quoted *Detroit News* reporter James Sweinhart of Mr. Ford. "Instead, somehow, he was getting madder and madder."

Mr. Ford made up his mind definitely on December 7, 1931, to produce the V-8. Before

Top folds relatively flat, leaves clear rear vision. Ash trays and armrests are pleasant touches.

hat, everything had been chaos—no one had been sure. Henry Ford spent only an hour in private consultation that day with Edsel, and when their meeting ended, the V-8 was set. It had, by that time, been developed to the point of very satisfactory running (in prototypes).

On December 19, the respected magazine *Automotive Industries* headlined a speculative article: "Make an Eight, Says Ford." This piece observed that the Ford Motor Co. had to be tooling for a new engine, most likely a V-8, and that the V-8 would go into an intermediate-sized car, probably on a 117-inch wheelbase.

Henry Ford let such rumors generate themselves, and by keeping his lips sealed, public curiosity built up of its own accord. Simple silence led several newspapers to call Mr. Ford a master of publicity—a *manipulator* of publicity. But Ford manipulated very little.

Prof. David L. Lewis, a Ford historian, writes, "Press and amateur photographers armed with cameras and telephoto lenses stalked Dearborn, and *Automotive Daily News* scored a beat after buying and publishing a shot of an authenticated V-8. Detroit's Hollywood Theater obtained 40 feet of movie film from a cameraman who had spent weeks in the brush alongside roads on which the new car was tested. Informed of the film, excited newsreel companies offered to 'pay handsomely' for it. The Ford Company hastily announced that it would 'match the top offer.' The theater surrendered the film to the company in exchange for a coveted opportunity to exhibit a V-8 in its lobby on the day of its first public showing."

On February 10, 1932, Mr. Ford granted a favored reporter, James Sweinhart of the *Detroit News*, an exclusive interview. Sweinhart's words were picked up by almost every paper in the country. Mr. Ford was perfectly candid—he told Sweinhart that the V-8 and the 4 would be interchangeable within the same body and chassis. This allayed the rumors that the 4 might be dropped.

"How certain are you that you have a market for your new cars?" asked Sweinhart.

"We're not certain," Ford replied. "But we're going to risk it. Someone has to risk something to get things started. And, you know, faith is catching; if we have confidence, others will, too. . . ." At the time of this interview, though, Henry Ford couldn't have been certain that a one-piece V-8 block could be mass produced for a low-priced car. He actually put himself out on a very long limb.

Everything was set, then, except the means for mass-producing the V-8 quickly and inexpensively. Henry Ford wasn't worried, and Larry Sheldrick tells us, "Sorensen, with his magic in the pattern shops and foundries, assured us it could be done, and it was done." The trick now, as Fred Thoms pointed out earlier, was to "put an 8 in a $550 car."

The first American production V-8 with a one-piece block came out in 1929 (see 1929 Olds Viking V-8 driveReport, *SIA* #10). In 1930, Oakland/Pontiac brought out another monobloc V-8. Both these cars, though, carried much higher price tags than Fords.

Charles E. (Cast-Iron Charlie) Sorensen was Ford's production boss and perhaps the second

Front seat folds forward as a unit. Capacious rear boasts plenty of leg room, small drive hump.

most powerful man in the organization. He had joined Ford in 1905 as a patternmaker, but he soon showed a genius for mass-production techniques. It was Sorensen who came up with a lot of the conveyors, assembly lines, and sub-assemblies that made the Model T so inexpensive. Sorensen had kept out of the V-8's early development, but now it was up to him and a few other men to make it a producible proposition.

Says Sorensen in his book *My Forty Years With Ford* (W.W. Norton, 1956), "The first major problem was a unit casting. All previous V-8s had been cast in more than one piece [this isn't so, as we've seen]. What we proposed to do was to cast whole a V-8 in a single, solid, rigid block.

We studied every move in the molding operation and mechanized its handling. The sand for each mold was shot into flasks from overhead chutes. Pattern and mold were then vibrated with a raise-and-drop movement which packed the prepared sand. This did away with all the sand handling by shovel, and heavy pounding of the sand by hand was eliminated."

Sorensen makes it sound so easy. William F. (Bill) Pioch, head of production engineering, recounts in his *Reminiscences* some of the headaches. "We set up the foundry to make the V-8 castings. . .the same as we had been doing on the 4-cylinder job. The result was that our scrap was about 50% [normal is 2%]. The main reason for that was that we'd get core shifts. The V-8 engine. . .had the exhaust [ports] going through the waterjacket of the cylinder block. These cores would shift and, of course, you would get scrap castings.

"This was the problem: The exhaust cores were loose cores, and the production men would just lay them in the mold, and the cores would shift on them. They would have to put them in there and judge proper placement with their eyes only. Well, that was no good because you get all kinds of people working down there. One good man would get you a good casting, but if your

man would be just a little bit careless in placing these cores, you would get a scrap casting.

"So we designed a fixture to place these cores and paste them and get them permanently set. That way you could just take anybody. . .and he couldn't go wrong, because he had to put these pieces exactly where they were supposed to be. It eliminated all that scrap and problem of repairs. From then on we didn't have any more trouble.

"When we went to the V-8 engine, it was a different type engine, and from our past experience we really went into high-production machinery, like for instance boring the block. We bored all the eight bores at one time. In fact, our machining time on the block wasn't much more than it was on the 4-cylinder engine. We had a lot more machining, but it didn't take much more time in labor."

Sorensen had arranged a pilot production line long before he had to. To quote Larry Sheldrick, "It was really an experimental production setup which Sorensen had arranged and set up. He must have foreseen what was coming, because he was pretty well ready. He actually had a pilot line ready before the announcement came on production. Between January and March, this thing was whipped into shape."

The Ford organization had learned a lot from the mistakes of switching from the Model T to the Model A. They might also have learned from Chevrolet's experience of putting the 6 into production. Unlike the A, which shut Ford down for seven months, the Chevy 6 cost only 45 days of downtime. Ironically it was ex-Ford-man William S. (Bill) Knudsen who rode herd on the Chevy 6 conversion.

But it wasn't too long before Ford's block-casting losses were down to 2%—with considerable hand welding on some of the more rescuable. "We produced the finished, machined block for less per pound," recalled Sorensen in his book, "than our previous (4-cylinder) cost."

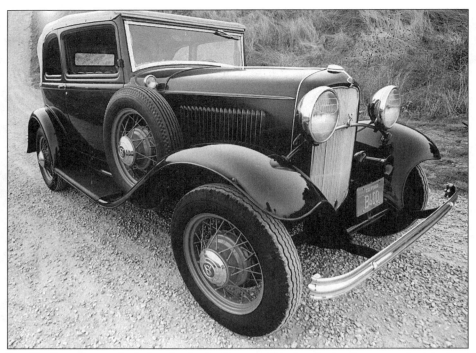

Beguiling Deuce has remained a heartbreaker for 42 years, still looks as fresh and young as when introduced in March 1932. Values are now sky high.

Amazingly little is known about the 1932 Ford's body styling. Edsel Ford and Joe Galamb oversaw the design from the factory's point of view, but it's been said that the Deuce's actual body and grille shape came from Briggs Mfg. Co., Ford's principal body supplier. The grille shape, word has it, had first been intended for the Plymouth. Others view the entire car as a scaled-down version of the 1932 Lincoln.

In most ways, the '32 Ford was simply an extension of the last Model A. Wheelbase was lengthened from 103.5 inches to 106, and the frame's central crossmember was gusseted. Brake drums grew an inch in diameter, and the gas tank left its complicated cavern in the cowl and now stood at the rear. The A's 2-bar bumpers gave way to the less expensive fluted design, and Ford was among the few major automakers who sidestepped hood doors. Voguish as they were, they cost money.

Inside, the 1932 Ford borrowed the Lincoln's instrument panel design, damascening and all. This oval cluster was centered in the dashboard so it could adapt to either left- or right-hand steering.

By March 5, three weeks before its introduction, Ford had received 75,000 firm orders for V-8-engined cars, all sight unseen. Another 100,000 orders arrived within a few days of the car's debut on March 31. Over 5.5 million people jammed Ford showrooms that day to see the car.

But the trials and tribulations of developing the V-8 weren't over yet. Buyers were snapping up Model I8s (V-8s) as quickly as they came down the line, but the first cars were still full of bugs.

"Edsel Ford was very much for this V-8," explains Larry Sheldrick in his *Reminiscences*, "but I think he was very fearful at the suddenness with which it was done—fearful of the lack of background, lack of experimentation and tests on it. He was fearful that we would have trouble, and we did have trouble.

"We were using the public as our testing crew.

The ignition system was a troublesome thing. We had coil breakdowns. The people in the field didn't know how to service this ignition. It required an entirely different routine in processing and adjusting. . .than any other distributor that was ever seen before. You couldn't just walk up to the car and take off the distributor cap to adjust the breaker points. You had to take the entire distributor off; unbolt it from the front of the engine and put it on a test setup. . .or give the man a replacement distributor to put on. In other words, you couldn't adjust it in a few minutes."

Clem Davis, a Ford tool- and die-maker, recalls in his *Reminiscences*: "When the V-8 came out, they had trouble with motors using oil. They came out with it in too much of a hurry. When they were using a quart of oil for 50 miles, you know what that meant. We were in piston difficulty there for quite a while. As soon as they would wear out a set of pistons, they would go back, and the dealer would replace the pistons. They would be good again for a little while, and then soon people would be in again. The company would reimburse the dealer for the labor and give them the pistons. . . . We gave away millions of pistons. . . . They had trouble with the pistons and also the bearings. The bearings just wouldn't hold up. They wouldn't take the pounding.

"They also had trouble with the cylinder blocks. They would crack very easily near the valve ports.

They fought that out, and they licked it, too."

Dale Roeder, head of truck engineering remembers that V-8s placed into trucks tended to overheat badly, so larger radiators were needed Roeder's *Reminiscences* also state, "There was tremendous amount of trouble on the early V-8 with condensation around the fuel pump. In winter, this condensation would freeze up the pump mechanism; then the engine couldn't be started Finally this objection to the condensation freezing and holding the diaphragm of the fuel pump in a fixed position. . .was overcome by baffling. . . and ventilation.

"There was quite a little trouble in the early V-8s on oil control. . .also cooling problems. The water pumps on the first V-8 engines were designed with the impeller at the top of the cylinder head instead of at the bottom. I think it wasn't until 1937 that the water pumps were located down in the cylinder block."

Back to Larry Sheldrick: "You simply cannot devise a firing order for a 90° V-8 with a 90° crankshaft with a single manifold that gives proper distribution to all cylinders. The manifold had to be broken up into two sections, half for each cylinder block feeding one stratum of the manifold. The #1 cylinder was always the orphan—the #1 cylinder on the right-hand bank.

"All sorts of firing orders were devised to try to overcome this without going to the extent of the over-and-under manifold. But that was the only cure then and it's the only cure today. All modern V-8s today are using the over-and-under manifold. . . . Dave Anderson of Bohn Aluminum Co. was very active with me on that job. Bohn Aluminum. . .was supplying pistons for the V-8 [plus] aluminum heads, distributor housings, and intake manifolds. So this man Anderson was a very accomplished engineer and he saw the need. . .and we worked together on it. We had to depend on suppliers for a great deal of our engineering. We would merely give the idea to the supplier and he would do the detail engineering for us. They were only too glad to do it. People like Kelsey Wheel, Budd Mfg. Co., Bohn Aluminum, and various carburetor companies the ignition companies, the brake companies Bendix was in the picture by that time."

The 1932 V-8 was only a start. It grew by quick steps, and by 1934 the Stromberg duplex carburetor, copper-lead bearing inserts, revamped pistons, and modified distributor made it a livable lovable engine. It would never be as inexpensive and trouble free as the Model A, which grossed much less in replacement parts and repairs than either the T or the V-8 (Ford grossed $10-12 million a month in T parts vs. $3-4 million per month for the A). But the V-8 won races and quickly became the favorite of bank robbers, bootleggers, and the public alike.

The British magazine *The Autocar* tested 1932 V-8 cabriolet that year in July, and they couldn't have been more enthusiastic. "For this innocent-looking vehicle, the new V eight-cylinder Ford, with its neat, trim lines and fairly short bonnet, conceals, as it were, a tremendous reserve of power. . . . The chassis is virtually that of the four-cylinder model. . . . It is the manoeuvrability of this Ford, coupled with really terrific acceleration, which makes it an exceptional car to handle. . . .

specifications

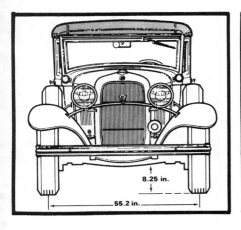

8.25 in.

55.2 in.

RUSS VON SAUERS, THE GRAPHIC AUTOMOBILE STUDIO

106.0 in.

1932 Ford V-8 Model 18 convertible sedan

Price when new	$650 f.o.b. Dearborn (1932).
Options	Dual sidemounts, trunk rack, leather upholstery, clock mirror, twin tail lamps.

ENGINE

Type	L-head V-8, cast-iron block, water-cooled, 3 mains, pressure and splash lubrication.
Bore & stroke	3.0625 x 3.750 in.
Displacement	221 cid.
Max. bhp @ rpm	65 @ 3400.
Max. torque @ rpm	130 @ 1250.
Compression ratio	5.5:1.
Induction system	1-bbl. downdraft carburetor, mechanical fuel pump.
Exhaust system	Cast-iron manifolds, crossover pipe, single muffler.
Electrical system	6-volt battery/coil.

CLUTCH

Type	Single dry plate, molded asbestos lining.
Diameter	9.0 in.
Actuation	Mechanical, foot pedal.

TRANSMISSION

Type	3-speed manual, floor lever, synchro 2-3, silent 2nd.
Ratios: 1st	2.82:1.
2nd	1.60:1.
3rd	1.00:1.
Reverse	3.38:1.

DIFFERENTIAL

Type	Torque-tube drive, spiral bevel gears.
Ratio	4.11:1.
Drive axles	¾-floating.

STEERING

Type	Semi-reversible worm & sector.
Turns lock to lock	3.1.
Ratio	13:1.
Turn circle	39.0 ft.

BRAKES

Type	4-wheel mechanical drums, rod activated.
Drum diameter	12.0 in.
Total lining area	186.0 sq. in.

CHASSIS & BODY

Frame	U-section steel, ladder type, 5 crossmembers.
Body construction	Composite wood & steel.
Body style	2-dr. 5-pass. convertible sedan.

SUSPENSION

Front	I-beam axle, transverse semi-elliptic leaf spring, hydraulic lever shock absorbers, wishbone radius rods.
Rear	Solid axle, transverse semi-elliptic leaf spring hydraulic lever shock absorbers, wishbone radius rods.

Tires	5.25 x 18 tube type.
Wheels	Welded spokes, drop-center rim, lug-bolted to brake drum.

WEIGHTS & MEASURES

Wheelbase	106.0 in.
Overall length	165.5 in.
Overall height	68.625 in.
Overall width	67.0 in.
Front tread	55.2 in.
Rear tread	56.7 in.
Ground clearance	8.25 in.
Shipping weight	2480 lb.

CAPACITIES

Crankcase	4 qt.
Cooling system	22 qt.
Fuel tank	14 gal.

FUEL CONSUMPTION

Best	22 mpg.
Average	18 mpg.

PERFORMANCE (from The Autocar, 7/8/32):

10-30 mph	4.6 sec.
20-40 mph	5.6 sec.
30-50 mph	8.8 sec.
Average top speed	78.26 mph.

I have always felt that Ford underrated horsepower. Even the 65-bhp V-8 feels stronger than it should. Its reputation for power soon became the Model I8's greatest selling point, and Ford outsold all competing makes between March and December 1932—one million V-8s by year's end.

"From the very commencement," continued *The Autocar*, "the driver is conscious of the unusual ratio of power to weight. . . . The gear ratios are high, yet the car can be started on second gear. . .or even on top [high] as an illustration of the smoothness of the pickup. There is a synchronising mechanism which eliminates the necessity for double-clutching. . . . Apart from the indirect gears, the acceleration on top is extraordinarily good, and the figure from 10 to 30 mph on top gear has seldom been matched by any other make or type of car, irrespective of price.

"Furthermore, acceleration is devoid of hesitation, the car veritably shooting forward the instant the throttle is depressed, [and] not accompanied by vibration. . . . Though the engine is not entirely silent, it is smooth, and there is little above an insistent drone when accelerating hard. . .known as power roar, which is not unpleasant. It is a car which gets along at a remarkably high speed without suggestion of effort. . . . A steady speed of 60 does not cause stress, and even 65 or 70 can be maintained should conditions permit.

"Anyone unacquainted with the car would not suspect that it had a transverse spring at front and rear. . . . In the past this arrangement usually permitted sideways roll on corners. The latest Ford. . .is a car which can be taken round curves fast with a feeling of safety, yet the springing is especially comfortable for the occupants."

The Autocar likewise found steering and braking light, and altogether its report became a total endorsement. The V-8, despite initial snags, was off to a good start, and it would soon become America's most popular engine, just as the Model T had been the country's most popular car. To many, both remain that today. ⌆

Sincere thanks to Henry E. Edmunds and his staff at the Ford Archives, Henry Ford Museum, Dearborn; Michael W.R. Davis, Technical and Product Information, and Ray Jackson of the Ford Motor Co., Dearborn; Prof David L. Lewis, Ann Arbor, Michigan; David L. Cole and members of the Ford V-8 Club of America, Box 2122, San Leandro. California 94577; Rudy Martinez, La Mirada. California; and John R. Bond, Newport Beach, California.

Two Look-Alikes

Ford & Citroen

The similarity seems to be more than purely coincidental.

by Michael Lamm, *Editor*

I've ALWAYS FELT that they look too much alike to be pure coincidence. It's not just their grilles and the fact that the 1934 Citroen reminds me of a channeled 1933-34 Ford. The similarities carry through to the smaller details: hood latches, door handles, and windshield outlines.

The bumpers, too, on some of the first front-wheel-drive Citroens have that same Ford dip in them. And the angles of windshield pillars, of door openings, hood louvers, and even the flow of the front fenders—I see more than a coincidental resemblance.

The idea, then, for this dual driveReport began when I asked myself, "Is there any real connec-

tion between the styling of the 1933-34 Ford and the 1934-57 Citroen? Was it something somebody planned?"

Andre Citroen called himself the Henry Ford of France. He enjoyed that epithet and even bragged about it. The newspapers and magazines picked it up and repeated it like a title after Citroen's name. Citroen admired Henry Ford greatly, and although you'd be hard put to find two more different men, they knew each other fairly well. Andre Citroen visited Henry Ford in Dearborn at least three times—in 1912, 1923, and 1931. It's Citroen's 1931 trip to this country that's significant here.

Henry Edmunds, director of the Ford Archives, writes: "In 1931, Citroen returned to Am-

erica to renew his friendship with Ford and to meet President Hoover. Again he was seeking ideas applicable to his own situation. He proclaimed himself an enthusiastic admirer of American business and Ford methods and called himself Henry Ford's disciple. In the Henry Ford Room there is a photograph inscribed by Citroen as follows: 'To Mr. Henry Ford, the builder of the World's Automobile Industry. —His French Admirer and Disciple, Andre Citroen, December 1931.'"

What struck me was the part about Citroen meeting with President Hoover. If Citroen went to Washington, he most likely stopped off in Philadelphia, too. Why Philly? Because that's the home of The Budd Co., and Citroen had, since 1925, built his auto bodies under Budd

1931 Budd/Ledwinka prototype used aluminum V-8, fwd, had Ford-like grille shape (not visible here). Andre Citroen saw car when he visited Budd in 1931, and it might well have inspired 1934 fwd Citroen.

British Ford Model Y debuted in Mar.-Apr. 1932, presaged lines of 1933 U.S. Ford. Citroen could easily have pirated general shape and details from this car, which would account for many styling similarities.

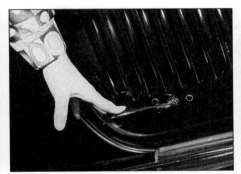

Can you tell which hood release belongs to 1934 Ford and which to 1937 Citroen? They work just alike. Attachments and louvers also show similarities. If you said Ford is left, you're right.

Citroen openly admired Ford, called himself the Ford of France. 1931 marked their last meeting.

license. More important, I had heard from various sources that the fwd 1934 Citroen's body structure was largely conceived in Budd's Philadelphia engineering shops.

To find out whether Citroen did indeed stop off at the Budd plant on his 1931 trip, I first phoned Joe Kelly in Budd's Detroit office. I knew Joe from previous articles, and he put me in touch with Al Maul, an engineer at Budd in Philadelphia.

Al confirmed that Budd did have quite a bit to do with developing—or at least tooling for—the fwd Citroen's sheet metal. He said that some of the research and development was done by Joseph Ledwinka, Budd's experimental engineering genius (and he *was* a genius; I'm not just using that word). Led, as they called him, together with William J. Muller, had, in 1930-31, created a small, fwd one-off sedan. Among this car's features were an aluminum V-8, front drive, and a frameless unitized body. One point to remember, too: its grille shell happened to look almost exactly like the 1933 Ford's.

It was common practice at Budd back then to build experimental one-offs like this to try to sell their ideas to prospective customers. Citroen had expressed interest in fwd and unitized bodies to Bill Muller when Muller visited him in Paris in 1928. (I learned this later when talking to Muller, who now lives in New Orleans. Citroen, by the way, spoke excellent English.)

Anyway, it now seemed even more likely that Andre Citroen would have stopped by Budd to look at this fwd one-off. Al Maul didn't know, so he put me in touch with Russell Leidy, Budd's former production manager. Mr. Leidy retired in

1957, and I found out that Joseph Ledwinka had been his stepfather.

I phoned Mr. Leidy at his home in Glenside, Pennsylvania, and he told me, yes, he remembers the fwd Citroen body tooling job, although not in great detail. While I had him on the phone, I thought he might be able to tell me about the time element involved in tooling for the Citroen, because that would have a bearing on the question of Citroen's copying Ford's styling. "Who styled the Citroen?" I asked Mr. Leidy.

"The French did the styling and the interior," he told me.

I then asked him, "If the French were responsible for the looks of this car, how late could they have waited to firm up the shape of, say, the grille shell? In other words, how long in all would it have taken Budd to make all the sheet-metal tooling for the 1934 Citroen body?"

"Right from scratch?" asked Mr. Leidy. "Tooling, from the time you get your preliminary engineering drawings until you get okayed stampings—I'd say 5-6 months. Tools alone can be built in about four months, but I'm talking about design and tryouts. You take some of the larger stampings like quarter panels, back panels, or a roof—you have those on a press at least 3-4 weeks getting all the kinks out."

"In other words," I said, "you could have shipped finished tooling over to France six months after you got the drawings?" Mr. Leidy said yes.

When I asked him whether he remembered Andre Citroen visiting Budd in 1931, he wasn't sure, but he put me in touch with George Trautvetter, Budd's chief draftsman at that time. I then

phoned Mr. Trautvetter in Jenkintown, Pennsylvania.

Mr. Trautvetter remembered the visit quite vividly, because Andre Citroen was handing out watches to Budd employees, and Mr. Trautvetter got one of them. "Mr. Citroen was broke," Mr. Trautvetter told me, "as he so often was, but he passed out watches. I remember his motorcade coming up Broad St. with a police escort. Mr. Citroen felt he needed a shave, so he stopped the motorcade and went into a barbershop and had a shave. Then he came on into the plant and spent several hours there."

I asked whether Mr. Trautvetter thought Citroen saw the Ledwinka prototype at that time, and Mr. Trautvetter said he probably did, but it's true, too, that there was a constant stream of Citroen engineers and management people coming and going through the Budd plants and offices. There was apparently very close liaison.

Knowing that E. T. (Bob) Gregorie had been responsible for styling the 1933 Ford, I next telephoned him in Daytona Beach. Bob told me that the American '33 Ford's styling had actually come by *scaling up* the design of the 1932 British and German Model Y Fords. Bob's first assignment at Dearborn under Edsel Ford had been to design the 1932 European Fords. These had the slightly heart-shaped, V'd grille shells, the suicide doors, and in every way looked like the 1933 U.S. Ford V-8. Edsel and Henry Ford liked the lines so well that they had them scaled up for the American Model 40 (1933 V-8). Bob Gregorie later went on to become Ford's director of design in 1935, a position he held until 1946. I asked Bob *when* he had designed the Dagenham and

Cologne Fords, and he said around mid-1931. I then asked him whether he'd ever seen the 1931 Ledwinka/Budd fwd prototype, and he said no, not that he recalled.

Michael Sedgwick, the British auto historian, meanwhile sent me a letter telling when the Dagenham Ford made its first appearance:

"The original Ford Model Y prototype was exhibited at Ford's London showrooms in Regent Street, London, in March or April 1932. I remember as a very small boy being taken by my father to see it. A revised grille and fender skirts were incorporated around June 1933. Citroen engineers could certainly have seen the finalised Ford shape by June or July 1932, and if they'd waited another month they could have seen it in every Ford dealership's showroom the length and breadth of the United Kingdom."

Dates and facts, then, were beginning to match up. If Andre Citroen had first seen the Ledwinka/Budd one-off, with its Ford-like grille, in December 1931 and then had seen the Dagenham/Cologne Ford itself in May 1932, it would surely not have been too late to incorporate details or general shapes into Citroen's *traction avant* (fwd to you), which made its first public appearance on March 3, 1934.

Mr. Leidy says that tooling would take 5-6 months. Giving another six months for shipping tools and dies across the Atlantic (a generous allowance) plus another half year setup time in Paris (generous again), that brings us back to about August 1932. This certainly gives Citroen plenty of time to copy any styling features he wanted from the European Fords.

The Citroen factory in Paris says flatly that the *traction avant* was conceived by Andre Citroen himself and actually engineered by two men: Maurice Sainturat and Andre Lefevre. I believe, though, that it involved the combined efforts of

Citroen and Budd working together so closely that total responsibility was mutual.

Now there's still considerable doubt in my mind as to whether Citroen actually did copy Ford styling. Perhaps not the entirely, but the little details, yes. The grille shape, yes, and the door handles, hood latches, bumpers, fender line, door shapes, windshield shape—things like that, yes. And why not? Ford was the world's most successful car at that time. Andre Citroen admired Henry Ford and envied his success.

As for the louvers, again yes, I'd say Citroen copied Ford, although the first 1934 Citroen 7CV used big doors in the hood instead of louvers. It wasn't until late 1935, with the 11CV's introduction, that Citroen adapted the narrow Ford-like louvers.

If imitation is the sincerest form of flattery, Andre Citroen's "ideal car" seems to be one of the ways he tried to flatter Henry Ford.

As I mentioned, you'd be hard put to find two more different men. Andre Gustave Citroen was short, bald, dapper, wore spats, a neatly trimmed mustache, and pince-nez glasses. Henry Ford was lanky, angular, loose-jointed, slightly weathered, and didn't care what he wore.

During his first visit to Dearborn in 1912, Citroen was chief engineer for Mors. He studied Ford's ways of building Model T's. Then the next year he applied The Method to the mass production of herringbone gears (from which came the chevron emblem on the Citroen's grille). During WW-I, Citroen's big coup was the mass production of shell casings.

Right after the war, in 1919, Citroen plunged into automaking. His avowed purpose was to build a "French Model T," a car for the masses. It looked more like the Chevrolet 490, but the

Citroen Type A sold for half the price of an other French car of that time, and Citroen's fir big problem became trying to keep supply u with demand.

Citroen lived his entire life on credit, and h was usually broke—just the opposite of For who insisted on paying cash for everything ar had millions in cash on hand. So right awa Citroen found himself in trouble with the bank Even as his first Type A's came rolling out of h Quai de Javel plant in Paris, he shot off telegram to Cast Iron Charlie Sorensen, Ford powerful production boss, saying, "Willing accept any financial cooperation with For either partnership or sleeping partner, or form tion of limited company. Shall be absolute mast of the French market and can also make very b exportations. The requirements of business a $10 million." Henry Ford liked Citroen, but n that much, so he had Sorensen wire back, "Im possible to secure Mr. Ford's aid in financir your company."

Citroen bailed himself out of that crisis ar managed to lead the banks a merry chase for years, enjoying every minute. He might hav been perpetually broke, but you'd never suspect to watch him. He lived high, both personally ar professionally, gambling in a big way during h younger years and also living the life of a pla boy socialite. He once broke the bank at Mon Carlo, and reports have it that one night he wc $700,000 at Deauville, soon afterward losir $400,000 of it again at the flip of a single car These shenanigans didn't leave him exact revered by his creditors. Citroen rented (but nev bought) a string of expensive chateaux, villa townhouses, and mansions.

Henry Ford, of course, wouldn't dream gambling. He could care less for high societ parties, fancy villas, and luxurious living. For enjoyed keeping his name before the press ar public, but Citroen absolutely loved notoriet He created it when it didn't flow his way natu rally. His name blazed in lights for years fro the top of the Eiffel Tower. CITROEN was th first word ever written in the Paris sky by sk writers. And he did all sorts of clever things keep his name before the French public.

Anthony Rhodes, in his book about Lou Renault, writes, "Another publicity device em ployed by Citroen was the use of his scrap she metal [from his stamping presses] for small to models of his cars. There was no question profit here, only of publicity. Models costing francs were sold for 20. In every family, the fir three words a child must learn were 'Pap Maman, and Citroen.'"

There's no doubt that both Citroen and For made extraordinarily good cars. The Model T legendary durability was certainly matched the early Citroen's. It seems that one of the fir Type A's to come off the line was driven 180,00 miles before it needed overhauling. When And Citroen heard of that, he made very sure ever Frenchman did, too.

Citroen organized fantastic expeditions ar endurance runs. Many international long-di tance speed records set in 1933 by Citroens st stand today (see box, this page). Factory-spo sored Citroens also crossed equatorial Afric trekked through the depths of Asia and Chin slogged up the Amazon, slipped and slithere

CITROEN'S ENDURANCE RUNS

By 1940, Citroen held 260 official World and International speed records, most of them of the endurance variety. Rear-drive Citroens—the Rosalie series—had racked up stupendous long-distance speed records between March and August 1933. Some of the 1933 Citroen records still stand today.

These pre-fwd Citroens ran flawlessly around the Montlhery track for half a year straight. The idea at first had been to go up to 150,000 miles, but the Yacco Oil-sponsored Citroens performed so beautifully that the distance was doubled. Before the runs ended, one of these cars, the Petite Rosalie. had covered 300,000 trouble-free miles of continuous running at an average speed of 58.08 mph.

When the first fwd Citroen appeared on March 3, 1934, Andre Citroen met with Francois Lecot, a veteran driver (then aged 56) and suggested he test the new model's endurance by driving it every day for a year on public roads at a rate of 1,100 km per day—a total of 400,000 km (just under 250,000 miles). Lecot agreed.

Lecot's home stood near Rochetaillee, halfway between Paris and Monte Carlo, which let him make a 2-way run to either city on successive days, yet return home each night. His car was a stock 11CV, modified only by adding an accelerator pedal for the left foot and setting the windshield upright for less chance of interior fogging.

The runs were monitored by the Automobile Club of France, and Lecot set off on July 22, 1935, at 3:30 a.m. The ACF representative went along and remained with him until the end of the run.

Lecot averaged four hours sleep a night. He kept fit by exercise and massage. But he could sleep anywhere, and a 10-minute nap sufficed to start him off again refreshed. He would eat a sandwich at noon while driving, then stop for a longer meal around 9:00 p.m.

In January 1936 he caught up with the Monte Carlo Rally, which started from Portugal. Figuring he had to be behind the wheel anyway, he thought he might as wall take part, but he didn't finish well. Then on June 7, he took off on a tour of European capitals.

Lecot's run ended the evening of July 24, 1936, at Monte Carlo, and the press heralded it as an unprecedented feat for both car and driver. Andre Citroen had died in the meantime, but Lecot lived until 1959.

1934 Ford rear passengers sit atop frame, over rear axle. This makes body tall, ride jouncy.

In Citroen's unit body, floor is well below the door-sills, and passengers sit ahead of rear axle.

Citroen's built-in trunk would be small if lid weren't ballooned. Sill stands comfortably low.

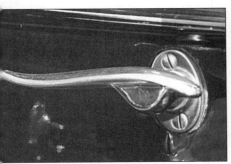

Again, care to guess which door handle opens the Ford and whicih opens Citroen? Both doors, of course, open from the front. Door shapes are amazingly similar. Ford handle is at left.

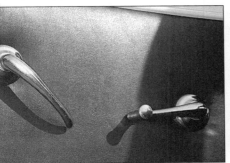

Even interior hardware shows uncanny similarity. Mrs. Rossigneux's Citroen is reupholstered in leather, but some models were originally done in Bedford cord, much like cloth used by Ford.

June Falk must lift suitcase high to get it into her Ford's accessory (Potter Mfg. Co.) trunk.

S.A. ANDRE CITROEN

With torsion bars, fwd, and independent front suspension, Citroen corners like a sports car.

Ford's transverse springs compensate for irregular road surface here, give stable cornering.

Lecot (left—see box, opposite page) drove '34 traction avant nearly 250,000 miles in a year.

Direct comparison shows front-end likenesses. Earlier Citroens had more Fordish bumper, with dip in the center. Citroen was extremely low for its day. Some models had plated grilles.

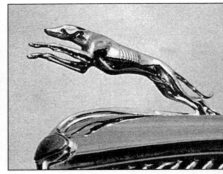

Greyhound graced early '30s Ford and Lincoln and this one is one of the originals, not a replica.

Gearshift pokes out of Citroen's dashboard, and gear change takes getting used to. Suspended pedals, pull-handle emergency brake at center, dash-mounted mirror are 20 years ahead of time.

Phoenix decorates trans hole, Chevron emblem symbolizes Citroen's use of herringbone gears.

Ford also groups gauges in front of driver, uses twist handle to open windshield. Both cars have flat floors, 2-passenger capacity up front. Ironically, Ford uses suspended accelerator pedal.

across the Alaskan tundra, and percolated around the perimeter of Australia.

Another way Andre Citroen kept his name before the public was to put up thousands of roadsigns and plaques all over France—name markers for towns and villages, churches, landmarks, museums, etc.—all free, but all with the discreet/bold legend, "Gift of Citroen."

Citroen, like Ford, believed in one model, the least expensive possible, pricing it low and keeping quantity and quality high. His cars gave Citroen his reputation, not his flamboyant ways, although those probably did help sell cars.

Ironically, the *traction avant* helped kill Andre Citroen. So did his gambling, his mounting debts, the Depression generally, and a nagging duodenal ulcer. The huge cost of developing and tooling for a car so totally different from anything before it—this coming at the worst possible economic time—greatly speeded Citroen's death.

Andre Citroen had lived most of his life on other people's money. The Depression made his creditors demand payment. At the same time, the

Michelin family, a very tidy and tough group of Auvergne peasants, made a deal with Andre Citroen that he could buy tires from them at a 10% discount if he could sell more than 80,000 cars a year. Citroen, forever the gambler and optimist, knew he could, but for several years during the Depression he barely managed to sell 70,000 a year. Michelin billed him at the full amount, but Citroen couldn't or didn't pay, perhaps figuring he'd wait until he got his discount and would then pay the whole amount.

The Michelins waited patiently as Citroen went deeper into the hole. Finally, on December 21, 1934, after piling up the staggering debts of tooling and setting up his plants to manufacture the first *traction avant*, Citroen went into receivership. Meanwhile, his ulcer had been greatly aggravated by these worries, and the ultimate blow came when his doctors found he had cancer. In his last months, Citroen wasted down from his normal 140 pounds to 70.

On July 3, 1935, the day of his death, the *New York Times* wrote, "Citroen, 'Ford of France,'

Dies of Grief Over Crash. Famed Automobile Magnate Once Had Been Leading Manufacturer of Europe." The obituary said in part: "Citroen biggest employer of labor in France and outstanding automobile manufacturer of Europe admitted openly that he copied Ford methods of production. He adopted American ideas of standardization of parts and chain methods of assembling, using American patents, machinery, and designs." Citroen was 57 at his death.

The French government immediately asked Michelin to take over running the Citroen works, and of course they did and have ever since.

Surely Citroen didn't copy Ford's engineering with the *traction avant*. Imagine, if you can, a 1934 Ford with front-wheel drive, hydraulic brakes, a frameless unitized body, stepdown floor, independent front suspension, and torsion bar springing at all four wheels. Inconceivable, right? Yet those are only some of the specifications for the 1934 Citroen.

Andre Citroen's hope, like Henry Ford's, was to build the "ideal car." Sounds good, but remember that the surest, quickest way for a carmaker to go out of business is to bring out something radically different. Ford took that chance with the V-8 of 1932, although the rest of his car was engineered very conservatively. Not everyone went along with the V-8. The vogue was to Straight 8, and here was Ford with the first V-8 in the low price field. It took some getting used to.

If Ford took a chance with the V-8, imagine the chance Citroen was taking with a model his admen called "Two Years Ahead of Current Motor Car Construction." The *traction avant* remained popular and basically unchanged through 1957, so the "Two Years" slogan meant about much as saying "Brigitte Bardot is female." Frenchmen, being much more willing than

*raction avant Citroen offered stylish roadster that
esembled channeled 1934 Ford hot rod.*

*Ford V-8 leaves 4-cylinder Citroen at stop lights, has slightly higher top speed, but winding roads give
Citroen the advantage. Citroen became a consistent rally winner after World War II.*

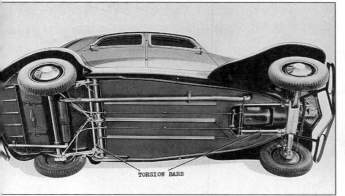

*mooth undercarriage of unitized Citroen body helps aerodynamics and low-
ess. Brake lines and wiring are protected by V-section conduits.*

*Citroen's "works in a drawer": power unit unbolted, slipped out for repairs. Unit
body was largely engineered, wholly tooled in Philadelphia.*

*Ford leapfrogged Chevrolet, bypassed 6, went from 4
o V-8—a radical departure for the day.*

*11CV's ohv 4 uses wet sleeves, sidedraft carb, lacks
brute power. Duct at side is for heater.*

*Citroen considered producing V-8 in 1934, built 100-
bhp prototypes using 2 4s joined together.*

*Citroen was one of few 1934 cars you could see over.
-window coupe accents long, low lines.*

*Citroen also offered 8-passenger limo on 129-in.
wheelbase. Same chassis led to station wagon.*

*Attempted Citroen V-8 (above) fit into this body. For
testing, factory used Ford V-8s.*

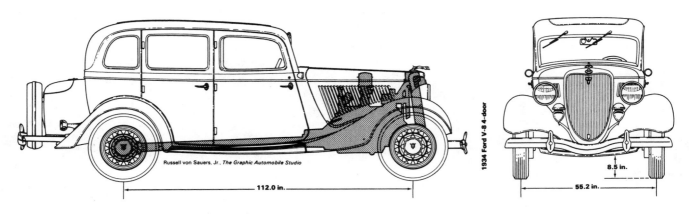

Russell von Sauers, Jr., *The Graphic Automobile Studio*

1934 Ford V-8 4-door

|← 112.0 in. →| |← 55.2 in. →| 8.5 in.

SPECIFICATIONS: 1934 Ford Deluxe 4-door sedan, Model 40 V-8

Price when new	$615 f.o.b. Dearborn (1934)	Ratios: 1st 2nd 3rd Reverse	2.820:1. 1.604:1. 1.000:1. 3.383:1.	Rear	Solid axle, semi-elliptic transverse spring, hydraulic lever shocks.
Current valuation*	Xlnt. $3,400; gd. $1,360			Tires	Tube-type 5.50 x 17, 4-ply, whitewalls.
Options	Clock, greyhound radiator ornament, Potter Mfg. Co. trunk, whitewalls.	**DIFFERENTIAL**		Wheels	Welded spoke, drop-center rims, lug-bolted to drums.
		Type	Spiral bevel gears, torque tube drive.		
		Ratio	4.11:1.	**WEIGHTS & MEASURES**	
ENGINE		Drive axles	3/4 floating.	Wheelbase	112.0 in.
Type	L-head V-8, water-cooled, cast-iron block, detachable aluminum heads, 3 mains, full pressure lubrication	**STEERING**		Overall length	182.9 in.
		Type	Worm & sector.	Overall height	68.0 in.
		Turns lock to lock	3.5.	Overall width	68.0 in.
Bore & stroke	3.0625 x 3.750 in.	Ratio	15:1.	Front tread	55.2 in.
Displacement	221.0 cid.	Turn circle	40.0 ft.	Rear tread	56.7 in.
Max. bhp@rpm	85 @ 3,800.			Ground clearance	8.5 in.
Max. torque @ rpm..	150 @ 2,200.	**BRAKES**		Curb weight	2,599 lb.
Compression ratio	6.3:1.	Type	4-wheel mechanical drums, internal expanding.		
Induction system	2-bbl. downdraft carb, mechanical fuel pump.			**CAPACITIES**	
		Drum diameter	12.0 in.	Crankcase	5.0 qt.
Exhaust system	Cast-iron manifolds, cross pipe, single muffler.	Total lining area	186.0 sq. in.	Cooling system	21.0 qt.
				Fuel tank	14.0 gal.
Electrical system	6-volt battery/coil.	**CHASSIS & BODY**			
		Frame	Channel-section steel, double dropped, central X-member.	**FUEL CONSUMPTION**	
CLUTCH				Best	23 mpg.
Type	Single dry plate, woven asbestos lining.			Average	16-19 mpg.
		Body construction	Wood and steel.		
Diameter	9.0 in.	Body style	4-dr., 5-pass. trunk sedan.	**PERFORMANCE** (from **The Autocar**, London. 7/6/34):	
Actuation	Mechanical, foot pedal.			0-50 mph	10.6 sec.
		SUSPENSION		0-60 mph	16.8 sec.
TRANSMISSION		Front	I-beam axle, semi-elliptic transverse spring, hydraulic lever shocks.	Top speed	81.82 mph.
Type	3-speed manual, floor lever, synchro 2-3.			*Courtesy **Antique Automobile Appraisal**.	

Americans to accept radical automotive innovations, took to the *traction avant* immediately. They particularly liked its low, rakish lines (it's a low car even by today's standards) and its excellent roadholding. Cops and robbers preferred it as a chase car, just as American cops and robbers preferred the early V-8 Ford, and you'll notice in old French movies on late-show TV that the good guys and the bad guys both always seem to be driving *traction avants*.

Like Ford, Citroen considered bringing out a V-8 for his 1934 model. No telling whether this engine was Ford-inspired, but it never got into production. It used two ohv 4-cylinder Citroen blocks joined to a common crankcase, hooked to a normal fwd setup. Called the 22CV, this engine delivered 100 bhp, and it's said that only six prototypes were built. For roadtesting, Citroen reportedly used stock Ford V-8s in place of the 22CV V-8, set backwards and driving a Citroen power train. The 22CV's body-work looked a good deal less Ford-like than production *traction avants*.

The first fwd Citroen was the 7CV (CV stands for horsepower, but the French rating system is quite unlike ours). Displacement was 1,302cc,

and at 32 bhp (U. S. rating), it was definitely a stone. Later in 1934, the 7CV went to 1,625cc and 36 bhp, and the first 11CV of 1935 displaced 1,911cc and rated 46 bhp.

The 11CV, our test car being a 1937 example, became Citroen's mainstay throughout the *traction avant*'s career. It came in three series and wheelbases: *Normale* ("normal" at 121.5 inches), *Legere* ("light," 114.5 inches), and the *Commerciale*, which, with jumpseats, became an 8-passenger limo. In 1953, the *Commerciale*'s rear sheet metal turned into a huge roof-hinged tailgate, making this series a station wagon. The *Commerciale*'s wheelbase was 129.0 inches. Body styles included a very handsome rumbleseat roadster and 3-window coupe, plus the 4-door sedan (with and without trunk) and limousine/wagon.

Citroen, under Michelin, made running improvements continuously—nothing dramatic, but the car had been dramatic enough to begin with. In late 1935, they added hydraulic shocks all around (fronts had been friction before), and in June 1936, Citroens got rack-&-pinion steering. For 1939, an optional 56-bhp 4 was added to the 11CV *Legere*. This had wet sleeves like the rest,

and like the rest also, the entire power unit coul be unbolted and rolled out from under the whee barrow horns of the unit body.

The first 6-cylinder *traction avant* bowed at th 1938 Paris salon, specifications being basicall the same as the 11CV, but this engine delivere 76 bhp. It had a downdraft carb instead of the 4' sidedraft Solex, a twin-plate clutch, plus shorte and thicker axleshafts. The 6 made low-spee steering so heavy that most women didn't dar drive the car.

From Michael Sedgwick's strange-but-tru files come these tidbits. "The 11CV engine wa used in a rear-drive model, the 11UA (1936-40 mounted back to front. This was a utility 7-pas senger sedan with the old Rosalie pre-fwd chas sis and mechanical brakes. Other automakers namely Chenard-Walcker and Licorne, also use 7CV and 11CV engines mounted back to front i conventional chassis, while Georges Irat an Rosengart used Citroen power units driving th right way around (fwd)."

This reminds me of all those flathead Ford V 8s used in experimental oddballs down throug the years, some fwd, some rear-engined, som

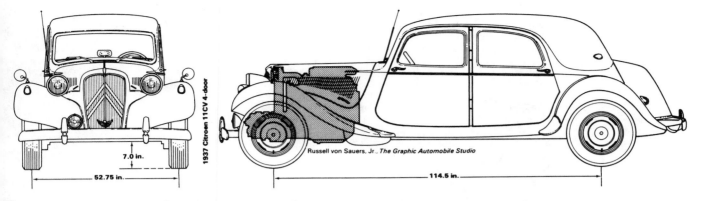

1937 Citroen 11CV 4-door

Russell von Sauers, Jr., *The Graphic Automobile Studio*

7.0 in.

52.75 in.

114.5 in.

SPECIFICATIONS: 1937 Citroen, Type 11CV, 4-door sedan

Price when new	Approx. $1,250 in France (1937)
Current valuation*	Xlnt. $2,160; gd. $670
Options	Radio, heater
ENGINE	
Type	In-line, ohv 4, water-cooled, removable wet sleeves, 3 mains, full pressure lubrication.
Bore & stroke	3.07 x 3.93 in.
Displacement	116.6 cid.
Max. bhp @ rpm	46 @ 3,800.
Max. torque @ rpm..	90.4 @ 2,200.
Compression ratio	5.9:1.
Induction system	Solex 1-bbl. sidedraft carb., mechanical fuel pump.
Exhaust system	Cast-iron manifold, single muffler.
Electrical system	6-volt battery/coil.
CLUTCH	
Type	Single dry plate, woven asbestos lining.
Diameter	N/A.
Actuation	Mechanical, foot pedal.
TRANSMISSION	
Type	3-speed manual, dashboard lever, synchro 2-3.
Ratios: 1st	3.05:1.
2nd	1.70:1.

3rd	1.00:1.
Reverse	N/A.
DIFFERENTIAL	
Type	Transaxle, beveled pinion & ring gear.
Ratio	5.00:1.
Drive axles	Independent, U-jointed at each end.
STEERING	
Type	Rack & pinion.
Turns lock to lock	2.25.
Ratio	12:1.
Turn circle	44.0 ft.
BRAKES	
Type	4-wheel drums, hydraulic; duo-servo.
Drum diameter	10.0 in.
Total swept area	N/A.
CHASSIS & BODY	
Frame	None
Body construction	Pressed steel, unit body/chassis.
Body style	4-dr., 5-pass. sedan.
SUSPENSION	
Front	Independent, longitudinal torsion bars, adjustable friction shock absorbers.
Rear	Tubular dead rear axle, transverse torsion bars,

	radius rods, hydraulic lever shock absorbers.
Tires	Michelin 5.50 x 16 tube type, 4-ply.
Wheels	Pressed steel, lug-bolted to brake drums.
WEIGHTS & MEASURES	
Wheelbase	114.5 in.
Overall length	168.0 in.
Overall height	59.5 in.
Overall width	63.75 in.
Front tread	52.75 in.
Rear tread	52.25 in.
Ground clearance	7.0 in.
Curb weight	2,350 lb.
CAPACITIES	
Crankcase	3.5 qt.
Cooling system	8.0 qt.
Fuel tank	13.0 gal.
FUEL CONSUMPTION	
Best	36.5 mpg.
Average	20.6 mpg.
PERFORMANCE (from **Road & Track**, Jan. 1953):	
0-30 mph	4.2 sec.
0-45 mph	13.5 sec.
0-60 mph	21.25 sec.
0-70 mph	39.0 sec.
Top speed	75.0 mph.

*Courtesy **Antique Automobile Appraisal**.

---

mid-engined. It seems the more popular a car becomes, the more its components are tapped for unusual mutants.

I realize I'm neglecting the V-8 Ford's history and development here, but I believe it's been so well chronicled that no one will greatly miss it.

Our two driveReport look-alikes happen to live very near each other in the town of Walnut Creek, California. The 1937 Citroen 11CV belongs to Mrs. Paul Rossigneux, who helps manage her son's Epicurean Shop in Lafayette, California; and the 1934 Ford's owner is Dick Falk, a professional restorer.

Mrs. Rossigneux has owned her Citroen for 15 years and also owns a 1964 Citroen DS convertible. "We've always had Citroens," she says, and she told me that during WW-II, the Nazis took an identical 11CV away from them. The Rossigneux family happened to be aboard an ocean liner when war broke out, and they just kept sailing for South America, not returning to France until well after the war. Paul Rossigneux was a vintner, which is what brought him to California.

Dick and June Falk bought their 1934 Ford

trunk sedan in August 1967. It was original and had 64,000 miles on it at the time (it has 82,000 now). Dick got it in pieces and had to put it back together, but it was (and is) original and mostly unrestored.

There's all the difference in the world driving these two cars. The Ford has a lot more snap and a bit higher top speed, but the Citroen will leave it on a winding road. As fantastically stable as the old arch-spring Ford is in cornering (and it's always amazed me now Henry Ford managed to sophisticate that primitive suspension system), the 11CV moves through turns with the agility and stick-to-it-ness of a true sports car. The *traction avant* had no business being family transportation. Family sedans of the 1930s—or even the '40s, '50s, and '60s—simply don't handle that well.

Citroen's rack-&-pinion steering takes only two turns lock to lock. It's quick but relatively heavy—heavier than the Ford's. And the Citroen's turning circle is unbelievably huge—it takes four full lanes to make a U-turn. Yet this car claws its way around corners at full throttle without the slightest lean or sway, and it's almost impossible to break away. Admittedly, the

engine's not very powerful, and actually the rest of the car is very well matched to its power; such items as gearing, drive mechanism, and brakes. Both cars stop about equally well despite the fact that the Ford's brakes are mechanical and the Citroen's hydraulic.

The fwd Citroen, except for a certain lack of oomph at low speeds, is completely modern in all engineering aspects even today. Not so, of course, the Ford. But then, as the French say, "Vive la différence!" ☙

Heartfelt thanks to SA Andre Citroen, Paris; The Budd Co., Automotive Div., Detroit and Philadelphia; Ford Archives, Henry Ford Museum, Dearborn, Michigan; Dick and June Falk and Mrs. Paul Rossigneux, Walnut Creek, California; William J. Muller, New Orleans; Russell Leidy, Glenside, Pennsylvania; George Trautvetter, Jenkintown, Pennsylvania; Harrah's Automobile Collection, an attraction of Harrah's Hotel/Casinos, Reno/Lake Tahoe; E. T. Gregorie, Daytona Beach; Michael Sedgwick, Midhurst, England; and Jean McDonnough, South Pasadena, California.

Competition was hot during the depressed market of 1934, and it was Chevrolet and Ford that dominated the scene. The two cars make an interesting comparison, for in a number of respects—size, price, and even in a general way, styling, they were very much alike. And yet, beneath their sheet metal there were, as we shall see, vast differences between the two.

Let's start by taking the wheel of each car and noting how they handle, perform and ride, comparing them back and forth as we go, and paying particular attention to special features that each car possesses. And let's start with Jack Day's Chevrolet, for Chevy outsold Ford that year (on a calendar year basis) by a margin of about ten percent.

The Chevrolet's starter is activated when the driver's foot comes down on the accelerator pedal; while the Ford's starter button is located on the floor, between the clutch and brake. The rationale behind the Chevy mechanism is obvious enough; but in the case of the Ford, the idea apparently is that when the clutch is depressed, the starter is within reach of the driver's left heel. Of course, this isn't much help to the lady driver, if she happens to be wearing high heels. But on the other hand, the Ford mechanism has proven, over the years, to be more fool-proof than the rather sophisticated Chevrole setup.

In this particular case, the Chevrole engine turns over slowly, almost relud tantly. This casts no reflection on th car; it's simply that this unit has bee driven no more than 300 miles since th engine was rebuilt, and it's very tigh The Ford's engine, on the other hand has been well broken-in, the car havin been driven well over 2,000 miles sinc the overhaul. This also puts the Chevy a something of a disadvantage vis-a-vi our comparisonReport Ford when comes to acceleration, obviously, bu then, the Chevy carries nearly 22 percer more weight per horsepower than th

Dominant Rivalries

Chevrolet or Ford:
Which was the better car of 1934?

by Arch Brown
photography by Bud Juneau

Ford; so in any case it could hardly be expected to keep pace, off-the-line, with its rival.

Clutch action is smooth in both cars, which is to be expected, since both clutches have recently been completely rebuilt. The Chevy may have a slight edge in this respect, but it also requires more pedal pressure than the Ford.

Gear changes are quick and easy on both cars. The Ford shifts with slightly greater precision than the Chevrolet, and synchronizers are marginally more effective. This, we suspect, has more to do with the condition of the gearbox than with its design, for every moving part in the Ford's gearbox has been replaced.

Steering the Chevy requires more muscle than the Ford. We found that surprising, since the Ford has the quicker ratio of the two. On the other hand, the Chevrolet turns in a much tighter circle than its competitor, a real convenience in many circumstances.

Both cars offer comfortable seats. Leg room is sufficient in front, even for the tall driver, and downright generous for rear seat passengers. Thanks to the cut of its front "suicide" doors, for those of us with big feet the Ford is easier to board. This is not to suggest that we prefer rear-hinged doors, which clearly pose a danger to the occupants.

With respect to riding qualities, it's simply no contest. The Chevrolet, thanks to its "Knee-Action" independent front suspension wins that one, hands down. Sound insulation is better, too. One of the major differences between Chevrolet and Ford in 1934 had to do with their bodies, with the Chevy retaining the traditional "composite" construction, comprised of steel over wood framing, while Ford had long since adopted all-steel construction. The wood framing is a mixed blessing, as many restorers have discovered, because over the years it tends to rot out. But there is little doubt that the Chevy's construction makes for a quieter ride. (Ultimately, of course, General Motors would follow Ford's and Chrysler's lead by adopting all-steel body construction, which had proved to be not only lighter, but also stronger and safer in the event of a serious accident.)

Both cars are fitted with internal mechanical brakes. Not until 1936 would Chevrolet go to hydraulics, to be followed three years later by Ford. In the case of these two cars, the brakes are set up in perfect working condition, and they do their job very well. Once again, the Chevrolet requires more pedal pressure than the Ford, yet we thought the Chevy brakes may have had a slight edge when it came to effectiveness.

While the two car owners drove their respective cars in rapid circles, standing on the sidelines, it was interesting to observe the difference between them. The Ford could be cornered much faster than the Chevrolet, for the Chevy's outboard "knee" tended to buckle under when the car was pushed very hard. Both cars leaned more than slightly, though both drivers maintained control without difficulty. Yet it seemed clear that the Ford would be harder to roll over than the Chevrolet.

Walter P. Chrysler used to say that the proper number of cylinders for a low-priced car was four. Evidently Henry Ford was of the same mind, for he is quoted as having declared that he had "no use for any car that has more spark plugs than a cow has teats." But the public didn't necessarily agree with them, and when the Hudson Motor Car Company came up with a reasonably priced six-cylinder Essex, it proved popular enough to propel that company, in just two short years, from eighth place to third in the sales race. (At its introduction, in 1924, the Essex coach, or two-door sedan, sold for $975, but by mid-1926 that figure had been cut to $695, just $50 higher than the four-cylinder Chevrolet.)

The message was not lost upon William S. "Big Bill" Knudsen, Chevrolet's astute general manager. Knudsen, who has been described as "the greatest production genius of modern times" had come to Chevrolet in 1922, after a falling out with Henry Ford. Chevrolet, at that time, was a deeply troubled division. The product, to put the matter as kindly as possible, was not as durable as it should have been. Ford was outselling it by a ratio of five and a half to one, and Chevrolet's dealer organization was dispirited. But when Knudsen was elevated to the position of General Manager, in 1924, in a speech to his dealer representatives he promised, in his heavy Danish accent,

Stylish design with its stately looking grille was well proportioned.

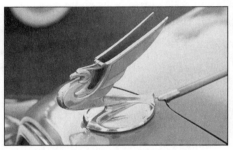

Sculptured hood ornament is pure art.

Chevy's dashboard nicely decorated.

PROS & CONS
1934 Chevrolet Master Sedan

PROS
1-Comfortable ride
2-Affordable price tag
3-Easy to work on

CONS
1-Down on power
2-Limited parts supply
3-Hard to find good examples

that they would match Ford "vun for vun." Which of course they did, and then some, for during 1927 and again in '28, the Chevrolet was America's (and the world's) Number One seller.

It was at that point, of course, that Henry Ford was forced to abandon his beloved Model T in favor of a much more powerful, better looking and generally more modern car, the Model A. And it was obvious to Bill Knudsen that in order to stay ahead of the game, he would have to come up with something dramatically different, something that Ford would be unable to match.

Beverly Rae Kimes recounts a story that has become almost legendary. "At a meeting when arguments for continuation of a four-cylinder engine were

pressed, Knudsen listened politely for a few minutes, then stood up and said, 'Gentlemen, we make a six'—and walked out." And so they did. Dubbed the International Series, it was introduced just before Thanksgiving, 1928. Chevy advertised it as "A Six for the Price of a Four."

Which indeed it was, for the best-selling Coach, which accounted for more than 43 percent of Chevrolet sales during the 1929 model run, was priced—at $595—just ten dollars higher than 1928's four-banger.

Powering this new Chevrolet was a newly developed, 194 cubic inch, overhead-valve engine, rated at 46 horsepower, a six horsepower advantage over the Model A, though the Ford's displacement was marginally greater. Of course, to make possible a six-cylinder car at a four cylinder price, a few corners had to be cut. Just three main bearings were fitted, for instance; not until 1937 would the Chevy have the advantage of a four-main crankshaft. Connecting rod bearings were lubricated by the splash method, while gravity feed took care of the main and camshaft bearings, continuing the practice employed by the old Chevy Fours. Perhaps most significantly, the aluminum alloy pistons used by 1928's four-cylinder "National" series were replaced by cast-iron pistons for the

"International" six, leading to the familiar sobriquet, "The Cast-Iron Wonder," and the use of slotted head bolts led to a second nickname, "The Stove-Bolt Six." It was not a flawless engine, to be sure, but it was good enough to remain in production with only minor changes as late as 1936, after which a re-designed Six was employed.

The Chevy "six" was a handsome car styled by Harley Earl, and its 107 inch wheelbase—three and a half inches longer than that of the Ford—enhanced its impressive appearance by making possible a relatively long hood. Twenty-inch disc wheels were used, in contrast to the 21-inch welded steel wires employed by Ford for the 1928-'29 Model A.

Thanks to a backlog of orders, which had accumulated while Ford's output was limited by the job of converting to production of the Model A, Ford regained the sales lead during 1929 and held it for 1930. But then, Chevrolet forged ahead and the sales race was on in earnest, each manufacturer trying to outdo the other.

So what was Henry Ford to do about this upstart six-cylinder Chevrolet? To have built a Six would have put him in the position of playing Follow the Leader, which would obviously have been intolerable. Besides, Henry didn't like Sixes. Between 1905 and 1907 Ford had produced a six-cylinder car, a big, powerful, expensive ($2,500) machine called the Model K, guaranteed to do sixty miles an hour. Unfortunately, the Model K, crippled by a totally inadequate two-speed transmission, proved to be a disaster both on the road and on the sales floor, and it is believed that it was this car that soured Henry Ford on six-cylinder engines.

The result, as every car enthusiast knows, was the Ford V-8, introduced on April 2, 1932. Rated at 65 horsepower, it held a theoretical advantage of five horsepower over the Chevrolet, which by that time—thanks to a higher compression ratio and a downdraft carburetor—produced 60 horsepower. (We say "theoretically" because there is reason to believe that the Ford's advertised 65 horsepower may have been a conservative figure.)

By 1933 Ford was using a 112-inch wheelbase. Chevrolet, meanwhile, em-

RESTORERS
1934 Ford Sedan

Classic Carriages
Dept. SIA-174
267 County Rd. 420
Athens, TN 37303
423-744-7496
Restoration and repair; specializing in 1932-53 flathead Ford engine rebuilds and conversions.

Shapely grille and flowing fenders gave a sportier appearance.

Leaping dog ornament very racy.

No-frills dashboard very simple.

[empl]oyed two chassis lengths. In response [to] the Depression, Chevy produced a [sm]aller model called the Standard [M]ercury (and later, simply the Standard) [se]ries, fitted to a 107-inch chassis. [M]eanwhile the larger cars, whose wheel[b]ase was stretched to 110 inches, were [gi]ven the Master Eagle title, later short[e]ned to simply the Master. By 1934 the [C]hevy Master—the series of which our [Co]mparisonReport Chevrolet is a mem[b]er, matched the 112-inch wheelbase of [th]e Ford.

Ford, too, had its "Standard" line, but [it] was simply a plain jane version of the [m]ore popular "Deluxe" series, priced at a [s]avings of about $50.00. And for the [ec]onomy-minded, Ford made available—[a]gain at a $50.00 price advantage—an [u]pdated, 50-horsepower four-cylinder [e]ngine, although 99.6 percent of 1934 [F]ord buyers opted for the V-8.

Thanks to an increase in the stroke [th]at brought its displacement to 206.8 [c]ubic inches, along with a higher com[p]ression ratio, Chevrolet could claim 80 [h]orsepower for its 1934 Master line, up [fr]om 65 the previous year. The Ford V-8, [m]eanwhile, was putting out at least 85 [h]orsepower, although 90 may have been [a] more accurate figure. And here is [w]here we can clearly see the difference in [c]oncept that separates the two cars. With [F]ord, the emphasis was on performance, [a]nd it was clearly the hottest thing in its

price class. At Chevrolet, on the other hand, the emphasis was on comfort and refinement. For instance, since 1933 the Chevy had featured Fisher "No-Draft" ventilation, and for 1934 the big news was independent front suspension, advertised as "Knee Action."

The front suspension employed by the top-of-the-line Chevrolets from 1934 through 1938 was called the Dubonnet system, having been developed by a

PROS & CONS
1934 Ford Sedan

PROS
1-Durable
2-Affordable
3-Huge parts supply

CONS
1-Harsh ride
2-Body usually rusted
3-Getting hard to find

member of the famed French wine-making family. It was based on coil sprung trailing arms and integral shock absorbers, and although it may not have been as durable a mechanism as one might wish, particularly if the owner failed to have it serviced at required intervals, there can be no doubt that it did wonders for the car's ride.

Ford, meanwhile, stuck with the tried-and-true I-beam axle, and its familiar transverse leaf springs. Asked why he retained a suspension system that was essentially the same as that of the Model T, Henry Ford is said to have replied testily, "We use transverse springs for the same reason we use round wheels—because we have found nothing better for the purpose."

Nearly identical in size and style, the Ford is clearly the sportier of the two.

Trunk extension and small upright rear window lend this sedan a formal look.

Five gauges keep driver very informed.

Brand identity advertised everywhere.

Chevrolet offered five body types in its Standard line: coupe, coach, sedan, roadster and phaeton, the sedan being a late entry, introduced during October. The Master series consisted of eight types, including a roadster, a cabriolet, coupes with and without rumble seat, coach, sedan, and two newcomers that would proved to be trend-setters: The "town sedan" was a coach with a built-in trunk, something of a novelty in 1934, while the "sport sedan" was a trunk-back four-door job.

Ford, while producing a wider variety of body types than Chevrolet, had no counterpart to the trunk-equipped Chevrolets, an omission that would be corrected when the 1935 models appeared. Unlike the Chevy, however, Ford offered a Victoria, a station wagon (considered part of the commercial line rather than a passenger car), five window coupes in either Standard or Deluxe trim, and three-window coupes with or without rumble seat. And as far as open cars were concerned Ford was ahead by a country mile, offering both phaetons and roadsters in a choice of Standard or Deluxe trim, as well as the option of four- or eight-cylinder power. And Ford's cabriolet, or convertible coupe, outsold its Chevrolet counterpart by nearly four and a half to one.

As we've noted, both Ford and Chevrolet used four-wheel internal mechanical brakes for their 1934 models. Both were fitted with 17-inch welded steel wire wheels, and both employed worm-and-sector steering, though—as noted above—the Ford's ratio was somewhat quicker than that of the Chevy.

Jack Day's first car was a 1934 Chevrolet Master sedan. He was a senior in high school at the time, and he was dating a freshman named Donna Russell. He married Donna when he was 20 and she was 16, and at this writing they are preparing to celebrate their 50th anniversary.

Jack had always been interested in Chevrolets, '34 Masters in particular, and he searched for a number of years for a '34 sedan like the one in which he had courted Donna. He found this one 18 years ago, sitting under a walnut tree, rotting away, but the owner wasn't interested in selling. Four years later the car was still sitting under the walnut tree, but in worse condition. Jack ap

continued on page 6

Color Gallery

1914 Model T Touring
With more than 165,000 models built, Ford's Model T Touring was by far its most popular offering in 1914. A 20hp, 176.7-cu.in. L-head Four was standard power for 1914 Fords. This was also the first year Ford went to an all-black-finish paint offering.

1926 Model T Touring
For the first time since 1911, The Model T Tourings that were produced in the U.S. came with a functional driver's-side door. They were also give much needed new sheet metal, though they retained the same 20hp, 176.7-cu.in. four-cylinder engine first used in 1909.

Photograph by David Newhardt

1929 Business Coupe

To much anticipation, the Ford Model A debuted for 1928. In addition to its new body styling and slightly longer, 103.5-inch wheelbase, the Model A received a larger, 40hp, 200.5-cu.in. four-cylinder. The 1929 Business Coupe was easily recognized by its oval quarter windows.

Photograph by Don Spiro

1930 Model A Sedan

New styling for 1930 included more flared fenders, a deeper radiator shell, and more pronounced body lines, but it continued to use the 40hp, 200.5-cu.in., in-line Four and selective-sliding three-speed transmission. By the end of the year, more than 4 million Model A's were sold.

Photograph by Marc Madow

1932 Convertible Sedan

V-8 power for the common man was what Ford gave automobile buyers in 1932. At a cost of $10 above the four-cylinder's price, 150,000 people opted for the 65hp, 221-cu.in. V-8. The $650 V-8-powered convertible sedan, which had a fold-down top that retained its roof rails, found 842 buyers.

1931 Model A Station Wagon

By 1931, A total of 19 models were offered by Ford, including wood-bodied station wagons. At 2,505-lbs. they were the heaviest of all Model A passenger cars this year. Standard power was still the 40hp, 200.5-cu.in. four, while side-mounted spare, external sunshade, rear luggage rack, and radiator ornament were optional.

1933 Tudor Seda[n]
Of all the Fords built in 1933, the fou[r] passenger Tudor was by far the mo[st] popular model sold this year. Standar[d] V-8 models accounted for more tha[n] 106,000 cars sold, while there were mo[re] than 48,000 DeLuxe V-8 models buil[t]. Options included a heater, clock, an[d] dual windshield wiper[s]

1934 Phaeton
Retaining the basic design introduced in 1933 albeit with more brightwork, Ford's 1934 passenger cars had a 112-inch wheelbase and more graceful styling. DeLuxe models had pinstriping, cowl light, twin horns, and two taillights. V-8 power output was up to 85 hp.

Photograph by Jim Tanji

1934 Five-Window coupe

Five-window coupes accounted for nearly 75,000 of the 563,921 Fords sold in 1934. While most had V-8 power, 23 five-window coupes were ordered with the 50hp, 200.5-cu.in. engine. A four-cylinder, five-window coupe had a base price of $465, while one with the Flathead V-8 cost $515.

Photograph by Josiah Work

1935 Five-window coupe

New styling for 1935 gave the Fords a heavier and sturdier look. Tudor and Fordor models were now available with a conventional trunk. Five-window coupes were also available with a trunk or, for $24 more, a rumble seat. Ford finally retired the old Four, and the 85hp, 221-cu.in. V-8 was the only engine available this year.

1936 Five-window coupe
Body changes for 1936 were limited to redesigned nose styling and new rear fenders. Pressed steel wheel replaced wire wheels, which were standard since 1927. Five-window coupes accounted for more than 100,000 Fords this year. Standard power was the 85hp, 221-cu.in. Flathead V-8.

1937 Convertible
Strongly influenced by the Lincoln Zephyr, the 1937 Fords were the first to have integral headlights mounted in the fenders, an all-steel roof, and one-piece cowl-hinged hood. The 85hp, 221-cu.in. V-8 was joined by a smaller 60hp, 136-cu.in. V-8, which came only in standard models.

Photograph by Bud Juneau

1938 Convertible

In 1938, two body styles differentiated the Standard and DeLuxe models. Standard bodies looked similar to the 1937s, while the DeLuxe versions had revised grille and separate side louvers. The 136-cu.in. V-8 was again available only in the Standard line, while the larger, 221-cu.in. V-8 came standard in the DeLuxe models.

Photograph by Vince Wright

1939 Fordor DeLuxe

Ford continued to offer two distinct Standard and DeLuxe models for 1939. Standard cars look similar to the 1938 models, whereas the DeLuxe examples had new front styling that included flush-fit headlights, lower grille, and a smoother body profile.

1939 Tudor Sedan DeLux[e]

Mechanically, the most significan[t]
innovation used in 1939 was four-whee[l]
hydraulic brakes. Standard models cam[e]
with the 60hp 136-cu.in. or the large[r]
221-cu.in. V-8. DeLuxe models cam[e]
only with the larger, 85hp engine. Wit[h]
more than 144,000 sold, the Tudo[r]
DeLuxe Sedan was Ford's bes[t]
seller in 193[9]

Photograph by Bud Juneau

1940 DeLuxe Convertible

Designed by Eugene Gregorie, the 1940 Ford DeLuxe had a three-section grille with
thin horizontal bars and sealed-beam headlights with chrome bezels. Standard models
look just like the 1939 DeLuxe versions. Nearly 24,000 buyers opted for the DeLuxe
convertible, which was priced at $850. Power was unchanged from the previous year.

Oval-shaped gauges look very elegant.

Ford's trim not as ornate as Chevy.

The lack of rear body overhang and slanted hood louvers provide spirited styling.

roached the owner once more, pointing out that the car was deteriorating so rapidly that in another year or so there wouldn't be anything left. At that point, the owner was persuaded to sell.

Jack did virtually the entire restoration himself, rebuilding the engine, clutch, transmission, rear end and brakes, and installing an upholstery kit. Paint and woodgraining were farmed out to specialists. The hardest part of the job, as any restorer would know, was re-creating the wooden body fram-

ing, which had largely rotted out during the years the car sat under the walnut tree.

The job is still not quite complete. Awaiting restoration and installation are two very popular Chevrolet options, a metal spare tire cover and a pair of fender skirts. An unusual piece of equipment on this car is its right-side taillamp. Both right and left lamps are fitted with the rare "blue dot" lenses. Jack, a metal worker by trade, had to fabricate the bracket for the right-side lamp.

PARTS SUPPLIERS
1934 Ford Sedan

Dennis Carpenter
Dept. SIA-174
P.O. Box 26398
Charlotte, NC 28221
704-786-8139
Large selection of weatherstripping, plastics, rubber, die-cast metal and mechanical parts and accessories.

Bob Drake Reproductions
Dept. SIA-174
1819 NW Washington Blvd.
Grants Pass, OR 97526
800-221-3673
www.bobdrake.com
Specializing in reproduction Ford body and trim parts for 1932-48 automobiles and 1932-66 pickups.

Early Ford V-8 Sales
Dept. SIA-174
Bldg. 37
Curtis Industrial Park
831 Route 67
Ballston Spa, NY 12020
518-884-2825
www.earlyford.com
Carries a complete line of mechanical, electrical, body and trim parts, plus flathead performance parts.

Mac's Antique Auto Parts
Dept. SIA-174
1051 Lincoln Ave.
Lockport, NY 14094
800-777-0948
www.macsutoparts.com
Offers a free catalog packed with mechanical, body and trim parts and accessories.

Obsolete Ford Parts
Dept. SIA-174
8701 S. Interstate 35
Oklahoma City, OK 73149
405-631-3933
www.ford-obsolete-parts.com
Stocks one of the largest inventories of antique and classic Ford parts in the USA. Catalog $3.00.

Dick Spadaro
Dept. SIA-174
P.O. Box 617, 6599 Rt. 158
Altamont, NY 12009
518-861-5367
www.dickspadaro.com
Supplier of quality accessories and replacement parts and sheetmetal repair panels. NOS and used parts always in stock.

Gerry Watson is hooked on 1934 Fords. He owns an award-winning Deluxe five-window coupe which he restored himself, and for five years he searched for a sedan to which he might give similar treatment. Surprisingly, in 1993 he found this one hidden away in a garage two blocks from his home. It had been a San Francisco car originally, and had been brought to Chico, in northern California, by its second owner, the man from whom Gerry eventually bought it. Some restoration work had been done back in 1983, including the paint job and new upholstery, but Gerry tore it down completely and rebuilt it mechanically, bolt-by-bolt. One of the previous owners had installed a 1937 Ford engine, but Gerry replaced it with the correct unit.

Since this car is intended for touring, rather than for show, Gerry installed a set of Kelsey-Hayes 16-inch wire wheels, and added a later-vintage Columbia axle, seat belts, turn signals and dual exhausts. The Ford had been in an acci-

SPECIFICATIONS: 1934 CHEVROLET MASTER vs. FORD V-8 DELUXE

	Chevrolet	Ford
Original price, 4-door sedan*	$645	$625
Engine	6 cylinder inline	V-8
Bore x stroke	3.3125" x 4"	3.0625" x 3.75"
Displacement (cu. in.)	206.8	221.0
Compression ratio	5.45:1	6.30:1
Horsepower @ rpm	80 @ 3,300	85 @ 3,800**
Taxable horsepower	26.3	30.0
Valve configuration	Ohv	L-head
Valve lifters	Mechanical	Mechanical
Main bearings	3	3
Lubrication system	Splash/pressure	Pressure
Carburetor	1-bbl downdraft	2-bbl downdraft
Fuel feed	Mechanical pump	Mechanical pump
Electrical system	6-volt battery/coil	6-volt battery/coil
Exhaust system	Single	Single
Cooling system	Centrifugal pump	Centrifugal pump
Clutch	Single dry plate	Single dry plate
Diameter	9"	9"
Transmission	3-speed, floor shift	3-speed, floor shift
Ratios, 1st/2nd speeds	3.02/1.70	2.82/1.60
Rear axle	Spiral bevel	Spiral bevel
Ratio	4.11:1	4.11:1
Drive axles	Semi-floating	3/4 floating
Torque medium	Torque tube	Torque tube
Steering	Worm/sector	Worm/sector
Ratio	16.0:1	15.0:1
Turning diameter	34' 10"	40' 0"
Turns of wheel, lock-to-lock	4	3
Brakes	Mechanical	Mechanical
Drum diameter	12"	12"
Effective area (sq. in.)	170.2	186.0
Construction	Body on frame	Body on frame
Frame	Channel section, 4 cross-members, YK sub-frame	Double-drop, curved side rails, X-member
Body construction	Composite	All-steel
Body type	4-door sedan	4-door sedan
Passenger capacity	5	5
Suspension: Front	Dubonnet "Knee action"	I-beam axle, transverse leaf spring
Rear	Rigid axle, semi-elliptic springs	Rigid axle, transverse leaf spring
Wheels	Welded steel wire	Welded steel wire
Tires	5.50/17	5.50/17 originally; now 6.00/16
Measurements and weights:		
Wheelbase	112"	112"
Overall length	175"	175.9"
Overall width	70.5"	67.4"
Overall height	68.5"	66.5"
Front track	56.5"	56.125"
Rear track	57.5625"	56.68"
Minimum road clearance	8.375"	9"
Shipping weight (lbs.)	3,080	2,684
Capacities:		
Crankcase (quarts)	5	5
Cooling system (quarts)	11	22
Fuel tank (gallons)	14	14
Transmission (lbs.)	2.5	2.5
Rear axle	4.5	2.25
Calculated data:		
Stroke/bore ratio	1.21:1	1.22:1
Engine revolutions per mile	3,160	3,165
Horsepower per cid	.387	.385
Weight (lbs.) per hp	38.5	31.6
Weight per cid	14.9	12.1
Weight per sq. in. (brakes)	18.1	13.9
Production	124,754	102,268

* Note: Since Ford did not offer a sedan with built-in trunk, comparable to our featured Chevrolet, sedans without trunks are use for this comparison. Our Chevrolet differs from the above only with respect to price ($675) and weight (3,155 lbs.) The difference in the above data table would be only fractional.

**Some sources say 90 hp

Options on feature Chevrolet: Radio (aftermarket), heater, locking cap for spare tire, dual tail lamps, locking gas cap (25 cents at a yard sale!), white sidewall tires, passenger-side visor, exhaust extension, clock mirror, fog lamps, left o/s mirror, two-tone paint

Options on feature Ford: Columbia axle, 16" Kelsey-Hayes wheels, white sidewall tires, îpeepî outside mirrors, greyhound radiator cap, grille guard, fog lamps, aftermarket ampere and oil pressure gauges, spare tire lock

dent at some point, and the front ax wasn't all that it should have been, that was replaced.

So, which to choose, Chevrolet Ford, if the calendar were turned bac to 1934 and we were in the market f a low-priced car? To tell the truth, if were up to this writer, neither. We opt instead for the Plymouth, for tw reasons: First, Plymouth was the on car at its price, in those days, to fea ture hydraulic brakes. And second, f that one year, the Deluxe Plymouth came with the superior "wishbone system of independent front suspen sion, something that the marqu would not feature again until 193 Both of these were highly significar advantages.

But of course, that's not being fai We're to choose here between Ford an Chevrolet. And here, it comes down to matter of priorities. If the buyer's prima ry interest was in passenger comfor the Chevy is the odds-on choice, whi for the performance enthusiast the no must go to the Ford. Probably the For also had a slight edge with respect durability, though the Chevrolet—a least as these cars were customari driven—had a small advantage in fu economy. Both cars represented tremendous advance over the mode offered just a few years earlier by the respective manufacturers. And eac offered a lot of automobile at an ama ingly reasonable price. ஃ

Chevy wheelbase: 112 inches

Chevy's straight-six was a rugged unit that developed 80 horsepower at 3,300 rpm.

Rear "suicide door" only on Chevy.

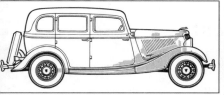
Ford wheelbase: 112 inches

Spacious interior is very comfortable.

Smooth Ford flathead V-8 made 85 horsepower.

1935 FORD MODEL 48

Originally published in Special Interest Autos #114, Nov.-Dec. 1989

by Josiah Work
photos by the author

THE SLEEPER AMONG FLATHEADS

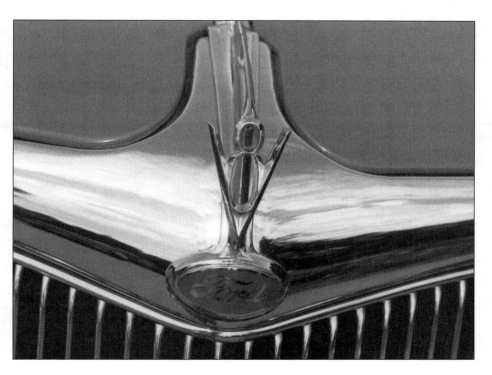

FOR years, the 1935 model was all but ignored by collectors of early Ford V-8s. Only recently has it come to be recognized for what it is: a handsome, well-built automobile; and a substantial improvement, in a number of respects, over its predecessors.

All of which seems strange, for back in 1935 the restyled Ford was clearly the smash hit of the low-priced field. Consider for a moment the production record of the Ford and its principal rivals — Chevrolet and Plymouth — for the first five years of what might be termed the "V-8 Era."

	Ford	Chevrolet	Plymouth
1932	287,285	306,716	121,468
1933	334,969	481,134	255,564
1934	563,921	620,726	351,113
1935	942,439	793,437	442,281
1936	791,812	975,238	527,177

Note the sudden surge in Ford sales during 1935, obviously at the expense of Chevrolet. There were a number of reasons, not the least of which was a prolonged strike at Chevy. But there was also the bulbous, ill-proportioned

Driving Impressions

We've never heard a quieter, smoother flathead V-8 than the engine in our driveReport car. The meticulous job that was done in balancing the mill is typical, we found, of the craftsmanship that went into the total, frame-off restoration of this fine little automobile.

The work was done by the Ford's previous owner, George Pezzolo, of El Sobrante, California. starting with what he described as a "basket case," George devoted his spare time to the task over a ten-year period, doing all the work himself apart from the upholstery and the pinstriping.

To illustrate just how meticulous George was: Twice the car was striped by acknowledged experts. Twice George was dissatisfied; after the painter departed, he wiped the car clean. The third time proved to be the charm, however; this pinstriping is flawless.

It can't be easy to part with an automobile after one has poured heart and soul into its restoration as Pezzolo did with this car. But in 1980 he sold the Ford to its present owners, Bill and Doris Cline, of Redwood City, California.

The Clines have toured in the Ford, traveling as far as Ventura, in Southern California. But basically, they treat it as a "show" car. It took first place trophies at both Hillsborough and Silverado in 1984. Twice it has captured the Early Ford V-8 Club's coveted Dearborn Award. And there have been two "firsts" at Walnut Creek, four at Palo Alto, and a number of other honors over the years. This is all the more remarkable in view of the fact that the Ford has been modified in one important respect: The brakes have been converted to hydraulics.

We applaud the alteration. The binders are very good.

It goes without saying that this is a nimble, lively car, fun to drive. The clutch is smooth, something that cannot be said of many of the early V-8s. Shifts are light and easy, though the synchro is (as usual, for these cars) only partially effective. Steering is lighter than we anticipated. Ford increased the ratio in 1936 in order to reduce the steering effort, but this one certainly doesn't require a lot of muscle. And the ride, while hardly flawless, is a good deal less choppy than that of earlier Fords.

The V-8 is at its best cruising down the freeway—at any speed up to the current legal maximum of 65. It leans over in the turns, perhaps more than one might wish, but the driver is still firmly in control. With its high-speed (1.60:1) second gear, this would be a great car to take up Meyers Grade, en route to South Lake Tahoe.

We have fond memories of the 1936 Ford DeLuxe coupe that we owned in our college days. And so, since the '35 and '36 models are so nearly alike, the preparation of this driveReport proved to be a particularly delightful experience.

drive report

Above: The car presents a good-looking appearance from almost every angle. Below: 1935 was the last year for externally mounted horns for Ford.

1935 FORD

appearance of the Master series Chevrolet, as well as the diminutive size of it Standard series companion. All thes were important factors.

To a considerable extent, though, th 1935 Ford was itself responsible for it own success.

Take styling, for instance.

Back when his sensational 1929 se ries was new (see *SIA* #103), Errett Lob ban Cord asked Frank Spring — the styling director for the Walter M Murphy Company of Pasadena, Califor nia — to develop some custom stylin proposals for the low-slung, front wheel-drive Cord chassis. Spring the laid down the parameters within whic his staff was expected to work. A num ber of sketches were made, but E. Cord, who had a keen and practiced ey and evidently an inherent sense of pr portion, rejected the lot.

However, it happened that on Fran Spring's staff were two gifted youn men, both destined for greatness a their careers developed. There wa Frank Hershey, best remembered toda as the designer of the smart little two passenger Thunderbirds of 1955-57 And there was Phil Wright, whose fabu lous Pierce Silver Arrow — designe especially for display at the 1933 Ch cago World's Fair — would soon ear him international recognition. (Se comparisonReport, *SIA* #114.) Workin at home, on their own time, each c

hese talented young stylists developed
 number of alternative designs, several
f which proved to be exactly what Cord
vanted.

History repeated itself. After the
ierce-Arrow assignment was complet-
d, Phil Wright went to work for the
Briggs Manufacturing Company. It hap-
ened that by that time, Briggs was well
under way with a styling proposal for
he 1935 Ford. But Wright. dissatisfied
vith what he saw, undertook to develop
n alternative rendering — again, at
ome, on his own time. He showed his
vork to Ralph Roberts, his superior at
Briggs. and Roberts, in turn, displayed
he drawings to a team of Ford officials
eaded by Edsel Ford.

The upshot was a parallel to the situa-
ion at Murphy, half a decade earlier.
he "official" Brlggs design was rejected.
vhile Wright's work was enthusiastical-
y accepted. As Paul Woudenberg re-
ounts the story, "Ford officials were so
leased, that the order went out to go to
 full-scale mock-up of wood, rather
han through the customary 1/24th-
cale clay models."

Phil Wright's design, beyond the V-8
mblem and the welded-steel wire
vheels, owed little to any previous Ford.
he engine was moved forward eight
nd a half inches, which helped to cre-
te a more aggressive appearance. This
nove had the further advantage of pro-
iding space for Wright's smoothly
apered rear-end styling. And most
mportant, following the lead of
Chrysler's Airflow, Ford was able to
ocate the rear seat ahead of the axle,
ather than directly over it — an enor-
nous contribution to riding comfort.

Above: Generous-sized cowl vent helped cool off the interior. **Below:** Hood vents have a racy appearance.

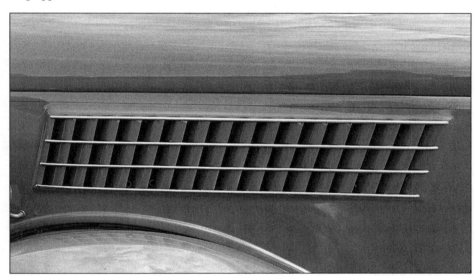

Comparison Table: 1935's "Low-Priced Three"

	Ford	Chevrolet*	Plymouth
Price, Deluxe Coupe w/rumble seat	$585	$600	$630
Wheelbase	112 inches	113 inches	113 inches
Shipping weight	2,643 pounds	2,940 pounds	2,730 pounds
Engine	V-8	6-cylinder	6-cylinder
Displacement	221.0 cubic inches	206.8 cubic inches	201.3 cubic inches
Horsepower/rpm	85/3,800	80/3,300	82/3,600
Compression ratio	6.30:1	5.45:1	6.70:1
Valve configuration	L-head	ohv	L-head
Clutch diameter	9 inches	9 inches	91A inches
Transmission ratios	2.82/1.60/1.00	3.02/1.70/1.00	2.57/1.55/1.00
Final drive ratio	4.11:1	4.11:1	4.13:1
Steering	Worm & sector	Worm & roller	Worm & roller
Brakes	Mechanical	Mechanical	Hydraulic
Drum diameter	12 inches	12 inches	10 inches
Effective area (square inches)	186.0	170.2	158.5
Independent front suspension	No	Optional	No
Tire size	6.00/16	5.50/17	6.00/16
Horsepower per c.i.d.	3.85	.387	.407
Pounds per horsepower	31.1	36.8	33.3

* Master series

illustrations by Russell von Sauers, The Graphic Automobile Studi...
© copyright 1989, Special Interest Aut...

specifications

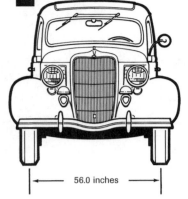

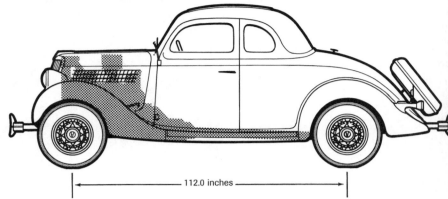

← 56.0 inches →

← 112.0 inches →

1935 Ford Model 48

Price	$585 f.o.b. factory (with rumble seat)
Standard equip. (deluxe models)	Twin horns, twin taillamps, dash panel including speedometer/odometer, fuel, oil pressure, engine temperature and amp gauges.
Options on dR car	White sidewall tires, "banjo" wheel, dual wipers. (Aftermarket accessory: left outside mirror).

ENGINE

Type	90° monobloc V-8
Bore x stroke	3-1/16 inches x 3-3/4 inches
Displacement	221.0- cubic inches
Compression ratio	6.30:1
Horsepower @ rpm	85 @ 3,800
Torque @ rpm	144 @ 2,200
Taxable horsepower	30.0
Valve configuration	L-head
Main bearings	3
Induction system	Stromberg EE1 dual downdraft carburetor, camshaft pump
Lubrication system	Pressure
Exhaust system	Single
Electrical system	6-volt

CLUTCH

Type	Single dry plate
Actuation	Mechanical, foot pedal

TRANSMISSION

Type	3-speed selective, synchronized 2nd and 3rd speeds, floor-mounted lever

Ratios:	1st	2.82:1
	2nd	1.60:1
	3rd	Direct
	Reverse	3.83:1

DIFFERENTIAL

Type	Spiral bevel
Ratio	4.11:1
Drive axles	3/4-floating

STEERING

Type	Gemmer worm and sector
Turns lock-to-lock	3.5
Ratio	15:1
Turning circle	40' 0" (curb/curb)

BRAKES

Type	4-wheel internal mechanical
Drum diameter	12 inches
Total swept area	186 square inches

CHASSIS & BODY

Construction	Body-on-frame
Body	All steel
Body style	Deluxe 5-window coupe with rumble seat

SUSPENSION

Front	38-11/16-inch transverse leaf springs; I-beam axle, radius rods
Rear	46-1/2-inch transverse leaf springs, conventional axle, radius rods
Shock absorbers	Lever hydraulic
Tires	6.00 x 16 inch 4-ply

Wheels	Welded steel wire spoke, drop-center rims

WEIGHTS AND MEASURES

Wheelbase	112 inches
Overall length	182.75 inches
Overall width	69.5 inches
Overall height	64.625 inches
Front track	56 inches
Rear track	58.25 inches
Ground clearance	8.5 inches (minimum)
Shipping weight	2,643 pounds

CAPACITIES

Crankcase	5 quarts
Cooling system	22 quarts
Fuel tank	14 gallons

CALCULATED DATA

HP/c.i.d.	.385
Lb/.Hp	31.1 pounds
Lb./c.i.d.	12.0 pounds

Lb. per sq. in. (brakes) 14.2

Color of dR car: Cordoba Gray with Poppy Red wheels and pinstriping.

Production, this body style (including standard and Deluxe cars, with and without rumble seat): 111,542. (Third most popular model.)

This page: *V-8 engine makes for a stubbier hood length than the competition.*
Facing page: *Rear window cranks down for cooling and for conversation with rumble-seat occupants.*

1935 FORD

Bodies were longer and wider, fenders were deeper and higher-crowned, wheels were smaller, tires fatter. Altogether the 1935 Ford appeared sleeker, smoother, more streamlined and certainly more impressive than any of its predecessors.

It was also, model-for-model, about 85 pounds heavier than its 1934 counterpart, and a few dollars more costly. But the Ford V-8 still would handily out-perform the competition, and it still held a slight price advantage over both Chevrolet and Plymouth.

There were other improvements:

• Under the hood there was a new, cast-alloy crankshaft, an improved camshaft, "directed flow" crankcase ventilation, and new copper-lead connecting-rod bearings. Horsepower was customarily rated at 85, same as before, though some sources quoted 88 or even 90 bhp.

• The frame was stronger, incorporating heavier bracing and more box sections. As a result the Ford felt (and indeed was) more solid than before.

• The redesigned clutch offered substantially reduced pedal pressure, with no loss of strength or durability.

• The front transverse spring was moved four inches ahead of the axle, while the rear spring was relocated four inches aft of the rear axle. Not only did this extend the spring base by eight inches, it also made possible the use of longer (by seven and a half inches) and softer springs. The resultant improvement in the car's riding qualities was substantial.

• Passenger accommodations were more spacious. Leg room was enhanced, and front seat width was increased by anywhere from four to five and a half inches, depending on the body style. In the five-passenger cars, the rear seats gained an inch and a half in width.

There were 17 distinct models to choose from, compared to 11 each from Chevrolet and Plymouth. Four of these came in Standard trim, featuring a painted grille and windshield frame, black wheels, single horn, inside visor and taillamp, and wide-wale Bedford Cord upholstery.

The others were Deluxe cars, featuring a chrome-plated grille and windshield frame, twin matched-tone horns, twin visors and taillamps, left front door armrest — among other amenities. Upholstery came in a choice of mohair or pin-striped broadcloth — genuine leather in the open models. And the wheels were brightly painted to contrast with the body color. Model for model, the Deluxe cars cost $65 more than the plain-Jane Standards. Most people evidently considered it money well spent.

Ford's advertising program, which carried the slogan "Greater Beauty, Greater Comfort, Greater Safety," attempted to make a virtue of Henry's antiquated mechanical brakes, stressing "The Safety of Steel from Pedal to Wheel." Transverse springing, the company maintained, "retains the important advantages of the solid axle and yet minimizes road shocks transmitted to frame and body." The claims weren't particularly impressive. The Ford sold well, not because but in spite of its outmoded suspension and brakes. Its appeal, rather, was based upon performance (meaning speed), looks, and price — probably in that order.

Reviewers on both sides of the Atlantic greeted the 1935 Ford with enthusiasm. James Dalton, writing in *MoToR*, noted that, "The Ford is longer, larger, more commodious and far more beautiful

Looking At All Three

Let's take a moment, just for the fun of it, to step back in time to 1935. And let's go shopping, in our imagination, for a low-priced car.

Of course we'll want to look at Chevrolet, the only car in its field with an overhead-valve engine.

That's a "plus." So is the seamless steel "turret" top, exclusive to Chevrolet in this price range during 1935. The Chevy's valve train tends to make the engine a little noisier than the competition, but the well-insulated, composite steel-and-wood body construction actually provides a quieter ride than either Ford or Plymouth. And if the car is equipped with the Dubonnet "Knee Action" front suspension, a $20.00 option, the Chevrolet ride is easily the smoothest of the lot.

Of course, those Dubonnet "knees" would give us some trouble in time to come, but perhaps in 1935 we don't know that. We do know, however, that the Chevrolet is relatively heavy, and its power-to-weight ratio leaves something to be desired. We also know that the brakes, like those of the Ford, are the old-style mechanicals. And if we're like most Americans, we have little enthusiasm for the Chevrolet's bulbous styling, its "suicide" doors, or its skinny, 5.50/17 tires.

Then there's the Plymouth, still regarded by some as the "new kid on the block." Its performance can't equal that of the Ford, but it's a good deal quicker than the Chevy. And with its hydraulic brakes it will stop a lot faster than either of its rivals. The engine — fitted with four main bearings, compared to three in the Chevrolet — is smooth and quiet, but the sound insulation isn't all that great. Road noises are sometimes altogether too audible. Styling, which — like that of the Ford — originated at Briggs, is attractive, but to most of us it's no match for the Ford's stunning good looks.

In a puzzling backward step, Plymouth has abandoned for 1935 the independent front suspension featured by the 1934 Deluxe PE series. The ride is still superior to that of the Ford, though it can't rival that of a Dubonnet-equipped Chevy.

So that brings us back to the Ford. Unquestionably it is the fastest, most nimble car of the three. It offers the widest choice of body styles, and it holds a small price advantage over the competition. It's stoutly built, and to most of us it is by far the best looking of the "low-priced three."

But on the other hand, the ride — while better than that of any previous Ford — can't quite match that of either of its rivals. Its brakes are nothing to brag about. And it is more likely than either the Chevrolet or the Plymouth to fall victim, some hot summer afternoon, to vapor lock.

So nobody's perfect. Each of these three industry leaders has its strong points, and each has its drawbacks. But all three represent an enormous advance over the low-priced cars of just five years earlier. And at prices hovering around the $600 mark, each is a phenomenal value for the money.

Above left: *'35 was also Ford's last year for wire wheels.* *Above right:* *Roof-mounted wipers were carried through 1939.* *Below:* *Instruments were the same in 1936 models.*

than ever before." And across the ocean, *The Autocar* declared, "Anyone who had not had previous experience of a car of this description could but be astounded by the ease of the running at 40 to 50 mph... and by the way in which the speedometer literally shoots across the dial."

All of which is not to say that there wasn't a downside. The superiority of hydraulic brakes had been convincingly demonstrated (to the satisfaction of nearly everyone except Henry Ford), long before 1935. And there were complaints of the Ford's brakes groaning, juddering, and occasionally pulling to one side. Nor was their effectiveness enhanced by the fact that the 1935 cars weighed 400 pounds more than their 1932 counterparts, while the effective braking area remained unchanged.

The V-8 engine, unique to Ford in its price class, was lively and responsive, but it was still subject to occasional problems of overheating and vapor lock. And the longer, softer, repositioned springs, though they represented a significant improvement, were still no match for the independent front suspension that was just then coming into general use. For that matter, even the welded steel wire wheels were out of date, in part because they contributed unnecessarily to unsprung weight.

Yet the fact remains that Ford offered an unparalleled combination of high performance and low price, in an automobile that was stoutly built, easy to drive, and handsome in appearance.

A combination like that is hard to beat. And in 1935, to judge by the sales figures, nobody managed to beat it. ◌

Acknowledgments and Bibliography
Automobile Trade Journal, March 1935; Automotive Industries, *February 23, 1935;* Ford Motor Company factory literature; Jerry Heasley, *The Production Figure Book for US Cars;* Beverly Rae Kimes, *The Cars That Henry Ford Built;* Beverly Rae Kimes and Henry Austin Clark, Jr. (eds.), *Standard Catalog of American Cars, 1805-1942;* David L. Lewis, Mike McCarville, and Lorin Sorensen, *Ford, 1903-1984;* MoToR, *January 1935;* Allan Nevins and Frank Ernest Hill, *Ford: Decline and Rebirth 1933-1962;* Paul R. Woudenberg, *Ford in the Thirties.*

Our thanks to Dave Brown, Durham, California; John Cavagnaro, Stockton, California; Dr. Lawrence Dirksen, Chairman, Hillsborough Concours d'Elegance, Hillsborough, California. Special thanks to Bill and Doris Cline, Redwood City, California.

1935 Ford Model 48 Prices and Weights

Body Style	Price	Weight
Standard Coupe, 5-window	$495	2,620 pounds
Standard Coupe, 5-window, rumble seat	$520	n/a
Standard Tudor Sedan	$510	2,717 pounds
Standard Fordor Sedan	$575	2,760 pounds
Deluxe Coupe, 5-window	$560	2,643 pounds
Deluxe Coupe, 5-window, rumble seat	$585	n/a
Deluxe Coupe, 3-window	$570	2,647 pounds
Deluxe Coupe, 3-window, rumble seat	$595	n/a
Deluxe Tudor Sedan	$575	2,737 pounds
Deluxe Tudor Touring Sedan	$595	2,772 pounds
Deluxe Fordor Sedan	$635	2,767 pounds
Deluxe Fordor Touring Sedan	$655	2,787 pounds
Deluxe Roadster, rumble seat	$550	2,597 pounds
Deluxe Phaeton	$580	2,667 pounds
Deluxe Cabriolet, rumble seat	$625	2,687 pounds
Deluxe Convertible Sedan	$750	2,827 pounds
Station Wagon	$670	2,896 pounds

Color Availability

Body	Striping	Wheels
Black	Apple Green	Apple Green
Cordoba Gray	Poppy Red	Poppy Red
Vineyard Green	Apple Green	Apple Green
Light Gunmetal*	Apple Green	Apple Green
Dearborn Blue*	Poppy Red	Poppy Red
*Deluxe models only		

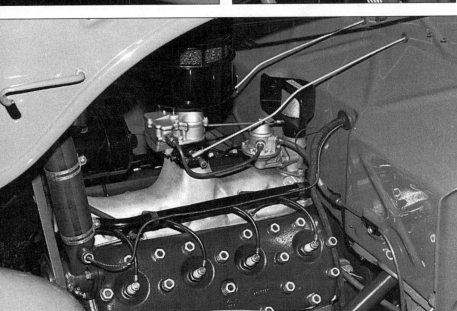

Above left: Ashtray and windshield crank occupy center of dash. *Above center:* Banjo-style steering wheel lends a sporty look. *Above:* Rear bumper shape complements body contours. *Left:* Flathead V-8 in driveReport car is smooth as whipped cream and whisper quiet.

1935: Neither The Best of Times, Nor Yet The Worst

• The Works Progress Administration (WPA) was established in May, providing jobs for two million unemployed Americans. Three months later the Social Security Act was signed into law. Both programs created distress among many conservatives, who pointed out that the public debt was already approaching $29 billion — more than $225 for every man, woman, and child in the country.

• In the world of aviation it was both a time of triumph and a time of tragedy. The $4,000,000 dirigible *Macon* broke up over the Pacific, fell into the sea, and sank. Miraculously, all but two of the 85 per-sons aboard were saved. And that summer, aviator Wiley Post and philoso-pher/ humorist Will Rogers were killed near Point Barrow, Alaska, when their plane crashed in a fog.

But on the other hand, 1935 was also the year in which Amelia Earhart flew solo from Pearl Harbor to San Francisco — "first" for a woman pilot. And that November Pan American inaugurated regular passenger service, via the China Clipper — the "super-plane" of its day — between San Francisco and Manila, with stops at Honolulu, Midway, Wake Island and Guam.

• Sinclair Lewis's *It Can't Happen Here*, Clarence Day's *Life With Father*, and John Steinbeck's *Tortilla Flat* were among the year's best-sellers; and on October 10 the premier performance of George Gershwin's opera, *Porgy and Bess*, was held in Boston.

• Broadway hosted what proved to be the first of 837 performances of the hilar-ious *Three Men on a Horse. Jumbo*, with a sparkling score by Rodgers and Hart, was the musical hit of the season; while Alfred Lunt and Lynn Fontanne revived Shakespeare's classic, *The Taming of the Shrew.*

• The movies were in their heyday, pro-viding outstanding shows ranging from *Top Hat* (starring Fred Astaire and Ginger Rogers) to *David Copperfield* (Lionel Barrymore, Edna Mae Oliver — and W.C. Fields in a rare dramatic role). Other top-flight pictures that year included *Mutiny on the Bounty* (Charles Laughton, Clark Gable), *Anna Karenina* (Greta Garbo), *Les Miserables* (Frederic March), and *Curly Top*, with Shirley Temple.

• And for popular music it was truly a vintage year. Cole Porters "Begin the Beguine," Duke Ellington's "In a Senti-mental Mood," Jerome Kern's "Lovely to Look At," Joe Burke's "Moon Over Miami," Richard Rodgers's "My Romance," Jimmy McHugh's "I'm in the Mood for Love." and Irving Berlin's "Isn't This a Lovely Day" were just a few of the many hit songs of the season that remain with us today as "standards."

• The economy, wracked for more than half a decade by the Depression, picked up a little. Automobile production, always a bellwether, stood at better than 80 percent of its pre-Depression level. But the picture was spotty. Buick's out-put for 1935 was less than half the figure for 1928, yet Oldsmobile sales more than doubled. Chrysler was down 69 percent, perhaps because buyers were defecting to Dodge, whose production more than tre-bled. Even Pontiac, despite a dramatic 276 percent increase over 1932's miser-able production record, had recovered only about 72 percent of its 1928 market.

But as a group it was the independents that were the most seriously hurt. Stude-baker's volume was down by 62 percent, comparing 1935 with 1928. Hudson fell by 64 percent. Nash by 68 percent. Auburn and Hupmobile, meanwhile, both struggling valiantly to survive, very nearly fell off the charts.

On the whole, however, things were looking up. And as a harbinger of things to come, on May 23 Cincinnati took on Philadelphia in the first night game in the history of major league baseball.

1939-40 Ford Spotter's Guide

WIPERS ABOVE WINDSHIELD ON SEDANS & COUPES — COWL-MOUNTED WIPERS ON OPEN CARS & WAGON. BRIGHT WINDSHIELD FRAMES ON BOTH SERIES.

1939 DELUXE FORD V-8 — (LEFT) DIFFERENT FROM 'STANDARD' W/NEW & UNIQUE HOOD, FRONT FENDERS, & HEADLAMPS. NEW BUMPER W/HORIZONTAL GROOVE - NEW GUARDS. NEW GRILLE W/BODY-COLOR VERTICAL BARS TRIMMED W/BRIGHT MLDGS. HORIZONTAL TRIM STRIPS ON HOOD ABOVE GRILLE. 'V-8' EMBLEM ON VERTICAL HOOD CENTER MLDG. 'FORD' & 'DELUXE' SCRIPT ON HOOD SIDES ABOVE GRILLE. TWO HORIZONTAL BRIGHT MLDGS. ON HOOD SIDES. BRIGHT HOOD CENTER MLDG.

1939 'STANDARD' FORD V-8 — (ABOVE) SIMILAR TO 1938 DELUXE WITH SAME FRONT FENDERS, HEADLAMPS, BUMPER, & GUARDS. NEW HOOD W/HORIZONTAL GRILLE LOUVRES & HORIZONTAL LOUVRES @ REAR EDGE W/TWO BRIGHT MLDGS. - ALSO BRIGHT HOOD-BELT MLDG. THREE BRIGHT HORIZONTAL GRILLE MLDGS. 'FORD' SCRIPT ON HOOD SIDES - 'V' & '8' ON HOOD PEAK - HORSEPOWER DESIGNATION ('60' OR '85') ON BRIGHT CENTER PEAK MLDG. ABOVE 'V-8'. BODY COLOR GRILLE LOUVRES.

1939 DELUXE TUDOR SEDAN — CARRYOVER 1938 DELUXE 2-DR. & 4-DR. SEDAN BODIES - NEW BODIES ON CONVERTIBLE SEDAN & CONVERTIBLE COUPE - LAST FORD CONVERTIBLE W/RUMBLE SEAT. NEW COUPE BODY

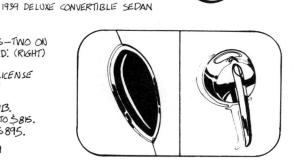

1939 DELUXE CONVERTIBLE SEDAN

DELUXE HUBCAP — BRIGHT W/CONCENTRIC RINGS. 'V-8' EMBLEM IN BLUE. WHEEL TRIM RINGS. STD. ON DELUXE CARS. BODY COLOR WHEELS.

'STANDARD' HUBCAP — PLAIN BRIGHT DISC W/'V-8' IN BLUE. BLACK WHEELS.

GODSHALL '76

CARRYOVER 1938 TAILLIGHTS — TWO ON DELUXE, ONE ON 'STANDARD'. (RIGHT)

NEW DECK LID HANDLE & LICENSE PLATE LIGHT. (FAR RIGHT)

ALL 1939 FORDS ON 112" WB. 'STANDARD' SERIES — $580 TO $815. DELUXE SERIES — $680 TO $895.

THANKS TO FORD EXPERT JIM WAGNER FOR HIS HELP!

1940 'STANDARD' FORD V·8 — (BELOW)
SIMILAR IN APPEARANCE TO 1939 DELUXE SERIES
W/CARRYOVER HOOD & MODIFIED FENDERS.
NEW GRILLE W/BODY·COLOR VERTICAL LOUVRES.
BRIGHT VERTICAL CENTER PANEL W/'V' & '8'
EMBLEM AT TOP. BRIGHT CENTER HOOD
MLDG. W/'FORD' IN VERTICAL LETTERS.
HORIZONTAL BRIGHT TRIM MLDG. ABOVE
GRILLE. NEW BUMPER & GUARDS. NEW
BRIGHT GROOVED HOOD·BELT MLDG·
BODY·COLOR HEADLAMP TRIM RINGS.
SEALED·BEAM HEADLAMPS — SEPARATE
PARKING LAMPS.

1940 DELUXE FORD V·8 — (ABOVE)
NEW UNIQUE HOOD, HORIZONTAL BRIGHT CENTER GRILLE, BODY·COLOR
FLANKING GRILLES W/THREE BRIGHT HORIZONTAL MLDGS. 'V' & '8' IN RED
IN VERTICAL CENTER MLDG. NEW BUMPER & GUARDS SHARED W/'STD.'
BRIGHT HEADLAMP TRIM RINGS W/SEALED BEAM HEADLAMPS &
SEPARATE PARKING LAMPS. NEW GROOVED BRIGHT HOOD·BELT MLDG.

ALL CARS HAD COWL-MOUNTED
WIPERS. BLACK RUBBER
WINDSHIELD FRAME W/BRIGHT
DIVIDER BAR ON ALL
COUPES & SEDANS.
BRIGHT FRAMES
ON DLX. CONVERTIBLE
& WAGON.

1940 DELUXE CONVERTIBLE COUPE W/CONVEN-
TIONAL DECK LID—NO RUMBLE SEAT. ALL OTHER
BODIES CARRY·OVER FROM 1939. VENT WINDOWS
ADDED TO FRONT DOORS. 112" WB.
1940 'STANDARD' FORD — $ 600 TO $850.
1940 DELUXE FORD — $ 700 TO $920.

1940 DELUXE FIVE-WINDOW COUPE

DELUXE HUBCAP—
PLAIN BRIGHT DISC
W/ 'FORD DELUXE'
IN RED. BRIGHT
TRIM RINGS STD.
BODY·COLOR
WHEELS.

'STANDARD'
HUBCAP—
BRIGHT DISC
W/CONCENTRIC
RINGS.
'V·8' IN BLUE.
BLACK WHEELS.

GODSHALL '76

NEW CHEVRON-STYLE
TAILLIGHTS—TWO ON
DELUXE, ONE ON 'STD.'

NEW DECK LID
HANDLE & LICENSE
PLATE LAMP.

DELUXE—
BRIGHT HEADLAMP
TRIM RINGS—SEPARATE
PARKING LAMP.

'STANDARD'—
BODY·COLOR HEAD-
LAMP TRIM RINGS—
SEP. PARKING LAMP.

1936 Ford Station Wagon

HENRY Ford didn't invent the station wagon, or the series production of station wagon bodies, or even the first cataloged station wagon from a major auto maker. Typically however, once he decided to get into the station-wagon business, he immediately made more of them than anyone else in the world. And the Ford Motor Company held that lead for 20 years.

Wooden-bodied "depot hacks" are almost as old as the automobile in America, dating back at least to 1899. Mostly they carried paying passengers to and from train stations. In the beginning, their operators bought "express" trucks or bare truck chassis and built wooden seats in the back themselves. later on, auto and truck dealers arranged with nearby furniture or cabinet manufacturers to custom-build wagon bodies for the commercial market. Most often these bodies had fixed roofs, but rarely glass windows; the station wagon was an "open" body style.

In the summer of 1908, while Henry Ford was perfecting his Model T, Freelan Stanley was building his first "Mountain Wagon" to haul guests and their luggage from the railroad in Loveland, Colorado, up 35 miles of rugged trail to his hotel in Estes Park. The Mountain Wagon appeared in Stanley catalogs for 1909, but with its touring car-style canvas top, it did not look anything like our modern conception of a station wagon.

By the early twenties, however, a number of specialist coachbuilders supplied station-wagon bodies, almost invariably with fixed roofs but curtain-style windows. There were York and Martin-Parry, both in York, Pennsylvania; J. T. Cantrell & Co. in Huntington, New York; H. H. Babcock in Watertown, New York—and also Ionia, Raulang, Cotton, Springfield, Seaman, Mifflinburg, and Hercules. These companies shipped knocked-down bodies to dealers, who assembled and installed them for customers. And the customers themselves were changing. Ads ap-

peared in *Fortune* and *Country Life* touting station wagons as rugged vehicles for hunting or fishing, or as ideal runabouts for servants and nannies. As a result, wagon bodies sometimes found their way onto some fairly prestigious chassis. For the most part, however, even this wealthy new clientele considered the wagon a working vehicle and specified more humble running gear—from Dodge, for example, or Chevrolet. In fact, the most popular chassis of all for station-wagon conversion was the Model T—probably because it was also the most popular chassis for just about everything else.

One might have expected wily old Henry Ford to capitalize on this situation with a station wagon of his own manufacture. But Billy Durant beat him to it. In 1922, the former GM mogul launched a Model T competitor called the Star; by 1923, the official Star model lineup included a station wagon. This was the first fixed-roof wagon ever cataloged by a significant manufacturer of automobile chassis, but it succumbed to the collapse of Durant's overextended empire in 1928. The following year, Chrysler's Fargo division cataloged steel-paneled wagons on both four- and six-cylinder commercial chassis. But by that time Ford had finally entered the game.

He certainly had the means to do it. In 1920, Henry had bought a million acres of maple near Iron Mountain, Michigan,

to assure an adequate supply of lumber for the Model T's composite body. He even built a plant on the site to cut and finish wooden body parts. But it wasn't until 1929—and the Model A—that Ford officially offered a station wagon. At $695, it cost $70 more than a four-door sedan. Naturally Iron Mountain produced the wooden parts, then shipped them to Murray in Detroit for assembly. Piano-hinged doors latched at the center post, and all windows were covered by canvas and isinglass curtains. Ford built 4,954 of these wagons for the calendar year—a modest percentage of 1.4 million Model A's, but more than enough to instantly establish Ford as the world's largest producer of station wagons.

Raulang as well as Murray assembled Ford wagon bodies in 1930, as custom builders began converting Ford wagons to more specialized functions—ambulances, for example, or campers. Unfortunately, the deepening Depression cut into all auto sales, and wagons were no exception. Total Model A production for the calendar year slipped to just a little over a million, including 3,510 station wagons; it slid to under a half-million and 2,848 wagons in '31.

Business conditions were so bad that even Henry Ford second-guessed himself. Instead of the new V-8 he had been developing since 1929, he cautiously entered 1932 with the four-cylinder Model B — then reversed his decision and launched the V-8 in April. The new engine was a technological breakthrough — with both banks of cylinders cast as a single unit — and a marketing breakthrough as well. Never before had so many cylinders powered such a low priced car.

The station wagon continued, although for a while the components no longer came from Iron Mountain. Instead, maple framing and birch panels for Model B and V-8 wagons were provided by the Mingel Company of Louisville, Kentucky, and assembled by Murray or Briggs. Clearly Ford saw

by John F. Katz
photos by Vince Wright

drive
report

Above left: Ford boasted new grille treatment for '36, more rounded and streamlined than predecessor. Right: Individual grilles were provided for horns.

something in the wagon body style that his competitors had missed. Chevrolet had purchased Martin-Parry in 1931 — and converted the plant to produce light trucks!

But if GM just didn't get it, Chrysler did, and in 1933 both Plymouth and Dodge released their own cataloged wagons. US Body and Forging Company of Tell City, Indiana, supplied the bodies, which featured full upholstery and roll-up windows in the front doors — a first for a production station wagon. (Cantrell continued to custom-build Dodge wagons for the *Country Life* set.)

But Ford still led the industry, selling

over 2,000 restyled wagons in 1933. This must have encouraged Henry, because he resumed component production at Iron Mountain with another significantly revised wagon body for 1935. Frames were still maple, but paneling could be maple or birch, and all the ribs now ran horizontally, eliminating the checker-board pattern of earlier wagons and creating a sleeker, longer line. And where the '33-34 wagons had suicide doors all around, the '35 returned to conventional doors in front and suicide doors in the rear — but now with roll-up glass windows in the front doors.

Still, canvas and isinglass curtains

remained standard equipment for the rest of the body. Dealers could install removable glass windows in the rear doors and quarters, but there was no such option for the tailgate. The station wagon remained an open car, sharing its cowl and fixed windshield with Ford's convertible coupe and convertible sedan. Ford wagons also carried the same radio as open models, with its speaker under the dash; on closed models the speaker was in the roof above the windshield. And while closed Fords featured adjustable seats, roadsters, phaetons, and wagons had fixed seats presumably the driver was expected to adjust.

Like Plymouth and Dodge, Ford still classified its wagon as a commercial vehicle. It did not appear in Ford's passenger-car sales book, but rather in the "commercial car" brochure, along with pickups, panel trucks, and the sedan delivery. Of these, only the wagon and the sedan delivery were built on passenger-car chassis — albeit with heavy-duty rear springs — and with passenger-car front-end sheet metal. Yet all Ford wagons featured full Deluxe trim and equipment.

'Thirty-five was a good year for Ford

Despite short nose and high profile, there's a certain honest grace in the wagon design that's pleasing to the eye.

Six passengers easily; eight in a pinch.

Steel disc wheels were new for 1936 Fords.

which had redesigned not just its wagon but its entire passenger-car line. The 1935 Ford looked rounder and heavier, but at the same time more modern and streamlined, with Ford's first integral trunk on "Touring Sedans." Ford had significantly altered the proportions of the car, shifting the engine ahead eight inches over the front axle, then moving the seats ahead as well, so the "back-seat passengers enjoy a front-seat ride." Ford called this its "Center-Poise" chassis. One year earlier, Chrysler had called a similar arrangement the Airflow, but Ford had pulled it off with more style.

The V-8 engine was now rated 90 bhp, with copper-lead conrod bearings, a cast-alloy camshaft, and forced-draft crankcase ventilation. The frame and rear end were stronger, the clutch and brakes improved as well. Dearborn actually promoted its mechanical brakes as a safety feature — and maybe Henry Ford sincerely believed that they were. Sales literature stressed the solid reliability of steel levers and cables, and reassured potential buyers that the system could not fail "in an emergency." For the first time since 1930, Ford outsold Chevrolet — although a strike at Chevrolet probably helped.

Unfortunately, Ford wasn't able to carry this momentum into 1936. Although billed as a "new" model, the '36 Ford had in fact changed very little. Refinements to the steering mechanism reduced steering effort 25 percent; while spiral-cut gears for first and reverse, revisions to the rear axle, and new sound-deadening insulation in the body all contributed to quieter running. For reasons which aren't entirely clear, Ford now claimed

only 85 bhp for the V-8. Styling changes consisted of a new hood and grille, fatter fenders, and a switch from wire to pressed-steel wheels. Chevrolet recaptured its lead, and held it until 1954.

The Ford wagon body continued virtually unchanged for '36, even retaining its 1935 rear fenders. Ford still ruled the wagon market, in spite of thickening competition. Hudson cataloged a wagon that year, and so did truck manufacturer International Harvester. Studebaker and Packard followed in '37.

Chevrolet had debuted the steel-sided Suburban Carryall in 1935, but it was a homely, two-door vehicle based on a half-ton truck chassis. (A four-door woody version appeared in '37, as did GMC editions of both wood and steel models.) Yet, even though a large percentage of Cantrell's custom-ordered bodies were being fitted to Chevrolet passenger-car chassis, General Motors didn't catalog a car-based wagon until 1939 — and then it released three of them, for Chevrolet, Pontiac, and Oldsmobile. Buick followed in 1940.

Meanwhile, Ford began to assemble its wagon bodies at Iron Mountain in 1937; for the first time a wagon was built entirely in-house by a major auto maker. Glass windows became a factory option rather than a dealer-installed accessory, and Ford made them standard in '38. Ford produced nearly 7,000 wagons that year; nearest rivals Plymouth and Dodge didn't sell 1,000 between them.

But it couldn't last forever — not with Henry Ford clinging to increasingly obsolete technology. Ford lost the wagon sales race for the first time in 1948, to arch-rival Chevrolet. And while Dearborn quickly regained the lead in '49, Chevrolet — and Plymouth, too — would remain serious rivals as the station wagon market exploded to six-digit proportions in the early fifties.

Driving Impressions

Walt Hansen bought our featured '36 Ford wagon 20 years ago, in rough but running condition. He enjoyed driving it for a few years, then started a complete restoration — which turned into a 13-year project. It was well worth the effort, however, because Walt's wagon has since won multiple AACA Preservation Awards, as well as a Dearborn Award from The Early Ford V-8 Club of America.

Ford offered five colors for 1936, but Cordova Tan was the only standard hue for a wagon. It was possible to special-order a wagon in one of the other colors, but even then the interior hardware — for example, the window-winder boxes on the insides of the front doors — were still painted Cordova Tan. Wagon seats were upholstered in brown vinyl, while other Fords came with the customer's choice of Bedford cord, mohair, or two different broadcloths.

The rear seats don't fold flat as they

specifications

illustrations by Russell von Sauers, The Graphic Automobile Studio
© copyright 1997, Special Interest Autos

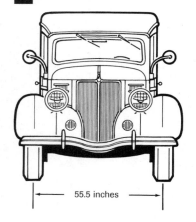

55.5 inches

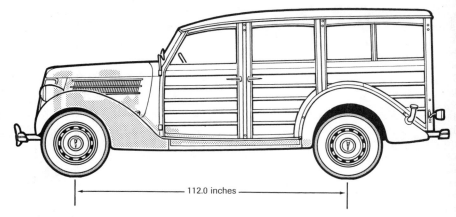

112.0 inches

1936 Ford Station Wagon

Base price	$670
Deluxe equip. incl.	Bright trim around grille, head-lights, and windshield; dual horns; dual taillights; gauges for fuel, oil, amps, and temperature; color-keyed floor mat; dual windshield wipers*; wheel trim rings*; clock*
Options on dR car	Radio, rear bumper, banjo steering wheel, glass side windows, Columbia 2-speed axle, outside mirrors.

*previously optional items which became standard on Deluxe models in June, the month our driveReport car was manufactured.

ENGINE
Type	V-8
Bore x stroke	3.0625 inches x 3.75 inches
Displacement	221 cubic inches
Compression ratio	6.3:1
Bhp @ rpm	85 @ 3,800
Torque @ rpm	148 @ 2,200
Taxable horsepower	30.0
Valve gear	L-head
Valve lifters	Mechanical
Main bearings	3
Induction	1 Stromberg 2-bbl downdraft
Fuel system	AC mechanical pump
Lubrication system	Pressure, gear-type pump
Cooling system	Pressure, centrifugal pump
Exhaust system	Single, 2-inch
Electrical system	6-volt

TRANSMISSION
Type	Three-speed manual, 2-3 synchronized

Ratios:	1st	2.82:1
	2nd	1.60:1
	3rd	1.00:1
	Reverse	3.83:1

CLUTCH
Type	Single dry disc
Diameter	9 inches

DIFFERENTIAL
Type	Spiral, 3/4 floating; incorporating Columbia 2-speed, vacuum-operated planetary overdrive
Ratios: Low	4.11:1
High	2.94:1

STEERING
Type	Gemmer worm and sector
Turns lock-to-lock	3.5
Ratio, overall	N/A
Turning circle	40 feet (curb/curb)

BRAKES
Type	4-wheel mechanical, internal-expanding drum
Size: front	12-inch drum
Rear	12-inch drum
Swept area	185.5 square inches
Parking brake	Mechanical, on all 4 service brakes

CHASSIS & BODY
Construction	Channel-section ladder frame with X-brace
Body	Wood, with welded steel cowl and fabric roof
Body style	7-seat station wagon

SUSPENSION
Front	I-beam axle, kingpins, radius rods, transverse leaf spring
Rear	Live axle with torque tube, radius rods, transverse leaf spring
Shock absorbers	Hydraulic, lever type, front and rear
Tires	Firestone 6.00 x 16
Wheels	Stamped steel disc

WEIGHTS AND MEASURES
Wheelbase	112 inches
Overall length	182.8 inches
Overall width	N/A
Overall height	N/A
Front track	55.5 inches
Rear track	58.2 inches
Min. road clearance	9.0 inches
Weight (w/out options)	3,020 pounds

CAPACITIES
Crankcase	5 quarts
Transmission	2.5 pounds
Rear axle	2.2 pounds
Cooling system	20 quarts
Fuel tank	14 gallons

CALCULATED DATA
Bhp/c.i.d.	0.38
Foot pounds/c.i.d.	0.67
Lb./bhp	35.5
Lb./sq. in. of swept brake area	16.3
Production total	7,044

Still good visibility for third seat passengers

would in a modern wagon, but they are removable: just tip them forward and then lift — although the weight of the rear bench might make you think twice about how badly you need that extra cargo space. The center seats come out the same way, and at least they're lighter. Removing both rows of seats leaves a rectangular box 76.875 inches long, 52.5 inches wide, and 45 inches high. That works out to 100 cubic feet of cargo space, or about mid-way between the 81.6 cubic feet in a '97 Explorer and the 118-cubic-foot capacity of an Expedition.

Installed, those seats are not one of the wagon's more lovable features. All three rows are too soft to support spines and too skimpy to support thighs. On top of that, the center-row buckets are narrow and the rearmost bench set low to the floor. That said, the passenger accommodations are still better than in many modern minivans, and even the driving position is not too bad. The front seat is bolted to the floor, but the place where it's bolted is just about right for my five feet and ten inches; even the backrest lies at a comfortable angle. The steering wheel is surprisingly small and tilts noticeably away from the driver — not at all the usual thirties helm.

The gauges have a simple, if oddly delicate, look; they are easy enough to read, but if they were just a hair smaller they wouldn't be. The headlight switch is conveniently located in the steering wheel hub, but other accessories are controlled by a lot of identical-looking and haphazardly labeled knobs.

A key releases the steering-column lock and allows the ignition switch to be flicked to the "on" position. The starter lives over by the clutch; Walt said you were supposed to be able to push the clutch in with your toe and depress the starter with your heel. I'm not quite that flexible, so I simply reach over with my right foot.

The engine idles quietly, and rumbles with a muffled V-8 rhythm once under way. A little rasp in the exhaust suggests power. It's no idle boast: Performance is plenty lively for a car of this era.

The clutch operates easily and engages smoothly, and the transmission runs quietly too, with little whine for a thirties unit. It shifts so clean and easy that it's tempting to try to hurry it. Crunch. Like most older machinery, the Ford much prefers a slow hand that pauses momentarily in neu-

Above left: Graceful accessory mirror is boon to safe driving. *Right:* No question where the gas goes. *Below:* Combination of curved and angular styling works well.

tral. Down-shifts are smooth, too, if timed precisely.

Despite the small wheel, the Ford

steers easily, maneuvering as handily as a compact in close quarters. On the road, the steering feels tight and informative. Walt quipped that the Ford handles as if it were "pivoted in the middle," which in a way it is. The body rolls considerably atop its transverse springs, even in gentle corners, but the tires grip the road securely. The sensation is similar to driving a Citroen 2CV, although not as extreme. A quick S-turn prompts a queasy moment, as the body rolls across the center, but the Ford quickly settles again, just leaning the other way. Understeer is minimal; if anything, the tail feels as if it might come around if I pushed it too hard.

The ride, while busy on secondary roads, is never uncomfortable. The wooden body creaks a bit over bumps, but again not as much as I expected, and Walt said it creaks even less in damp weather when the wood swells.

The mechanical brakes, too, were a pleasant surprise. Sure, they feel rubbery and require a bit of muscle, but they do their job as well as most mid-thirties systems, maybe even a bit better than some

Prewar Wagon Production at Ford

Calendar year	Total passenger cars	Station wagons	Percent Wagons
1929	1,378,151	4,954	0.36
1930	1,024,579	3,510	0.34
1931	481,754	2,848	0.59
1932	287,285	N/A	N/A
1933	334,969	2,013	0.60
1934	563,921	3,000	0.53
1935	942,439	4,536	0.48
1936	791,812	7,044	0.89
1937	848,608	9,304	1.10
1938	410,048	6,944	1.70
1939	532,152	9,432	1.77
1940	599,175	13,199	2.20
1941	600,814	15,601	2.60
1942	43,407	6,050	13.94

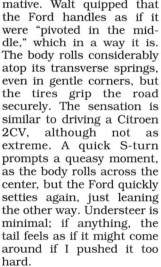

early hydraulic setups. And the[s] showed no signs of fade, even afte[r] repeated use during our action photog[raphy]. No wonder ol' Henry was in n[o] hurry to switch over to juice-typ[e] binders.

During the restoration, Walt added [a] rare and desirable Columbia two-spee[d] axle. With the axle in Low — which corre[sponds] to the Ford's standard ratio —th[e] engine sounds like it's starting to work [at] 45, and at 50 it's working hard. But shi[ft] into High, and the old V-8 cruises as qu[ietly]

Top left: *Rear woodwork is so simple it looks like it could be produced with a handsaw.* **Center:** *Door hardware is minimalist but effe[c]tive.* **Right:** *Banjo steering wheel lends sporty air.* **Above left:** *Central-mount radio allows easy tuning. Above right: Flathead V-8 wa[s] rated at 85 bhp in 1936.*

Hail, Columbia

One of the most interesting period accessories on our driveReport car is the Columbia rear axle, which shifts the final drive ratio from a vintage 4.11:1 to a thoroughly modern 2.94. Ford Motor Company never actually authorized the installation of Columbia axles in Fords and Mercurys (Zephyrs are another story; read on). Still, the device is so obviously useful to the modern driver/collector that both the Early Ford V-8 Club of America and the Antique Automobile Club of America accept it as authentic equipment. Author Dave Cole recounted its story in the May-June 1992 issue of *V-8 Times*.

In 1932, the year the Ford V-8 appeared, the Columbia Axle Company belonged to the Cord Corporation and made a "dual ratio" axle for both eight- and twelve-cylinder Auburns. Like the axles later built for Ford, these incorporated a two-speed planetary gearset into the ring gear of the differential, shifted by a vacuum cylinder when the clutch was depressed.

Columbia supplied axles for Auburns right up to the end in 1936, but someone in the company must have seen the end

coming, because they released a version for the Ford V-8, too, in August 1934. In principle, this worked the same as the Auburn axle, but differed considerably in actual mechanical detail. The Ford unit used a stock center section and left axle half, but replaced the right half with a housing and gearset made by Columbia. According to *Ford Dealer & Service Field*, the Columbia axle could be installed in '34 Fords and retro-fitted to '33s. In December 1934, Columbia debuted a completely redesigned unit for the '35 Ford.

Columbia offered a mechanically identical kit for the Zephyr; the only difference was a push-pull knob rather than a switch for the dash. (The Ford kit used the push-pull knob, too, from '37 on.) The Columbia axle actually proved even more popular on Zephyrs than on Fords, and in April '37 Dearborn made it a factory option—but only on the Zephyr.

Beginning in May 1940, however, the Zephyr offered the Borg-Warner "automatic" overdrive as an alternative to the Columbia. First seen on the '34 Chrysler Airflow, the Warner unit bolted up behind

the transmission and was controlled by the gas pedal: Lifting off the gas engaged the High range, stomping down on the pedal kicked it back to Low. Columbia responded in May '41, doubling the number of teeth on its synchro clutch (from 12 to 24) to make down-shifting easier.

Still, Columbia production seems to have ceased late in 1941. Perhaps the company converted early to military contracts; no one seems to know for sure. But it returned to the overdrive business late in 1946 with "Skyway Drive," which was essentially the pre-war axle with new electrical controls. Now the axle automatically shifted back into Low whenever the driver stepped on the clutch—to down-shift for a hill, for example, or to stop at a traffic light. But the kit never did enjoy Ford's official blessing, and production ceased with the introduction of Ford's '49 models—which offered the more sophisticated Warner overdrive as a factory option.

Kaplan Auto Parts Distributing Company, of Cleveland, bought the remaining parts stock from Columbia and continued to sell them through 1968.

bove left: Wagon's roof has the feel of a ship's cabin. **Above right:** Tailgate is held by chains. **Below:** Mirror-mounted clock was standard on Deluxe models as of mid-year '36. **Bottom:** Now you know why that outside mirror is needed!

tly as a car from the fifties or sixties. To shift the axle, simply flick the dash-mounted pre-selector switch from Low to High. The speedometer jumps as its own little gearbox shifts, then drops about 15 mph — but nothing else happens until you step on the clutch. Then, with a faint thunk from the back of the car (akin to the sound of a Chrysler Fluid-Matic shifting itself, but a touch louder and sooner), the axle shifts into overdrive. Then simply re-engage the clutch as you would for any other gear.

Walter cautioned me against shifting back into Low until I had come to a complete stop, as the lower gear may not engage while the car is rolling. Of course, you can still downshift the transmission into second or even first gear with the axle left in High. Performance doesn't suffer as much as I expected, although throttle response gets a bit soggy in the lower gears. But we were driving on mostly level ground, and Walt said that he wouldn't want to drive in hilly country with the overdrive engaged.

On the whole, the '36 Ford drives significantly better than some of the more "advanced" cars available at that time. Even with the heaviest body in the catalog, the wagon feels light and lively, with a surprising level of refinement for a low-priced car. Anyone who traded his Model A for a '36 would have been surprised at how far Ford had come in just five years. ᦂ

cknowledgments and Bibliography

Dave Cole, "Some Historical Notes on olumbia 2-Speed Axles," V-8 Times ay-June 1992; George H. Dammann, lustrated History of Ford; Beverly Rae imes, The Cars That Henry Ford Built; everly Rae Kimes and Henry Austin lark, Jr., Standard Catalog of American ars 1805-1942; Donald J. Narus, Great merican Woodies & Wagons.

Thanks to Kim M. Miller of the AACA Li-rary and Research Center, and special hanks, of course, to owner Walter Han-en.

Fabulous Flathead

Roaring through Pennsylvania behind the wheel of a 1939 Ford DeLuxe convertible

By John Katz
Photography by Vince Wright

The deep, smooth, low-rpm rumble of the Ford V-8 has become a familiar experience. Spirited, yet flexible, Henry's flathead pulls smoothly in third from as little as 10 mph — which means you can pretty much shift up into third and leave it there, as long as you aren't in any hurry. Yet the Ford accelerates briskly up to 65 mph, accompanied by a hearty, hot-rod rrrrippp.

Cruising along on a fairly rough back-country road on a sultry, drippy, 95-degree day, hot-footing through twisting bends, the thermometer-style temperature gauge

The first Ford with low-profile, grinning front-end and headlights integrated into fenders.

reads a worrisome 200 degrees. But owner George Mitchell, riding shotgun beside me, assures me that the radiator won't boil "as long as you can see daylight at the top of the gauge." I've got one eye fixed on the tiny glimpse of white that remains as I set up for the corner again.

I am always impressed by how well these transverse-sprung, solid-axle Fords ride and handle, particularly on rough or broken surfaces. The road jostles George and me, and flexes the willowy, open body, but the chassis tracks right where I point it, totally unperturbed. Of course it leans hard into the corner. But the old Ford understeers only minimally, and the quick, easy steering returns just enough feedback to inspire confidence. The oddly small— by 1930s measure—and horizontal wheel only adds to the handy, manageable feel of the car.

Back on a relatively smooth county highway, the 3.78 rear allows more

relaxed cruising than the 4.11 gears of earlier Fords. And I'm still impressed by the ride. Ol' Henry designed his transverse springs for bouncing across plowed fields without twisting the frame, but they perform pretty well in the civilized world, too. The Ford rides softly, albeit with a bit too much float, although its directional stability on the highway could match some independently sprung cars from the Sixties.

Thirty-nine was the last year for a floor shift in a Ford. The transmission is synchronized in second and third, but it still prefers a slow, deliberate hand, almost like shifting a pre-synchro unit. A quick double-clutch and a gentle blip on the throttle help ease it down from third to second. Fortunately, neither the clutch nor the shifter demands much physical effort.

Ford's first hydraulic brakes feel remarkably like Ford's last mechanical brakes—all rubbery, as if you were stretching a cable. They fade a bit with

repeated use, but they recover quickly. Effort and modulation aren't too bad, but stops are still best planned in advance.

Compared to the '36 Ford wagon I drove for SIA #163, this '39 convertible sedan has softer, more generously proportioned seats. I find myself sinking low, surrounded by a high rim of sheet metal well above elbow level. It's a little like sitting in an antique bath tub, or in a very large Porsche 356. The convertible top, with its tiny round window, rather seriously restricts vision out the back, and the small round mirrors don't help much at all. Up front, that long, pointed hood blocks the forward view when cresting steep hills—particularly disconcerting if the hill coincides with a curve.

Inside, at least, the instruments are large, straightforward, and complete save for a tach. The "Roto-Matic" radio is a little strange though, controlled by two nearly hidden thumbwheels for volume and tuning and a single button that sequences through five pre-set stations. Big, rectangular tabs around the speaker handle the choking, throttling, ash-catching, and cigarette-lighting functions. And the pop-up cowl vent pours a hurricane of cool air into the footwells at speeds as slow as 30 mph.

By the late Thirties, this combination of performance and refinement attracted a new kind of buyer to Ford's DeLuxe V-8s—wealthy buyers who sometimes sought security behind the middle-class facade of a Ford. The Depression had brought not only poverty, but also demand for change. Strikes exploded

 Originally published in Special Interest Autos #178, Jul.-Aug. 2000

Even with the top up, the convertible sedan had a handsome, if chunky, look. Rearward visibility was obviously restricted.

across the country in 1937. Accepting the inevitable, GM and Chrysler recognized the legitimacy of the UAW. But Henry Ford would not. While he preached pacifism and isolationism regarding conflicts abroad, his hired thugs fought bloody battles against labor organizers at home. The man who had once led the industry with $5-a-day wages now paid his workers a dime an hour less than his two major competitors.

For Ford, 1938 was a year of both trial and triumph. Henry suffered his first stroke, and celebrated his 50th wedding anniversary. Production dropped 52 percent for the calendar year, to just 410,048 cars, due mostly to a backsliding economy. Perhaps some of the blame belonged to the peculiar heart-shaped grille of the '38 Ford Deluxe, or to the stubby notchback body of the standard Ford. Or perhaps not. Chevrolet production fell 44 percent in the same period.

Certainly, 1938 was a full year for Ford exploits around the globe. Two men drove a '35 Ford wagon 7,700 miles from Buenos Aires to Caracas, a route never before conquered by car. Dutchmen Bakker Schut and Klaas Barendrecht pressed their '37 Ford V-8 to victory in the 2,300-mile Monte Carlo Rally, and four more Fords followed in the next six places. A Ford also won the misnamed Argentina Grand Prix, which was really a 4,000-mile stock-car race. Fifty-four cars started. Twelve of the 18 finishers were Fords. And despite the slowdown in sales, Henry built his five-millionth V-8 since the engine's spectacular introduction in April 1932.

Then, on November 4, Ford released the restyled 1939 models. So the Ford automobile entered 1939 with not only an impressive record of accomplishment, but a more appealing countenance as well. Design chief Bob Gregorie gave the '39 Deluxe a low, curved grille that looked charmingly like a chromi-

um-plated grin, and fully integrated the headlights into the new front fenders. The reshaped grille required a lower, wider radiator, which increased cooling area and forced Ford to relocate the engine fan from the generator pulley to the crankshaft. More than ever, the Deluxe Ford looked like a little Lincoln Zephyr. Even the standard Ford now shared the streamlined, fastback body of the Deluxe, although from the front it looked something like the '38 model—much as the '38 Standard had resembled a '37 Deluxe. Style probably mattered less at that end of the market.

Deluxe models and wagons were powered exclusively by Ford's larger, 221-cu.in. V-8, fortified for '39 with a heftier crank, rods, and bearings. A new carburetor and slightly higher compression boosted torque to 155-lb.-ft. at 2,200 rpm, up from 146 at 2,000 in 1938—although Ford still listed horsepower at 85, as it had since 1936, when the engine was mysteriously down-rated from the 90-hp claimed in '35. Standard models—other than wagons—came with either the big V-8 or the little 136-cu.in. 60-hp "V8/60." Either way, Standards stayed cool with the older, taller radiator and generator-mounted fan.

More significant was Ford's belated acceptance of hydraulic brakes. For years Dearborn had stubbornly resisted this inevitable advance, promoting instead "the safety of steel from toe to wheel." Henry had played his last, desperate variation on the mechanical-brake theme in 1937, specifying softer linings and replacing the brake rods with cables pulling through conduits. These "controlled self-energization" binders required about 30 percent less effort—and they did stop the car sooner—but the soft linings wore rapidly. Ford retained the system for '38 but substituted a harder lining material.

THE FORD FAMILY FOR '39

Standard Models	Price	Weight	Production
Coupe		$640	2,710
38,197			
Tudor Sedan	$680	2,830	124,866
Fordor Sedan	$730	2,850	na
Station Wagon	$840	3,080	3,277
Deluxe Models	**Price**	**Weight**	**Production**
Coupe		$700	2,752
33,326			
Tudor Sedan	$745	2,867	144,333
Fordor Sedan	$790	2,898	na
Convertible Coupe	$790	2,840	10,422
Convertible Sedan	$920	2,935	3,561
Station Wagon	$920	3,095	6,155

Sharp bend in second gear causes Ford to lean quite a bit, but understeer is under control. Transverse-sprung chassis works well on rough roads.

Amber "road lights" option costs $5 each.

V-8 emblem swings up to release hood…

… secondary hood release pops out of grille.

So when the Lockheed hydraulics finally arrived for '39, Ford did little to promote them. If Henry had to admit that he was wrong, he was going to do it as quietly as possible. The '39 dealer sales book grudgingly allowed that, "People have expressed a preference for this type of brake actuation, and in the Ford cars for 1939 they find it in a fully proved and thoroughly satisfactory form." The new Ford system featured cast-iron drums riveted onto steel hubs.

The drums still measured 12 inches all around just like the mechanical units they replaced, although the actual lining area was reduced, from 186 to 162 square inches.

The sales book lavished as much attention on Ford's new seat-cushion construction, with springs sewn into individual fabric pockets and a "flexible roll edge" that was supposed to eliminate the hard ridge at the perimeter.

In all fairness to Henry, we should note that Ettore Bugatti had surrendered to hydraulic brakes only months before. Both old masters still shunned independent front suspension—although Ford's transverse-sprung front axle was arguably more clever and defensible than the more conventional setup favored by Bugatti. Ford sales literature noted, accurately, that the crosswise springs could be tuned very soft because they only supported the weight of the car, they did not "take the drive from the rear axle, or push the front axle." Furthermore, Ford mounted the front spring slightly ahead of the front axle and the rear spring slightly behind the rear axle, for an effective "spring base" of 123 inches, or 11 inches longer than the wheelbase. This feature, combined with four-wheel hydraulic shocks and the new seats, provided what Ford called "Triple-Cushioned Comfort." Britain's *The Autocar* magazine judged the Ford suspension as good as any independent system, and in those days it probably was.

The '39 model lineup included two convertibles—coupe and sedan—available in Deluxe trim only. There was nothing unusual, of course, about a convertible coupe, and Ford had offered one in its lineup continuously since 1929. But the convertible sedan was a rarity among low-priced cars. Plymouth had one in '39 too, but it was a one-year anomaly, built on an extended wheelbase to accommodate a hand-me-down

Divided windshield is heavily framed.

Couch-like rear has built-in armrests.

Interior is handsome and functional.

Takes two to lower and fold heavy top.

Big trunk handle really fills your fist.

Locking gas cap was a $1.25 option.

The Ownership Experience

George Mitchell owns 35 Fords, most of them pre-1949 models. He has 15 pre-war V-8s at his private museum, Fords R Us, in Punta Gorda, Florida. But he keeps our featured '39 convertible sedan at his summer home in central Pennsylvania. It was probably someone's summer car originally, since it was ordered with such frills as a radio and spider wheel covers but without a heater or defroster. The body is painted Folkstone Gray and sports the tan leather upholstery that came standard on Ford convertibles.

For George, Fords represent the sentimental choice among collectible cars. More people seem to relate to Fords than any other historic automobile. "For guys my age after the war," he reminisced, "this was what was available. When I was a teenager in the late Forties, good-running Model A's were $5-$15, and V-8's were $15-$35. Of course a '39 convertible was maybe $250, and that was out of my reach."

Owner George Mitchell (left) and feature car with Ray Carr's '39 convertible sedan two months before the Peking-Paris rally.

You could hardly name an easier car to restore. "A person with basic mechanical ability can completely restore a Ford. There are catalogs available that will show you every nut and bolt. And parts for a Ford, well, you can practically build any Ford from the replacement parts that are available today. But

you're better off buying an older restoration and redoing it."

Before buying an old Ford, George recommends obtaining a judging sheet from The Early Ford V-8 Club of America, and using it as a guide to every detail; "You can't just look at it and see everything. Break it down; look at the wear on the seat edges and floor mats, and the fit of the doors, the paint, the fenders, the beading, the chrome; all that stuff is the difference between a mediocre car and a good one.

"And after you buy it, enjoy it. The Early Ford V-8 Club holds regional events all over the country—shows, tours, picnics. The best thing about owning such a popular car is that you'll meet so many people. The real fun of it is the small shows where people come around and say, 'My uncle had one.' And you meet nice people who have the same interest as you, and you look forward to seeing them again and again."

specifications

illustrations by Russell von Sauers, The Graphic Automobile Stu...

© copyright 1999, Special Interest A...

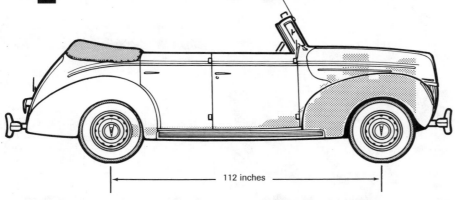

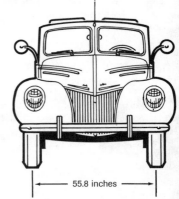

112 inches

55.8 inches

1939 Ford DeLuxe convertible

Base price	$920
Deluxe equip. inc.	Dual taillights, stainless steel wheel trim rings, dual sun visors, locking glove box with clock, banjo steering wheel, voltmeter, rear ash trays.
Options on dR car	Air cleaner, Roto-Matic radio, "spider" wheel covers, whitewall tires, dual outside mirrors, amber "road lights."
Est. price as equipped	$1,010

ENGINE

Type	V-8
Bore x stroke	3.0625 inches x 3.75 inches
Displacement	221 cubic inches
Compression ratio	6.15:1
Bhp @ rpm	85 @ 3,800
Torque @ rpm	155 @ 2,200
Taxable horsepower	30
Valve gear	L-head
Valve lifters	Mechanical
Main bearings	3
Induction	1 Stromberg 2-bbl downdraft
Fuel system	Mechanical pump
Lubrication system	Pressure, gear-type pump
Cooling system	Pressure, dual centrifugal pumps
Exhaust system	Single
Electrical system	6-volt

TRANSMISSION

Type	3-speed manual, 2-3 synchronized
Ratios	1st: 2.82:1; 2nd: 1.60:1; 3rd: 1.00:1; Reverse: 3.62:1
Overdrive	0.72:1

CLUTCH

Type	Single dry disc, semi-centrifugal
Diameter	9 inches

REAR AXLE

Type	Spiral, 3/4 floating
Ratio	3.78:1

STEERING

Type	Worm and roller
Ratio, gear	18.2:1
Turns lock-to-lock	3.5
Turning circle	38.2 feet curb-to-curb

BRAKES

Type	Lockheed 4-wheel hydraulic
Drum diameter	12 inches front and rear
Lining area	162 square inches
Parking brake	Mechanical, on rear service brakes

CHASSIS & BODY

Construction	Channel-section ladder frame with x-brace
Body	Welded steel stampings
Body style	6-seat convertible sedan

SUSPENSION

Front	I-beam axle, kingpins, radius rods, transverse leaf spring
Rear	Live axle with torque tube, radius rods, transverse leaf spring
Shock absorbers	Double-acting hydraulic, leve... type
Tires	Ford Universal 4-ply rayon
Wheels	Stamped steel spokes, 16x4 i...

WEIGHTS AND MEASURES

Wheelbase	112 inches
Overall length	186.3 inches
Overall width	69.5 inches
Overall height	67.2 inches
Front track	55.8 inches
Rear track	58.2 inches
Min. road clearance	8.0 inches
Weight	2,935 pounds (without option...

CAPACITIES

Crankcase	5 quarts
Transmission	2.5 pounds
Rear axle	2.2 pounds
Cooling system	21 quarts
Fuel tank	14 gallons

CALCULATED DATA

Bhp/c.i.d.	0.38
Lb. ft./c.i.d.	0.70
Lb./bhp	34.5
Lb. per sq. in. (brakes)	18.1
Production total	3,561

Spoke steering wheel unique to Deluxe Fords; speedo reads 100 mph.

Ford built 5 million flathead V-8s by '39; oil-bath air cleaner option...

Chrysler body. Chevrolet never cata-oged one at all.

Whereas Ford had first offered a con-vertible sedan in 1931—a two-door model with fixed window frames, and not altogether an aesthetic success with the top open—this body nonetheless survived the transition from Model A to V-8 and then disappeared at the end of 1932. But Ford re-introduced a convert-ible sedan for '35—done properly this time, with four doors, frameless win-dows, and removable center posts. At $750, it was the most expensive model in the Ford line—significantly pricier, even, than the rakish $580 Phaeton.

The "Convertible Touring Sedan" of 1936 was the first Ford with a modern-style trunk opening and a concealed spare tire. The '39 edition featured a larg-er, redesigned top and a sleek, fastback tail, more like Ford's steel-topped sedans. Already, however, the days of the open car were fading. Ford offered its last road-ster in '37, its final phaeton in '38, and its last rumble-seat convertible in '39. Nineteen thirty-nine would be the final year for the convertible sedan as well, although it would make a cameo appear-ance in the Mercury lineup for 1940.

With 3.78 gears, it's plenty lively to 65 mph.

Spare uses lots of space in 18.6-cu.ft. trunk.

Ford sales rebounded encouragingly for '39, with 532,152 cars produced during the calendar year. But that was still more than 100,000 units behind Chevrolet. And with 417,529 sales for the model year, Plymouth was closing in fast.

Nineteen-forty brought only minimal revisions to Ford styling. But technical advances included sealed-beam head-lamps, a column-mounted gearshift, disc-type wheels, and refinements to both the suspension and the brakes. A five-seat convertible coupe was the only open-top model. ॐ

221-cu.in. V-8 makes 155-lb.-ft. of torque.

PEKING TO PARIS IN A '39

As a way to torture old cars and their own-ers, Great Britain's Classic Rally Association decided to re-enact the 1907 Peking-to-Paris race 90 years later, pounding 10,241 miles, from a legendary Asian capital to a legendary European one. In the 1997 race which left Beijing, there were 94 cars; among them a '39 Ford Convertible Sedan driven by 72-year-old Ray Carr.

Ray would have to carry his mechanic, Mike Wyka, and everything else he needed in the Ford. He started with a fresh, NOS engine block; and replaced all bearings, seals, the transmission, rear end, and wheels with new-but-stock-specification parts. The rally orga-nizers allowed any radiator that would fit the original mounting, so Ray had one made without a crank hole for additional cooling capacity. He fitted a 27-gallon fuel tank, gas-filled shocks, and converted the electrical system from six volts to twelve so he could add an electric cooling fan and fuel pump.

"I brought belts, spark plugs, points, con-densers, coils, relays, thermostats, hoses, three fuel pumps, two distributors, a carburetor, left and right water pumps, an axle, and all the miscella-neous things that you think could go bad"—including a clutch, pressure plate, tools, and a jack. "I brought air filters. We had a sandstorm in Iran and Pakistan that lasted four hours.

"I had Sun Oil make a drum of 70 octane fuel, and I tuned it to 70 octane. That's what you get in China and Tibet. And I never had to adjust the carburetor." Repainted its original Dartmouth Green, the Ford was the only car in the rally with wide whitewalls. It looked good, and Ray made an effort to keep it that way. "The English people called it the 'slick little Ford.'"

Forty-three days after leaving Beijing, Ray's journey was relatively uneventful. "The car per-formed nicely," he reported. "There were only two cars in the rally that did not require assistance at one time or another from the rally mechanics, and they were my car and an Aston Martin." But the Aston blew seven tires, while Ray's Lesters per-formed flawlessly.

Ray did suffer a few frustrations. "We changed shocks in Katmandu," he remembered. "They were totally gone." He also had to change spark plugs and the voltage reducer going to the points—although the points themselves lasted. Ironically, the electric fuel pump quit in the Himalayas, so he made the rest of the trip on the mechanical pump that Henry Ford had thought-fully provided. Then the valves started tapping as Ray left Italy for Austria. "By the time I had driven that far, every sound was recognizable. I knew I had a problem, and eventually diagnosed that it was in the valve train. I had to baby my way to Paris, because when I reached 42 mph in high gear the noise was substantial." It took three frus-trating days to reach Paris, trundling slowly instead of making up time over the best roads on the route.

Still, Ray finished second in the Antique category. "I had no idea until that night in Paris when they called my name out," he told us. "I didn't try for a place, I only wanted to get to Paris. When they called my name out I was flabbergasted and overjoyed." On the whole, it had been a good day for Fords. A '42 Ford-built Jeep finished first overall, fol-lowed by a '50 Ford coupe, a '65 Cortina, and another '50 Ford.

Ray was also recognized as the oldest man on the rally. He attributes his unexpect-ed success to his gentle driving style, and not trying to win. "My experience on three previ-ous cross-country trips had a lot to do with how I drove and prepared the car. Most of the drivers ran like crazy to make their times, but I played the tortoise. People passed me, but I was not going to beat it to pieces." The strategy proved critical in the Iranian desert, where the ambient temperature soared to a scorching 118 degrees. Ray noticed that "if I drove over 52-53 mph, the temperature started to inch up. I just kept it below 52, so I didn't overheat."

And that wasn't the worst of it. "We camped in Tibet and went over the Friendship Bridge to Katmandu. It took me 12 hours to negotiate 78 miles. We drove on areas—you couldn't call them roads, they were just a mountain pass with rocks and rubble, under waterfalls and through rivers and streams. We dodged boulders, mud, and ruts...and dizzying heights with no guardrails."

Why a '39 Ford? "I chose the car because I could get new parts," Ray answered. "You can replace anything on a '39 Ford; you can get parts somewhere. And anybody in the antique and classic car clubs has great respect for that flat-head V-8. It has a proven track record—and once again, it did it."

1939 Ford Woody

by Ken Gross, *Feature Editor*
photos by Russell von Sauers

Henry's Lovable Lumber Wagon

FOR Ford Motor Co., 1939 marked the end of an era for some anachronistic features and two very special body styles. The rumble seat convertible was offered for the last time, and the lovely convertible sedan ended its production span. Three-speed floor shifts, bulb headlights, crank-out windshields, and spoke-type steel wheels would be followed in 1940 by a modern column shift, sealed beams, and disc wheels. Thankfully, one appealing link with the past still remained.

Up at Iron Mountain, Michigan, Ford employees were busy screwing, gluing and varnishing...station wagons were still made of wood—gloriously finished, brilliantly varnished, leather uphol-stered-—their lustrous paint often set off with wide whitewall tires. They were a special breed of car—even then.

North of Boston, we called them "beach wagons"—a beach wagon didn't have to be a woody but, in the late 1940s, it nearly always was. New ones with golden yellow varnished birch and birdseye maple contrasted with the greyed driftwood-like finish of neglected prewar cars. Most often, they were Fords.

Out my way. the wagons belonged to the wealthy old Yankee families on Little's Point, Marblehead Neck, Beverly Farms—always a station car, an estate hack—never primary transportation. That was the province of a Cadillac, a Lincoln, sometimes a Packard.

The people who owned these cars lived in imposing, Gatsby-like houses with huge garages or carriage houses. I was 16, fascinated with old cars, and had an after-school job delivering premium-quality S.S. Pierce groceries in a broken-down Ford woody for a long-gone little local establishment called The Farm Store. The owner was Frank Hall, or "Babe," as he was popularly known. Babe took most orders by telephone, punctuating his day with endless cups of coffee. I filled the cartons with gro-ceries, he selected the wine and cut the meat to order. Then we'd work out a delivery route, load the cartons into the woody—and off I'd go. Sometimes, I'd deliberately take my time so I could look under the tarpaulins in those big garages. In one of them, a majestic P-III Rolls languished on blocks, in another, a Hispano waited patiently.... I never looked in all the garages, but I was cer-tain each unexplored carriage house held its own four-wheeled treasure.

The loaded woody lurched along Puri-tan Road; with over-stressed cart springs and lots of steering play, curves were a real handful. Characteristically, the woody never faltered. It lugged the groceries, with wood groaning and creaking, until finally one day it just wore out. Its replacement, a step-down Hudson which doubled as the Hall's family transportation, while quicker. was never quite the same as that old Ford.

That was after the war, of course. Our driveReport deals with an earlier time. America, the sleeping giant, was rousing herself from the Depression, shrugging off the economic doldrums, and begin-ning to assume, for better or for worse, a place of responsibility in the world. Overseas, loyalist Spain had fallen, and Hitler, despite Chamberlain's appease-ment, was preparing for the Polish blitzkrieg. At home, recovery *seemed* to be in evidence.

"Business is not just coming back," exclaimed *The Ford News* in December 1938, "it will have to be brought back. That is now becoming well understood

Originally published in Special Interest Autos #63, May-June 1981

this country. Manufacturers, sellers, nd buyers will cooperate to bring back ne business that is waiting to be rought back."

With those words, a Depression-weary ord sales management cheerfully announced the company's 1939 models. ord shows nationwide hosted nine million people in just two days. The sales mphasis bears a familiar ring today. ord stressed quality and proudly nnounced the new Mercury's debut ee *Special Interest Autos* #23), for nose up-and-comers with a bit more to pend. While the new car's styling and ze may have been a disappointment or those expecting perhaps a much bigger automobile with a more distinctive nape, many clearly saw the intended mily resemblance to the new '39 ords—and attributed even more value the firm's bread-and-butter line.

Everybody in the industry was optiistic. At Chrysler, the ebullient K.T. eller predicted a 50 percent increase in ne demand for new cars. Announcing at his company had invested $15 million in tooling and dies for the '39 mods, Chrysler's president prophetically ated, "The year 1939, I am sure, will e one in which people will buy what ney *want* and not merely what they *ust have.*"

GM wasn't watching idly. William S. nudsen, the "Chrome Colossus" presient, noted an improvement in used car les that would spark a demand for ew cars. declaring that, "...GM was ady to meet the market's requirents." It didn't take a crystal ball to ee the winds of change. In 1938, autoobile operating mortality exceeded ew car sales by 150,351 unit~with the pply balance down, dealers could ford to be optimistic.

Ford's news wasn't confined to the ercury launch. The Auto King had nally succumbed to persistent dealer d public clamor for improved brakes. eluctantly, the old man abandoned he safety of steel, from pedal to wheel" r a new hydraulic-brake design. After , Chrysler pioneered mass-produced ice brakes as far back as 1924, and M had swiftly followed. Ford's long restance finally crumbled after countless periments. Henry tried many alterna-e mechanical systems—even all-metal ydraulics—in an effort to do it *his* way. Because they'd bad-mouthed hyraulics for so long, the company could arcely *rediscover* an improved braking stem. Still, showroom literature did erald the new brakes with phrases like precision-built," and "easy, velvety tion." Ford's hydraulic brake hoses ere sheathed in protective steel pres-re tubing—a distinctive but relatively nnecessary feature. The new brakes' fectiveness was evident in the reduc-on of brake lining area from 186 to 163 quare inches—a decrease of 12 percent.

Ford's smooth V-8 was still a big selling point. Competitors Chevrolet and Plymouth still used what Henry felt were "unbalanced" sixes. Meanwhile, the elder Ford, as a sop to dealer and customer requests for a six, experimented with a really unbalanced motor, an abortive in-line five. Ford dealers countered competitive claims of better gas mileage with a unique promotional booklet, in 1939, called "What's under the hood?"

The cover of the brochure had a cleverly designed Ford passenger-car hood which actually lifted (with a die-cut fold) to show the V-8 and explain key features. Economy freaks could still opt for the underpowered but thrifty V-8/60 (see *Special Interest Autos* #55), but most buyers bought the bigger V-8—which had a number of improvements for '39. Twenty-four-stud heads, a late 1938 phase-in, were continued. The crankshaft's main bearings were enlarged to 2.5 inches, while heavier rods and a bigger crankshaft improved lower-end rigidity. Compression was raised slightly to 6.2:1, and torque increased to 155 lbs./ft.

Gross horsepower, without the fan and muffler, was actually 93, but the engine was advertised as 85-bhp. On Deluxe cars, the fan was now crankshaft-driven like the Mercury—Standard models continued with a genera-

tor-driven fan—for better cooling, and a new, larger radiator was also available in the more expensive series.

The cooling system changes dovetailed with the '39's styling improvements. Standard models retained the basic 1938 grille, so they could utilize last year's radiator. Deluxe cars, with their extensive front-end restyling, needed a new low radiator. While capacity was reduced one quart to 21, frontal area was increased to 384 square inches. A six-blade fan, mounted low in the chassis, was crankshaft-driven—and became the source of two annoying problems.

The engine required a torsional damper to compensate for the lack of a fan belt, which had previously served as a flexible coupling. In extremely rugged terrain, the fan had a tendency to windmill into the radiator. Although Ford engineers began work on an electric fan, later restyling in 1942 would require a new radiator once more, and the fan was relocated and once again belt-driven.

Ford styling for 1939 marked the second year of a much more pleasingly proportioned Ford motor car. *Special Interest Autos* readers will recall that the lengthened wheelbase of the 1935-36 models (see *Special Interest Autos* #36) lent a graceful, sweeping effect to the rear sections of the coupes and roadsters, but a relatively stubby frontal

Left: *Hood latch forms integral part of nose trim.* **Above:** *'39 Fords were first ones to use spoke-type steel wheels. 6.50 x 16 tires were optional on woodies.* **Below:** *Simple, straightforward body design marks '39 and '40 Ford woodies.*

Above left: Woody uses regular passenger car sheet metal and trim up front. Above right: Single taillamp was standard equipment eve[n] on Deluxe models. Below left: Woody's top blends nicely into sheet metal. Below right: Sliding windows keep things warm or cool [in] the back.

appearance which continued in 1937 was also part of the package. While the 1938 design went a long way toward recovering proportions, the 1939 Deluxe hood and fender lines, closely related to the new Mercury, were just the refinement Ford needed to compete aesthetically in the low-price field.

Copywriters extolled the update, writing that the new Fords had "... brilliant, streamlined beauty inspired by the Lincoln-Zephyr—the acknowledged style leader among modern motor cars." Certainly the '39's good looks are an integral part of the model's present-day popularity.

Standard Fords, in keeping with what would be practice through 1940, used an adaptation of the previous year Deluxe model's front sheet metal; sedan bodies were enlarged to be identical with the Deluxe series—2.06 inches, longer overall than the 1938's, with four inches more body length. Coupe bodies were entirely new in both series.

Headlamps on Deluxe cars were now flush-mounted in the fenders themselves. The new, wider location sealed beams greatly improved night visibility. Interior selections included broadcloth or mohair, while convertibles and station wagons featured a light russet shade of leather. Deluxe cars used a golden grain mahogany finished instrument panel with circular dials—a new battery condition indicator replaced the ammeter.

Standard models came in three basic flavors plus a station wagon—they were the fordor and tudor sedans and the coupe. Deluxe cars included those four selections and added the two and four-door convertibles. In a reflection of the economy and manufacturing efficiencies, the line did not include a Deluxe convertible club coupe and a club coupe. These would return in 1940 and 1941, respectively. The open-windowed phaeton, with its drafty side curtains, had been dropped for 1939—not surprisingly, with a sales level in its final year of only 1,169 units.

The convertible sedan received a trunk section similar to the regular sedan's and a redesigned, bigger, canvas top. This lovely car would be dropped from the Ford line after 1939, but curiously was offered in the Mercury selection for 1940 before disappearing for all time. Perhaps the most romantic hangover, the rumble seat, was in its last year—sadly, the club convertible of 1940 made this old tradition redundant.

In mid-1939, the 27 millionth Ford ever, a Deluxe green tudor sedan, left the Golden Gate International Exposition in San Francisco for a round-trip trans-continental tour, which included a one week stop at the New York World's Fair. The car had been built at Ford's Richmond, California, plant in February. As the anniversary Ford proceeded from state to state, special license plates commemorating its trip were attached above and below the bumpers. (See *Special Interest Autos* #58.)

The tudor reached the New York fa[ir] on June 16th, just in time for the Fo[rd] Motor Company's 36th birthday an[d] Official Ford Day at the fair. The com[-]pany's presence at the exposition wasn['t] limited to its milestone car—the For[d] exhibit, including the very popula[r] "Road of Tomorrow," featured contin[u-]ous rides in full-sized cars from all thr[ee] Ford lines. When the fair ended, near[ly] two million visitors had ridden in t[he] Fords, Mercurys and Zephyrs.

The excitement of the anniversary ca[r] and the Mercury launch eclipsed all b[ut] a passing reference in *Automobile Topi[cs]* concerning the development of a For[d] small car. The magazine quoted un[-]named Ford executives who justifie[d] dropping the project because the initi[al] sales target of a million units seeme[d] unrealistic. The program, according [to] the article, was to be deferred for 1[8] months.

However, the development of Ford['s] six-cylinder engine was seriously und[er] way in early 1939 for a 1941 introduc[-]tion (see *Special Interest Autos* #41[).] Edsel Ford and the company's chi[ef] engineer, Laurence Sheldrick, were pi[t-]ted by Henry Ford against his laborato[-]ry team headed by Eugene Farkas. She[l-]drick's engine, a conventional L-head [6,] was far more practical than Farkas['s] ohc experiment and was adopted tw[o] years later. The introduction of Stude[-]baker's Champion inspired Edsel For[d] to order development of a smaller si[x-]cylinder engine, but by mid-year th[e] effort was abandoned.

For the first time, in 1939, both For[d] station wagons were available in th[e] Standard and Deluxe series—in prev[i-]ous years they were considered "com[-]mercial cars"—now they were classifie[d] with the other Ford passenger car[s.] Ford still planned the Standard serie[s] basically for commercial use. Literatu[re] for sales personnel indicated that offe[r-]ing the station wagon at two price leve[ls] "... should materially widen its market[."] The Deluxe car, according to the ve[ry] complex Ford sales manual, "...is intended particularly for the services it has filled in the past, namely for estates, summer resorts, country and golf clubs, where guests and members are to be carried with their baggage." In both models, the center and rear seats could be removed, leaving a long loading space measuring 72 x 44 x 42.5 inches. With the tailgate down, another two feet of length was available.

A number of improvements in 1939 added to the Deluxe wagon's appeal. These included chrome-plated carriage bolts and a high luster varnish rub applied on the hard maple body. Seats were "genuine" Spanish leather. The armrest on the right side of the middle seat was chrome plated, and all four doors, properly weatherstripped for 1939, had new stainless steel scuff plates.

Spare tires were mounted behind the front seat on both models—Deluxe cars had a tire lock and a metal tire cover. Colors varied from Standard to Deluxe. The factory offered Coach Maroon as the basic Deluxe woody color, but six other selections were available. Standard cars came principally in business-like Wren Tan with three other no-cost options.

6.00 x 16 blackwalls and the 85-bhp V-8 were standard on both series—6.50 x 16 six-plys could be specified, however, and the bluebloods could order wide-white sidewalls. A single left-side taillight was all you got with either Standard or Deluxe—except in states which required two taillights by law. It was a drum type lamp and nowhere as attractive as the graceful tear-drop light, carried over from 1938, used on the rest of the passenger car line.

Many restorers today use an identical right-hand taillight accessory with custom cast-iron bracket that looks just as though it came that way from the factory. Ed Clarke, of Larchmont, New York, the owner of our driveReport woody, sells these lights and other woody goodies—like top material, special screws, bolts, interior hardware, and trim items.

A word about wooden bodies is in order here, although *Special Interest Autos* has touched on the subject in past articles and driveReports—particularly in *Special Interest Autos* #17, in an article called, "Lumber Wagons." Most major manufacturers sold wooden bodied station wagons as production items, but under commercial catalogues. Ford was the acknowledged leader from the beginning and the first to initiate its own manufacturing facility. GM, Chrysler and the independents used proprietary bodies built by firms such as Cantrell, Hercules, Ionia and US Body & Forge, to name just a few.

Ford initially bought its Model T depot hack bodies from a number of companies, including the Seaman Co., in Kenosha, Wisconsin, a firm which later

became a major Nash supplier.

The 1929 Model A line included Ford's first factory-catalogued station wagon, and bodies were built by long-time Ford suppliers Briggs Mfg. Co., and Murray Corp. of America—both in Detroit. The actual wood came from a furniture company, the Mengel Co. of Louisville, Kentucky. But by 1935, woodies were big business at Ford and, in keeping with Henry's desire to do everything possible within his own company, Ford ceased using Mengel and instead called upon its own forests and woodworking facilities at Iron Mountain, Michigan, to supply and pre-form the wood before shipping the components to Briggs and Murray for final assembly.

The Iron Mountain timber acreage grew maple, birch, gum, and basswood, and these requirements became pretty much standard for woodies by 1932. Woodies were always more expensive than passenger cars, despite the best of

Ford and other manufacturers' cost-cutting attempts. Although the wood was relatively inexpensive, the intensive labor required to shape, cure and fit the furniture together—plus the finishing costs for all those coats of varnish—was always more expensive than the automated lines which poured out metal panels in Detroit

In 1935, Ford made glass windows an option—drafty side curtains had been standard woody fare in the preceding year—and finally, in 1938, glass all around was standardized. To help keep costs down, Ford used basically the same wagon body from 1935-38 and a different one with fewer horizontal strips and broader plywood panels from 1939-48, with some trim variations. The '39 woody is the last of the angular bodies, and the 1940, its replacement, dropped the '39's suicide rear doors and has a more gracefully rounded front roof section. Mercurys shared the same bodies

*Above left: Even passengers in the third seat had sliding windows for their comfort. **Above right:** Wood inside as well as out. Window crank is mounted through metal escutcheon plate; door latch looks like it could do a nasty job on clothing. **Below:** Thanks to Ford's "primitive" transverse leaf spring and beam axle, woodie offers good handling through corners.*

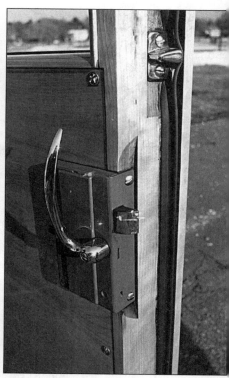

Above: Angular body is somewhat relieved by subtle arches on top of window frames. *Right:* Inside door latches are mounted in an awkward spot for ease of use. *Below left:* Rear-end styling couldn't be much simpler, but it's attractive nonetheless: *Below right:* With removable third seat installed, carrying capacity is just about nonexistent unless tailgate is used.

from 1941-48. During the war, Ford put the Iron Mountain facility to good use making gliders.

When the war ended, Ford developed the lovely Sportsman (see *Special Interest Autos* #10) as a quick and relatively inexpensive (in terms of tooling) way to add some excitement to a product line which still used basically prewar bodies. Chrysler's Town & Country, which bowed before the war, continued in 1946 with wooden bodies supplied and trimmed by the Pekin Wood Products Co., in Helena, Arkansas. These efforts and the inclusion of woodies in competitive lines kept the furniture fashion alive through 1949, but thereafter, less-expensive, all-steel bodies took over. Ever the diehard, Ford didn't give up on woodies until 1952.

Another reason for the demise of the woody was the degree of care needed to keep the bodies looking great. In a Ford factory pamphlet, it stated blandly that the original finish "...gives the body ample protection for about *one year* under ordinary circumstances." Thereafter, the factory recommended stripping, sanding, bleaching, and revarnishing on an *annual* basis to preserve the cars. While this might be fine for a business or country club, most private owners found the task disagreeable, at best Today, woody restorers can find wood available for many early Ford and Chevrolet models, and some firms will custom-make the cabinetry for the later cars. Modern technology with plastic

resin finishes hasn't helped woody folk—the experts recommend careful sanding and finishing the old-fashioned way, with good quality marine spar varnish. Fitting finger joints, bleaching wood to match, and carefully applying a snug boot top are all difficult efforts, but the finished product is a traffic stopper—and a recipient of countless "...they sure don't build 'em like they used to's."

Original accessories on restored cars are very popular today and, in the last few years, a number of restoration firms have been making some excellent reproductions. Many of the popular Ford 1939 extras, such as road lights (at $5.00 then), a locking gas cap ($1.25) and chrome spider hubcaps ($3.75 each) are all available today, but at greatly increased prices, of course.

Still, the high-point-seeking restorer can go on a treasure hunt for draft deflectors (originally a $10.75 accessory, in lieu of windwings), a matching three-piece set of Ford luggage ($41.00 then), or genuine Ford teardrop fender skirts (they were only $9.00 in 1939!).

Heaters and radios were the most frequently purchased 1939 accessories, according to the Ford sales manual. Buyers could choose from hot air or hot water—and both units featured illuminated switches, built-in defrosters, and adjustable heat control—you took your pick at $18.75. The radio was a new, for 1939, six-tube superheterodyne "...actually comparable to an eight-tube set."

With Ford's automatic tuning feature, single Roto-Matic control, you could pre-select any one of five local stations and use a second control for distant broadcasts. The roof-mounted antenna was located just above the center windshield divider. It stayed down for local stations and could be rotated vertically from within the car for better long distance reception. Buyers cheerfully paid $45.00 for their entertainment—installation was extra.

Under the hood, accessory selections included the usual Ford lineup of oil-bath air cleaners (hat-type and heavy-duty), an oil filter, and the electrically operated speed governor. The latter was sometimes specified for commercial use. The Columbia two-speed rear axle was a dealer-installed extra, highly prized by restorers today. "Cruise at 60 with your engine loafing at 43," proclaimed the Columbia brochure. The installation actually provided six forward speeds, but most owners simply used it for top gear economy.

None of the American motoring magazines of the period conducted "road tests" in 1939, but overseas, in its May issue, Britain's *The Autocar* put a '39 fordor through its paces. British road tests of the thirties are very businesslike and quite laconic—but an occasional burst of emotion creeps through.

Calling the Ford redesign, "strikingly modern," the editors stiltedly commented, "...when acquaintance is renewed with the V-8, the top-gear abilities never fail to be impressive." *The Autocar* testers weren't simply impressed with the Ford's acceleration, they also liked the car's ability to accelerate smoothly upward from four or live mph in high

rear. "Acceleration," the report continued, "was of an exciting order."

Surprisingly, the magazine found little fault with the Ford's semi-elliptic cart springs. "There is little or no tendency to pitching on normal roads, and whilst some leaning over occurs if high speeds are held round appreciable bends, the general impression is of sufficient stability for quite fast driving." Besides, the editors reasoned, the V-8's brisk acceleration would make up for ground lost slowing for curves.

While reasonably accepting of the car's suspension, the road testers criticized the Ford's rather vague steering. "No definite feel of the front wheels," was *the Autocar's* judgment. The new Ford hydraulics, however, received high marks. The export version of Ford's '39 Deluxe sedan was upholstered in leather, a £7 option overseas. Although it's not generally known, leather upholstery could be specified as a very special order for Ford closed cars at home, too—probably for dealers who just didn't want to lose a sale to wealthy customers.

The perennial sales battle in the low-price field was still a hot war in 1939. Although the Ford styling effort, now coupled with hydraulics, scored some points, it was up against a smartly re-vamped Chevrolet with independent front suspension—an unequal-length wishbone system that replaced the troublesome Dubonnet suspension. Chevy also had a vacuum-assisted column

Above left: Despite its square-rigged body styling, '39 Ford woody has a very pleasing appearance in profile. In fact, it looks positively voluptuous from this angle. Above right: Rear window flips up, tailgate comes down for scads of carrying space.

shift. Plymouth. too, came in for a restyling (see *Special Interest Autos #22*), was in its second year with a column shift, and had an effective new independent front suspension to match Chevrolet's.

The sales year started off well for Ford. Sales manager John R. Davis, working to improve his sales force, asked branch managers for suggestions that could be passed along to Ford engineering—a radical departure from the days when no criticism, even constructive, had been permitted. The reports for March indicated 75,400 units had been moved, the best sales month since July 1937. Spurred by this effort, Davis offered generous incentive prizes in a summer sales drive. He spoke enthusiastically to his managers, saying, "Is this the kind of help a factory should furnish dealers? if not, what?" Davis armed his men with

facts from *Consumers' Research* reports dating from 1934 onward showing Chevrolet had many weaknesses.

Sadly, the popular Davis would not be able to continue his momentum. He had a fight with "notorious" Harry Bennett at the September sales meeting at the Dearborn Country Club, and his dismissal soon followed. Ford historians Nevins and Hill wrote that Davis's departure "...checked the momentum of the Ford organization." Davis's replacement, Henry K. Doss, was a capable man, but he, too, found it difficult to overtake Chevrolet despite continued improvements in the product line.

When the dust settled at year's end, Ford had improved over its 1938 totals, but at 481,496 units, Ford trailed Chevrolet's 598,341 cars. Plymouth was still behind Ford with sales of 348,807. Rarest of the '39s?—not the convertible

Tips For Tops

The downfall of many woody restorers is that they don't take the necessary preparation time in the roof structure before putting on the cover.

Just as in painting, it's the effort put into repairing metal, sanding, priming, etc., before the top paint coat that counts. All nails and screws must be secured. All joints where the different sections of wood butt up against each other must be smooth and at the same level. Fill all open joints and bolt holes with auto body filler and sand holes and joints with a belt sander.

Follow this up with an air or electric oscillating sander. If equipment is not available, use a hand block sander. Now take your hand and run it over the front, rear, and side headers. It should be one continuous, well-shaped, smooth contour.

Sometimes the slats that run fore and aft are warped. It is not necessary to replace the entire slat. A new piece can be sectioned in between the bows. Varnish before installing. When you think you have it perfect, check by taking a bed sheet, placing a person at each corner of the roof, and having them pull the sheet taut. Sight the roof from all angles. Any irregularities should show up.

Seal top work structure with varnish. At this point I cheat a bit, as I don't like the coarse side of the top material showing through the slats. I place a piece of pink beige headliner material fuzzy side down over the roof first. Make it taut and staple or tack it about 1/2-inch from the edge of the top material, and trim excess.

I have available black and brown top material in long and short grain in 63-64-inch width. Position the material on top of the roof in the sunlight. The heat will assist you greatly in the pulling and stretching, particularly in the corners.

Start at the rear of the car. Call your helpers back on the job, as it will be very difficult or almost impossible to do it yourself. While someone holds the material on the outside opposite rear corner, place a few tacks or staples to hold the material in place. Now place a few tacks on the other side where your helper has been holding the material very taut. While your helper is pulling the material on one side towards the front

of the car, you should be pulling the material to the rear and down, working out the wrinkles in the corner on the same side.

Now, work on the other corner, tacking in each direction. This is the most important part of the job. If you are using tacks, don't drive them all the way home in the beginning, as you will find that you will have to remove some and readjust the material as you proceed.

At this point the corners should be well rounded, with no wrinkles, and the tacks should be spread towards the front about six to eight inches and along the rear header from the corner about six to eight inches. Don't place the tacks too close to the edge of the roof, as it may split the wood. If you place them too high they will still show after you replace the gutters. About 1/2-inch from the edge will do fine. I use an air staple gun, only because it's faster. Copper tacks are best to use; they won't rust.

Pulling the material down and forward, tack up one side about eight inches while your helper is pulling on the other side. Keep pulling the material down as you work forward. Only tack about eight inches at a time, then go over to the other side. Pull down material and tack. Back to the other side. Back and forth, tugging down and slightly forward as you tack and move towards the front of the car.

Never try to tack up one side completely. Work from one side to the other, about eight inches at a time. First thing you know you will be up to the front header. The front corners are a breeze compared to the rear. You will have to tug the material a little more for the front corners, and may even undo the tacks over the front doors to get all the wrinkles out. Pull and tack the front header. Pull and complete the tacking of the rear header.

Stand back and view the entire top from all sides. Stand on a chair and make sure the top's without a wrinkle and tight as a drum. If so, drive all tacks or staples home and trim excess material. Repair, sand, paint, and install front moulding, then side gutters. Install corner finishing pieces. Stand back, baby, to view a woody which has been topped with truly the crowning glory it deserves.

Ed Clarke

specifications

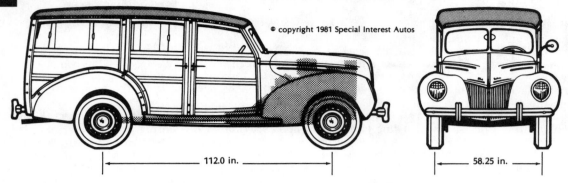

© copyright 1981 Special Interest Autos

112.0 in.   58.25 in.

1939 Ford Deluxe Station Wagon

Price when new	$920 Detroit
Std. equip.	85-hp V-8 engine, bumper guards, genuine leather seats, clock, cigar lighter, ash tray
Options on dR car	Whitewall tires, hub and spoke covers, wheel trim rings, outside mirrors, visor vanity mirror, spot light, road light, radio, hot air or hot water heater, center mount bumper guard, seat covers, speed governor, oil filter.

ENGINE

Type	L-head, 90-degree V-8, water-cooled, cast-iron block, 3 mains, full pressure lubrication
Bore x stroke	3.062 inches x 3.75 inches
Displacement	221.0 cubic inches
Max. bhp @ rpm	85 @ 3,800
Max. torque @ rpm	155 @ 2,200
Compression ratio	6.15:1
Induction system	Downdraft 2-bbl. carburetor, mechanical fuel pump
Electrical system	6-volt battery/coil

TRANSMISSION

Type	3-speed manual, floor shift
Ratios: 1st	2.820:1
2nd	1.604:1
3rd	1.000:1
Reverse	3.625:1

CLUTCH

Type	Single dry plate, molded asbestos lining
Disc diameter	9.0 inches
Actuation	Mechanical, foot pedal

DIFFERENTIAL

Type	Spiral bevel gears, torque tube drive
Ratio	3.78:1 (4.11:1 optional)
Drive axles	3/4-floating

STEERING

Type	Gemmer worm and roller
Ratio	18.2:1
Turns lock-to-lock	4.5
Turn circle	38 ft., 2 in.

BRAKES

Type	4-wheel, hydraulic drums
Drum diameter	12.0 inches
Total swept area	162.0 square inches

CHASSIS & BODY

Frame	Channel and box section steel, central X-member, 4 cross-members
Body construction	Wood and steel
Body style	4-door, 8-passenger station wagon

SUSPENSION

Front	I-beam axle, transverse, semi-elliptic leaf spring, lever hydraulic shocks, radius rods
Rear	Rigid axle, transverse, semi-elliptic leaf spring, lever hydraulic shocks, radius rods
Tires	6.500 x 16, 6-ply (6.50 x 16 6 ply optional)
Wheels	Pressed steel, 4.0-inch drop center rims, lug-bolted to brake drums

WEIGHTS AND MEASURES

Wheelbase	112.0 inches
Overall length	188.7 inches
Overall width	69.5 inches
Overall height	69.1 inches
Front track	58.25 inches
Ground clearance	8.0 inches
Curb weight	3,231 pounds

CAPACITIES

Crankcase	5.0 quarts
Cooling system	21.0 quarts
Fuel tank	14.0 gallons

FUEL CONSUMPTION

Best	18-20 mpg
Average	14-16 mpg

PERFORMANCE

0-30	4.9 seconds
0-50	12.2 seconds
0-60	18.2 seconds
0-70	25.7 seconds
Top speed	88-90 miles per hour (from *The Autocar*, 5/12/39)

MARQUE CLUBS

Early Ford V-8 Club of America
48 2nd St.
San Francisco, CA 94105

National Woodie Club
5522 West 140th St.
Hawthorne, CA 90250

sedan with 3,561 units, but the Standard wagon, which totaled just 3,277 cars produced. There were 6,155 Deluxe woodies, for a lumber wagon total of 9,432—double the sedan deliveries and nearly as many as the convertible coupes.

The '39 Ford is highly priced by collectors today—it represents continual refinements on Ford's thirties theme, and the improved braking and pleasing lines are a plus over earlier models. It's remarkable that the Ford company, with an aging, obstinate, certainly reactionary Henry at the helm, was able to develop cars that have such lasting pop-

ularity today. The Ford empire was struggling with union problems, internal management dissension, a product line which lagged behind the competition and the universally poor economic situation. The cars today bear an unmistakable stamp of individuality—but then, that was Henry Ford's trademark. There's a quote of the elder Ford's in the 1939 sales brochure that, characteristically, sums up his feelings:

"There are some things we refuse to do to sell a car. We like sales, but fair dealing and the confidence of our customers are desirable too.

"We refuse to keep dinning in your

ears that the Ford is the best, most ec nomical, lowest-priced car. Obviously, cannot be true of all. There comes point where claims and adjectives ar all advertising hysteria disappear their own fog. Personally, I prefer fact

"We say that the new Fords are th best we have ever made."

Driving Impressions

Our driveReport car, a beautiful Je ferson Blue '39 Deluxe woody, belong to Ed Clarke of Larchmont, New Yor Ed found his car at the Chatham, Ma sachusetts, Country Club, where it ha

Above left: Thanks to V-8 power and relatively light weight, woody will scamper along easily at modern speeds. *Below left:* Second seat passengers share space with spare tire and wheel. *Below right:* Regular '39 Ford woodgrain dash and window trim help carry the wood theme throughout the interior.

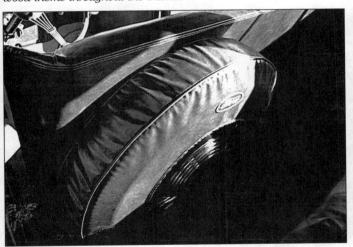

served for nearly 20 years, just as its makers intended, as a stylish but practical workhorse. The Cape Cod summer sun's ravages were erased each year when the Club had the woody revarnished—as a result, Ed commented, "The wood was all original and in pretty good shape considering the car's age." That didn't keep Ed from doing a full-scale, 32-month restoration, however, and the end result has won a number of Early Ford V-8 Club of America National awards. "The car originally had a 4.44 rear end," Ed told me. "It must have been used for some heavy hauling. I replaced the rear end with a 3.54:1 (not original) and added an extra tooth to first gear—now the car cruises quite nicely." As mentioned earlier, Ed is a terrific source for hard-to-get woody trim parts, and he's a friendly fellow who'll gladly give a caller the benefit of his extensive experience.

Driving a '39 woody, even in modern traffic, takes you back to what it was like over 40 years ago. The engine spins freely with that characteristic Ford starter cough and settles quickly into an almost imperceptible idle. Getting under way, you pull the long, curved shift lever back into first and accelerate briskly through second into top.

Then, wind your way through a gently curving country road. The Ford purrs contentedly in third, with enough low-end torque to tackle all but the steepest hills without shifting. The gleaming yellow body creaks perceptibly, but one's overall impression is that of strength—high above the street, pointing the graceful prow at the centerline and relaxing with the soft undulations of the long springs. On rough surfaces, there's a little axle tramp but, with the Philco radio humming a big band tune, you can almost pretend it's 1939. ⌘

Acknowledgments and Bibliography

Automobile Topics, *Sept. 5, 1938, Aug. 29, 1938, Nov. 7, 1938, Nov. 14, 1938, Feb. 20, 1939, and June 5, 1939;* Automotive Industries, *Nov. 5, 1938;* Motor, November 1938; The Autocar, *May 12, 1939;* Ford News, *Dec. 1938;* The V-8 Times, *May/June and Nov/Dec. 1960;* Ford Sales Literature; Ford in the Thirties, *by Paul R. Woudenberg;* Ford: Decline and Rebirth, *by Allan Nevins and Frank Ernest Hill;* The Production Figure Book for US Cars, *by Jerry Heasley;* The V-8 Affair, *by Glenn Embree and Ray Miller;* Special-Interest American Cars, *Spence Murray (Ed.);* Great American Woodies & Wagons, *by Donald J. Narus;* Vintage Station Wagon Shop Service, *by Thomas B. Garrett.*

Our thanks to the late Jim Bradley, former curator of the National Automotive History Collection in Detroit. For this, and many previous articles, Jim's resourceful help and friendly encouragement was invaluable. Thanks also to Alan Darr, Longview, Washington; E.T. "Bob" Gregorie, Daytona Beach, Florida; Will O'Neil, National Woodie Club, Hawthorne, California; and members of the Early Ford V-8 Club of America.

Special thanks to Ed Clarke, "Woodieologist," 67 Rockland Avenue, Larchmont, NY 10538.

1940 FORD–The Deliverer

by Ken Gross, *Managing Editor*

drive
report

Darryl Norenberg Photos

Spare tire hides beneath 1940 Ford sedan delivery's cargo floor, so with 36 x 36-inch rear door locked, spare compartment is theftproof.

Owner Ron Peduzzi checks spacious rear cavern. Fiberboard lines walls and ceiling. Hardwood flooring incorporates metal skids.

Ford Motor Co. found itself in near-chaos in 1940, but you'd never know it by the timeless cars they built.

Some of my best friends were 1940 Fords, because during the '50s of my high school days, reworked '40 coupes reigned absolutely. For my part, I drove and loved a much modified 1940 Ford opera coupe, and in my crowd Paul Bourque and Mickey Maguire shoehorned Olds V-8s into theirs; Steve Lane ran a mean 265 Chevy in his; and John Knowles tooled a Z-framed, rechromed version of a hot 3/8 x 3/8 flathead.

I'm sorry now for all those great cars we chopped up back then, but it took a certain sophistication to realize we were right about the '40. The 1940 Ford's smooth lines, light weight, and low cost made it a natural teenager's car, and you rarely saw a stock example. It's only recently that restorers have started remodifying modified '40s and transforming them back to stock.

The year 1940 was a great one for Detroit, second only to 1929 in total sales. The typical 1940 car represented a great improvement over those of the '30s. Sealed-Beam headlights, hydraulic brakes, column shifts, stronger engines, and smooth body lines with all-steel roofs all served to entice buyers. Some people even anticipated the coming of war and elected to buy a new car "for the duration."

Ford's and Chevrolet's perennial contest for No.1 wasn't really a sales battle at all, because Ford sold only two cars to every three of Chevrolet's. And when you consider the conflict that marked Dearborn's top management in the late 1930s and early '40s, it's a wonder Ford dealers even had cars for their showrooms.

Ford's labor union problems (*SIA* #29, p.13) were the first act in a titanic struggle for company control. The elder Henry Ford, aged 77, resisted what he felt were union efforts to seize his company. He was still lucid at that time, but the elder Ford was stubborn, ornery, close-minded, and difficult to deal with. By 1943 he would have periods of senility.

His son Edsel, overshadowed by his father and badgered mercilessly by Harry Bennett, often found himself in conflict with the Old Man. Along with production chief Charles (Cast-Iron Charlie) Sorensen, general sales manager John R. Davis, and Davis's successor Henry Clay Doss, Edsel tried valiantly to juggle Ford, Mercury, and Lincoln into a balanced, competitive line.

Nevins and Hill, in the second volume of their definitive history, *Ford; Decline and Rebirth*, refer to the firm in the late 1930s as "...a company in the doldrums." Little wonder. Harry Bennett had become Henry Ford's right hand. The elder Ford admired Bennett, rightly believing he'd found someone who shared his outspoken views and would immediately and unflinchingly carry out his orders. Edsel lacked "toughness," or so thought Henry, while Bennett, an ex-prize fighter, personified it. Even Sorensen, who hated Bennett, called him a man of "fearless personal courage."

Feisty, rude, and with underworld connections, Bennett headed Ford's internal security squad—a force made up partly of ex-cons, ex-pugs, and general assorted toughs. Although nominally confined to labor and personnel problems, Harry Bennett oozed into every area of the company. He kept the rank and file assembly workers in line with his security squad, and he also campaigned vigorously to curry favor with Henry Ford, ousting the best men in Ford's upper levels in the process. He and Edsel were silent enemies, and Bennett's constant

pressuring surely must have aggravated Edsel's ulcers.

In Bennett's own biography, however, Bennett states that he was never motivated by a drive for power. Instead, he insists in *We Never Called Him Henry* that he was simply carrying out Mr. Ford's wishes so that Edsel might become a rugged individualist in his father's image. Harry Bennett was tossed out of the company by Henry Ford II and Clara Ford two years after Edsel's death.

Outside the company, Henry Ford's widely published opinions managed to alienate unionists, New Dealers, Jews, and prospective customers sympathetic with these groups. That accounted in part for Chevrolet's 3:2 sales strength. But the elder Ford still had his loyal following, as he has even today.

At the time of the 1940 Ford's development, Mr. Ford's hobbies—Greenfield Village and the Henry Ford Museum, tiny hydroelectric plants, tractors, farming, soybean and plastics experiments, and schools—kept him out of the mainstream of passenger-car development. That might have been a relief to chief engineer Laurence (Larry) Sheldrick, but the cars certainly suffered a certain engineering freeze. Henry Ford's conservatism wielded a strong influence over engineering despite some smoke-screening experimental "advances."

Ford automobiles clung to their traditional solid axles and, by 1940, were only in their second year of hydraulic brakes. Ford dealers lobbied for a Ford 6, yet Henry tinkered with an inline 5 along with other blue-sky engine and chassis combinations. It was, finally, through the efforts of Sheldrick and Edsel that the flathead Ford 6 arrived for 1941 to replace the venerable Ford 4 and V-8-60.

Henry Ford kept a finger in engineering, but his influence on styling was almost nil. According to former design chief Eugene T. (Bob) Gregorie, very little of Bennett's mixing in and the elder Ford's opinions affected the styling of 1940 models. "We dealt with Edsel," says Gregorie. "Mr. Ford would come into the styling area from time to time, but he never made actual design suggestions. He wasn't at all conversant with styling. To him, redesigning a car had only a nuisance value. He couldn't see why it was necessary."

Gregorie continues: "Our design staff was very small—only 19 people—and considering the range of work we produced, I believe we did pretty well. We were fortunately not hampered by committees and elaborate ceremonial presentations as in some of the other companies. Decisions were prompt and casual. Mr. Edsel Ford took a personal interest in design, of course, and he was an excellent critic. We always had his full backing and cooperation, and we enjoyed a mutual regard for each other's judgment. If there were differences, they were always worked out to the satisfaction of all involved.

"Ford styling of that era seems generally to have grown old gracefully. Comparing our efforts with GM's and others', their results were more a composite, while ours perhaps had a certain purity, a directness and simplicity. That's not to throw any peas and beans at GM and the rest—they did pretty well, too, after all, but we worked along different lines. I think that the older Ford cars, as you look back at them, had a little more of a lasting attraction."

When asked whether there was much of an influx of stylists from Chrysler or GM, Gregorie recalls, "No, we worked very separately at Ford and almost never hired from GM and Chrysler. I didn't know what the others were doing and didn't care particularly. We were over in Dearborn, so Ford people rarely socialized with people from the other auto companies in Detroit."

Gregorie didn't spend a great quantity of time on the 1940 models, but the time spent had quality. Early 1940 styling exercises, dated 1937-38, showed the basic 1939 Ford lines, from still-chromed, crank-out windshield frame and overhead wipers to smoothly rounded tail section. Forward, the 1940's distinctive alligator hood and 4-section grille were beginning to take shape. Production

Only the driver's seat came as standard equipment— the passenger's bucket was optional. Twin door mirrors compensate for blind spots.

Gas filler emerges just behind driver's door. '40 Ford locking gas cap was dealer option.

Rich-looking oval headlamp bezel incorporates parkers. Sealed Beams were new in 1940.

1940 sedan deliveries came in DeLuxe series only, included twin wipers/visors/ashtrays, a clock, contrasting plastic gauge panel.

Both buckets fold for access and added storage space. Tank rests behind driver. There's a bin under floor behind passenger's seat.

Unlike other '40 Ford DeLuxes, sedan delivery use round raillamp instead of twin chevrons.

cars eliminated the plated windshield frame and crank-out glass and dropped the wipers to the cowl. Some transitional models seem to have been built, though, because James Parker of Suffolk, Virginia, presently owns a 1940 coupe with uncrankable chromed windshield framing, cowl wipers, and 1940 DeLuxe front sheetmetal.

The 1940's styling represents the last link in a patterned run that began in 1935 and saw steady refinement over a 6-year period. "It doesn't surprise me," Gregorie comments, "that the 1940 Fords are more popular with collectors than 1940 Chevrolets. We had to stay with what was basically the same midship shell for years. It was a matter of finances and sales. So our cars were carefully facelifted year to year. We had more delicacy, less razzmatazz than Chevrolet."

With the industry's decision to go to Sealed-Beam headlamps for 1940 (an increase from 27 to 40 candlepower) came Willys P. Wagner's classic 1940 egg-shaped headlight rims. Designer Wagner was also the man on Gregorie's staff responsible for the 1940 bumpers and chevron taillights. "Contrary to popular belief," Wagner told me, "the taillights weren't modeled after corporal's chevrons. The war had no impact on our thoughts at the time."

Along with retouched styling, the 1940 Ford offered a number of refinements over 1939. Ford ads heralded 22 important improvements, including column shift. This item was considered far out enough to warrant complete instructions on a special hang tag in each car. Also new were redesigned brake drums and more conventional 5-bolt wheels to replace 1939's 10-1/4-inch bolt-center types.

Controlled ventilation (new ventipane front windows), "Floating Edge" seat cushions, a front torsion bar to counter roll and stabilize ride (on 85-bhp models), and a bigger battery and generator were also included.

To squelch rumors of internal company strife, Ford ads of 1940 added, "This constant progress, under unified management, reaches a new peak in the new models for 1940." And Ford salesmen were quick to point out that their DeLuxe models came with a remarkable amount of standard equipment. Top-of-the-line Fords had a stem-wind clock set in the locking glovebox, a battery condition indicator, electric cigar lighter, bumper guards, twin ashtrays/wipers/sunvisors/horns/tail lights. Also included in the price of 1940 Fords were 10 prepaid chassis lubes.

Those buyers who wanted even more could order a spotlight, seatcovers, stainless steel wheelcovers and trim rings, fender skirts, dual fog lights, side and vanity mirrors, special guards for the bumper center and ends (the latter highly prized today by restorers), and a locking gas cap. Under the hood you could get a hot-air manifold heater, oil filter, oil-bath air cleaner, plus an engine speed governor.

Edsel Ford and Bob Gregorie chose six basic colors for the '40s. "We'd set up a rack of colored panels and choose among them," states Gregorie. "As was the case with upholstery, we tried to follow the Lincoln trend in Ford-priced paint and materials." The Standards came in black, Lyon Blue, and Cloudmist Gray only, but the DeLuxes added Folkestone gray, Yosemite green, and Mandarin maroon. Vermilion became a color for commercial units.

Our driveReport car, a gorgeous Cloudmist Gray 1940 sedan delivery, belongs to Ron Peduzzi of Pomona, California. This car's odometer shows fewer than 40,000 miles, and it belonged to its original owner for 25 years. The car was restored 10 years ago and is original except for optional 6.50 x 16 rear tires and a front passenger seat (standard equipment was a single seat for the driver, with the passenger's bucket optional).

The Ford sedan delivery concept dates back to the Model A and was called

"...the aristocrat of the Ford commercial line, the natural choice of shops tha cater to an exclusive clientele, widely used by salesmen who carry sampl kits..." in Ford sales literature.

For 1940, all 5,325 Ford sedan deliveries produced were DeLuxes, and thes came with three engine choices: 60, 85, and 95 bhp. Of these, 4,451 carried th 85 bhp V-8, 758 the V-8-60, and 116 had the 95-bhp truck engine. Sedan deliveries were assembled not only in the U.S. but in Mexico City, Buenos Aires, an Canada as well, and in Amsterdam the Ford plant put together seven seda deliveries before the war closed it down.

Ford sedan deliveries traditionally shared front-end sheet metal with passen ger cars, DeLuxe for 1940 but the 1940 Standard in 1941 (the '41 sedan deliv ery looked very much like the entire '40 Ford line). Transmissions had a optional low, 3.534:1 first gear ratio (vs. 2.819:1 in passenger cars) and an 1 inch clutch disc instead of the 9-inch regular disc. Peduzzi's car also carries th Columbia 2-speed rear axle.

For 1940, Ford sedan deliveries were redesigned to give 10 more inches o cargo deck length (to 74.6 inches), and capacity went to 86.6 cubic feet. Th spare tire stores underneath the rear floor below door level, so it can't be stole with the rear door locked, even if the front doors are left open. To accommodat the new tire compartment, a special 17-gallon gas tank had to be relocate behind the driver. This tank has its filler in the side panel behind the driver door.

The body's interior is lined in fiberboard. Tongue-in-groove hardwood floor ing with steel skids provides a rugged, almost waterproof loading base. The 9 square-foot rear door accommodates wide loads, and a door check holds th door wide open. Front doors share the 4-door sedan's new-for-1940 ventipane

Ron's sedan delivery is a delight to drive: no rattles, no drumming, just th quiet purr of the flathead V-8. Front vision is excellent, but the hood gives a fee ing of exaggerated length. Visibility to the rear and sides is terrible, even with out a load, and twin side mirrors become as much a necessity as the steerin wheel. The Columbia axle cuts down considerably on engine noise at cruisin speeds.

The 1940's brakes feel firm and stop smoothly. Although there's some tram from the solid front axle, the overall impression is one of a well mannered ca I didn't test the sedan delivery with a full load, but I judge that it can easil accept a well distributed 500 pounds before the springs would begin to dip. An an optional roll-down rear window would be a welcome accessory on hot day.

Sedan deliveries are among the rarest of 1940 Ford body styles today. Lon prized by surfers, street rodders, and customizers, Ford's rugged commercia cars command outrageous prices in the collector's market. The 28-million Ford rolled off the assembly line on April 8, 1940, and for a generation of 194 Ford V-8 fans, including this one, they could have frozen the design right there ᐁ

Our thanks to James J. Bradley, National Automotive History Collectio Detroit Public Library, Detroit; Henry Edmunds and David Crippen of the For Archives, Henry Ford Museum, Dearborn; Michael W.R. Davis and John Najja Ford Motor Co., Dearborn; Prof. David L. Lewis, Ann Arbor, Michigan; E. Gregorie, Daytona Beach, Florida; Willys P. Wagner, Tiburon, California; Ro Cousins, Bloomfield Hills, Michigan; Alan Darr, Early V-8 Club of America Box 2122, San Leandro, California; Lorin Sorensen, Silverado Publishing C St. Helena, California.; James E. Parker, Suffolk, Virginia; and special thanks Ron Peduzzi, Pomona, California.

specifications

55.75 in.

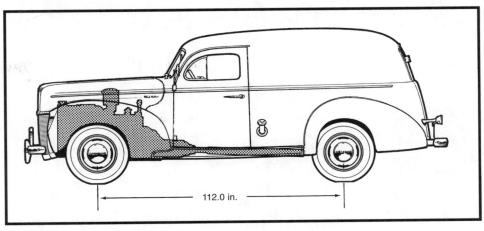

112.0 in.

1940 Ford DeLuxe sedan delivery

Price when new	$7,221 f.o.b. Dearborn, Michigan (1940)	**DIFFERENTIAL**		**SUSPENSION**	
		Type	Spiral bevel gears, torque-tube drive.	Front	I-beam axle, transverse semi-elliptic leaf spring, lever hydraulic shocks, radius rods.
ENGINE		Ratio	3.78:1.		
Type	L-head, 90° V-8, watercooled, cast-iron block, 3 mains, pressure lubrication.	Drive axles	3/4-floating.	Rear	Rigid axle, transverse semi-elliptic leaf spring, lever hydraulic shocks, radius rods.
Bore & stroke	3.082 x 3.750 in.	**STEERING**		Tires	6.00 x 16, tube-type, 4-ply.
Displacement	221.0 c.i.d.	Type	Gemmer worm & roller.	Wheels	Pressed-steel, drop-center rims, lug-bolted to brake drums.
Max. bhp @ rpm	85 @ 3,800.	Turns lock to lock	4.5.		
Max. torque @ rpm	148 @ 2,200.	Ratio	18.2:1.		
Compression ratio	6.15:1.	Turn circle	38.2 ft.		
Induction system	Downdraft 2-bbl. carburetor, mechanical fuel pump.			**WEIGHTS & MEASURES**	
Exhaust system	Cast-iron manifolds, single muffler.	**BRAKES**		Wheelbase	112.0 in.
Electrical system	6-volt battery/coil.	Type	4-wheel hydraulic drums, internal expanding.	Overall length	188.25 in.
				Overall height	69.75 in.
CLUTCH		Drum diameter	12.0 in.	Overall width	60.10 in.
Type	Single dry plate, molded asbestos lining.	Total lining area	162.0 sq. in.	Front tread	55.75 in.
				Rear tread	58.25 in.
Diameter	9.0 in.			Ground clearance	8.2 in.
Actuation	Mechanical, foot pedal.			Curb weight	2,056 lb.
TRANSMISSION		**CHASSIS & BODY**			
Type	3-speed manual, column shift, synchromesh 2-3.	Frame	Channel & box section steel, central X-member, 2 cross-members.	**CAPACITIES**	
				Crankcase	5.0 qt.
Ratios: 1st	3.534:1.	Body construction	All steel.	Cooling system	22.0 qt.
2nd	1.770:1.	Body style	2-door, 2-passenger delivery van	Fuel tank	17.0 gal.
3rd	1.000:1.				
Reverse	4.000:1.				

1940 sedan deliveries could be ordered with 60-, 85-, or 95-bhp V-8s. Peduzzi's has the 85 and also boasts Columbia 2-speed axle.

Fine performance, good looks, respectable handling and ride combine to make the 1940 Ford one of America's all-time great automobiles.

Spotter's Guide to Forties Fords

BY JEFF GODSHALL

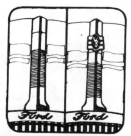

HOOD MLDG. ON EARLY SUP. DLX. & SPL. CARS WAS PLAIN. LATER CARS HAD 'V-8' OR '6' EMBLEMS IN BLUE BACKGROUND.

HOOD MLDG. ON EARLY DLX. CARS HAD 'DELUXE' NAME IN BLUE. LATER CARS ADDED 'V-8' OR '6' EMBLEM IN BLUE BACKGROUND.

—SHOWN ABOVE IS FRONT END TREATMENT ON DELUXE & SPECIAL CARS. CENTER GRILLE WAS BRIGHT BUT SIDE GRILLES WERE BODY COLOR. LICENSE PLATE WAS OFFSET TO RIGHT. PLAIN, SMOOTH BUMPER HAD GUARDS ON DLX., NONE ON SPL.

WHEELS—BODY COLOR WITH 3 PAINT STRIPES & TRIM RING ON SUP. DLX. CARS; BLACK W/O STRIPES ON DLX. & SPL. CARS. FORD SCRIPT IN BLUE ON HUBCAP.

1941 FORD—
ALL-NEW BODY ON 114" WB. PARKING LIGHTS ATOP FENDERS. MULTI-PIECE FRONT FENDER WITH HORIZONTAL PARTING LINE. SUPER DELUXE FRONT (ABOVE) HAD BRIGHT CENTER & SIDE GRILLES. 'SUP. DLX.' NAME IN SCRIPT ON LEFT FRONT FENDER. SUP. DLX. HAD UNIQUE FRONT & REAR BUMPERS WITH RIDGE ALONG BOTTOM—GUARDS STD. FRONT LICENSE PLATE IN CENTER WITH UNIQUE SUPPORT PIECE. BRIGHT HEADLIGHT TRIM BEZELS & HOOD CENTER MLDG. ON ALL MODELS.

EARLY CARS WERE ALL V-8's—'SIX' INTRODUCED MID-YEAR. HOOD MLDG. WAS CHANGED TO INCLUDE ENGINE DESIGNATION AS SHOWN ABOVE, RIGHT.

1941 FORD CARS PRICED FROM $689 TO $1017.

THREE SERIES OF CARS—'SUPER DELUXE' IN SIX BODY TYPES, 'DELUXE' IN FIVE BODY TYPES, 'SPECIAL' IN THREE BODY TYPES. 'SPECIAL' CARS WERE PAINTED BLACK ONLY W/PAINTED HOOD & BELT MLDG.

IN LATE MARCH 1941, THESE TRIM ITEMS WERE ADDED TO SUP. DLX. CARS (SHOWN BELOW)— BRIGHT FRONT & REAR FENDER MLDGS. BRIGHT WINDSHIELD & REAR WINDOW MLDGS. BRIGHT SIDE WINDOW SURROUND MLDGS.

SINGLE LEFT-SIDE TAILLIGHT ON 'SPECIAL' CARS.

TAILLIGHTS—BRIGHT ON SUP. DLX., BODY COLOR ON DLX. & SPL. W/BRIGHT GROOVED TRIM TOP & BOTTOM.

GODSHALL.

1941 SUPER DELUXE FORDOR SDN. W/LATE TRIM MLDGS.

Originally published in Special Interest Autos #29, Jul.-Aug. 1975

ON DELUXE CARS A 'DELUXE' NAMEPLATE WAS ATTACHED TO THE VERTICAL GRILLE CENTER PANEL. BRIGHT LETTERS ON BLUE BACKGROUND.

HOOD ENGINE DESIGNATION EMBLEMS - BLUE & BRIGHT

WHEELS - BODY COLOR W/THREE PAINT STRIPES & TRIM RING ON SUPER DELUXE CARS.

1942 FORD —
CARRYOVER BODIES WITH CONCEALED RUNNING BOARDS. NEW FRONT FENDERS & HOOD. NEW GRILLE & TAILLIGHTS. FRONT & REAR BUMPER STONE SHIELDS.

SUPER DELUXE FRONT END (SHOWN ABOVE). SIDE GRILLES, VERTICAL CENTER PANEL & GRILLE FRAME WERE BRIGHT W/BLUE PAINT IN GROOVES. SUP. DLX. CARS USED UNIQUE FRONT & REAR BUMPERS W/RIDGE ALONG UPPER SURFACE - GUARDS STD. 'SUPER DELUXE' NAMEPLATE IN SCRIPT ON LEFT FENDER.

ALL MODELS HAD NEW HOOD MLDG & ORNAMENT.

PARKING LIGHTS ABOVE GRILLE INBOARD OF HEADLIGHTS.

1942 FORDS PRICED FROM $830 TO $1193.

THREE SERIES OF CARS - 'SUPER DELUXE' IN SIX BODY TYPES. 'DELUXE' IN FOUR BODY TYPES; 'SPECIAL' IN THREE BODY TYPES. NEW HOOD & BELT MLDS. & BLACK RUBBER REAR FENDER GRAVEL SHIELDS.

BRIGHT FENDER MLDGS. WINDSHIELD & REAR WINDOW MLDGS., SILL MLDG. & SIDE WINDOW SURROUND MLDGS. ON 'SUPER DELUXE' ONLY.

SIX-CYLINDER ENGINE AVAILABLE ON ALL CARS. V-8 ON DLX. & SUP. DLX. ONLY

BECAUSE OF WWII, MANY TRIM ITEMS ON LATE CARS WERE PAINTED A CONTRASTING COLOR OR BODY COLOR. LAST CIVILIAN FORD CAR BUILT FEB. 10, 1942.

DELUXE & SPECIAL CARS HAD BRIGHT SIDE GRILLES & BRIGHT VERTICAL CENTER PANEL. GRILLE FRAME WAS PAINTED BODY COLOR. DLX. & SPL. USED 1941 SUP. DLX. BUMPERS, W/GUARDS ON DLX.

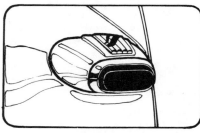

TAILLIGHT - USED ON ALL 1942-1948 CARS EXCEPT WAGON & SPORTSMAN. BRIGHT GROOVED TRIM PLATE ON SUPER DELUXE ONLY.

WHEELS - BODY COLOR ON DELUXE CARS, BLACK ON SPECIAL. NO STRIPING OR TRIM RING. FORD SCRIPT IN BLUE ON HUBCAP.

GODSHALL.

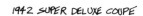

1942 SUPER DELUXE COUPE

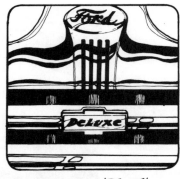

ON DELUXE CARS A 'DELUXE' NAMEPLATE WAS ATTACHED TO THE FIRST GRILLE BAR BELOW THE GRILLE HEADER. RED LETTERS ON BRIGHT BACKGROUND.

1946 FORD — CARRYOVER BODIES, FENDERS, MOULDINGS, & SUP. DLX. BUMPERS (ALSO USED ON DLX. CARS). NEW PARKING LIGHTS (SAME LOCATION). NEW HOOD AND GRILLE ASS'Y. GRILLE HEADER BAR HAD FORD SCRIPT & VERTICAL STRIPES IN RED. GRILLE BARS HAD HORIZONTAL STRIPE IN RED. NEW 'SUPER DELUXE' NAMEPLATE IN BRIGHT & RED ON LEFT FRONT FENDER. SAME FRONT END ON ALL CARS. TWO SERIES OF CARS - DELUXE '6' & V-8' IN 3 MODELS; SUP. DLX. '6' IN 5 MODELS; SUP. DLX. 'V8' IN 7 MODELS.

ABOVE — 1946 WOOD-BODIED SPORTSMAN CONVERTIBLE COUPE PRICED @ $2041. 'V8' ONLY.

WHEELS — BODY COLOR WITH 3 PAINT STRIPES. TRIM RING ON SUP. DLX. ONLY. 'FORD' BLOCK LETTERS & HASH MARKS IN RED ON HUBCAP.

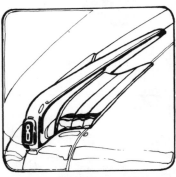

NEW HOOD ORNAMENT — '6' OR '8' ENGINE DESIGNATION IN BRIGHT W/RED BACKGROUND. NO HOOD CENTER MLDG.

ALL CARS HAD HOOD & BELT MLDGS, FENDER MLDGS, SILL MLDGS, SIDE WINDOW SURROUND MLDGS. ON SDNS. & COUPES, & RUBBER GRAVEL SHIELDS ON REAR FENDER. BRIGHT WINDSHIELD & REAR WINDOW REVEAL MLDGS ON SUP. DLX. ONLY.

1946 FORD CARS PRICED FROM $1110 TO $2041.

GOODSHALL.

TWO HORIZONTAL BRIGHT TRIM MLDGS. ON ALL DECK LIDS EXCEPT WAGON & SPORTSMAN. FORD SCRIPT & OVAL IN RED ON ALL REAR BUMPERS EXCEPT WAGON. '41-42 BUMPERS HAD FORD SCRIPT IN BLUE (EXCEPT '41 DLX. & SPL. & ALL WAGONS.)

1946 SUPER DELUXE CONVERTIBLE COUPE

HOOD EMBLEMS- 'SUPER DELUXE' IN BRIGHT LETTERS -BLUE BACK- GROUND. 'DELUXE' IN BLUE LETTERS ON BRIGHT. '6' OR '8' IN BLUE DE- PENDING ON ENGINE.

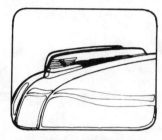

HOOD ORNAMENT APPEARED ON LATE 1947 AND ALL 1948 CARS. BRIGHT WITH TRANSPARENT PLASTIC INSERT ALONG TOP. NO HOOD CENTER MLDG.

1947-48 FORD— CARRYOVER BODIES, FENDERS, HOOD & BUMPERS. NEW LARGER BUMPER GUARDS. NEW CIRCULAR PARKING LIGHTS BENEATH HEADLIGHTS. NEW HOOD EMBLEMS. NEW, SMOOTH GRILLE HEADER BAR & GRILLE BARS. FORD SCRIPT & GROOVES IN BLUE. SAME FRONT END ON ALL CARS. TWO SERIES OF CARS— 'SUP. DLX.' & 'DLX'.-SAME MODELS AS 1946.

ALL CARS HAD FENDER MLDGS., NEW SMOOTH HOOD & BELT MLDG., RUB- BER GRAVEL SHIELDS ON REAR FENDER & SILL MLDG. WHICH EXTENDED ONTO FRONT FENDER. BRIGHT WINDSHIELD REVEAL MLDGS. ON SUP. DLX. ONLY. SIDE WINDOW SURROUND MLDG. ELIMINATED ON 1947-48 CARS.

FENDER MLDGS. WERE PLACED BELOW FENDER CHARACTER LINE IN- STEAD OF ATOP THE LINE AS ON EARLIER YEARS.

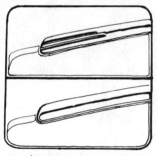

EARLY 1947 CARS HAD SMOOTH HOOD SIDE MLDG. WITH 2 GROOVES AT FRONT EDGE (TOP). LATE 1947 CARS & ALL 1948'S HAD SMOOTH MLDG. W/O GROOVES (BOTTOM).

ABOVE-1947-48 SPORTSMAN. ALL SPORTSMANS USED 1941 SUP. DLX. TAILLIGHTS. 'SPORTSMAN' NAME PLATES ON DECK LID & HOOD ON 1947-48 CARS. SPORTSMAN DISCONTINUED IN NOV., 1947

1947-48 FORD CARS PRICED FROM $1154 TO $2282.

WHEELS- BODY COLOR WITH THREE PAINT STRIPES. TRIM RING ON SUP. DLX. ONLY. 'FORD' BLOCK LETTERS IN BLUE ON HUB CAP.

NEW DECK LID ORNAMENT- 'FORD' IN BLOCK LETTERS IN BLUE. NEW BUMPER GUARDS. SMOOTH BUMPER W/O FORD OVAL.

1947-48 SUPER DELUXE TUDOR SEDAN

Godshall.

SIA comparisonReport

1941 Chevrolet, Ford, and Plymouth

by Arch Brown
photos by Vince Manocchi

BY The time America's 1941 cars were unveiled in the fall of 1940, Europe had been at war for a full year; and to the East the Sino-Japanese conflict had been raging a good deal longer than that. Congress had instituted the nation's first peace-time draft, and industries of virtually every kind were gearing up for what was euphemistically called "defense" production.

War was coming.

The American economy, after a decade of stagnation, reacted to the awarding of military contracts like a furnace operating under a forced draft. Once again the factories were humming, and workers had money in their pockets. And nowhere was the return of prosperity more obvious than in the automobile industry. 1941 had been Detroit's second-best year since the crash of '29, trailing 1937 by the narrowest of margins. ('Thirty-seven had been the year of the veterans' bonus, when literally thousands of World War I "doughboys" had invested their one-time legacy in a new set of wheels.)

Nineteen-forty-one promised to be even better; and indeed it was. And if prosperity made it possible for Americans to replace their aging chariots, prudence made it almost mandatory to do so; for it was obvious to anyone with eyes to see that it would be a long time before the opportunity to buy a new car would come again.

The medium-priced car was making something of a comeback. In 1934 the "low-priced three"—Chevrolet, Ford and Plymouth—had accounted for more than 72 percent of all new car sales, a figure that had dropped to less than 54 percent by 1940 and would dip again, to 51.9 percent, in 1941. Still, it was the low-priced automobiles that dominated the market, as John J. Everyman toured the showrooms to select the car that would see him through the difficult years ahead.

In an effort to turn back the calendar and recreate the scene, picturing the choice that our motorist of 41 years ago was about to make, *Special Interest Autos* brought together three 1941 coupes, representative of the nation's (and the world's) best-sellers of that long-gone day.

Let's consider each in turn, taking them in ascending order of their popularity.

Plymouth sold 452,178 cars during 1941, accounting for 12.1 percent of the US car market. Unlike its rivals, both of which featured restyled bodies that year, Chrysler Corporation's bread-and-butter car was carried over from 1940 with little alteration, apart from a new grille that someone has likened to a "chrome-plated bib." Mounted on the longest wheelbase in its class (117 inches—one inch longer than that of the Chevrolet, three inches longer than the Ford), it was nevertheless the lightest of the group and was powered by the smallest engine. Ads touted Chrysler's superior engineering; the smoothness of "floating power" was featured, and the comfort of Plymouth's chair-height seats was stressed. New for 1941 was the "Powermatic shift," a vacuum-assisted mechanism offered as an optional extra.

Ford advertised, "Now! Size to match

Left and below: General shapes of Ford and Plymouth are rather similar, while Chevy is distinguished by longer, sleeker greenhouse. **Bottom:** Ford and Chevy use combo stop/taillamp. Plymouth stoplamp is mounted in center of rear deck.

ts power!" Sharing the Mercury body hell for the first time, the Ford had icked up some 300 pounds over the veight of the 1940 model. The car's ride vas improved as a result, but inevitably ts lively performance was tempered omewhat. With 602,013 new car registrations for the year, Ford garnered 16.1 ercent of the 1941 market, stretching ts lead over Plymouth by a percentage oint or so, and even gaining a little on ront-running Chevrolet The solid front xle and transverse leaf springs were ontinued, in contrast to the independent front suspension featured by the ompetition. And although a new six-ylinder engine was introduced at mid-ear, Ford continued to emphasize the -8. The six, priced just $15 below the opular V-8, was actually the larger and nore powerful of the two engines,

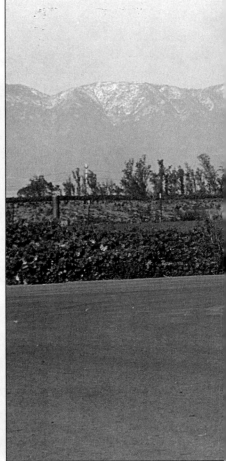

comparisonReport

though the margin was narrow (see *Special Interest Autos* #41). This fact—together with the Chevrolet's advertised 90 horsepower—caused Ford to decide, sometime in the spring of 1941, that their V-8 really developed 90 horsepower, rather than the 85 they had previously claimed.

Chevrolet entered the 1941 season with the confidence of a proven winner. Its horsepower was boosted from 85 to 90, giving the marque a temporary lead in that department. Smartly styled new bodies were shared with the smaller Pontiacs and the "60" series Oldsmobiles, but in most respects the new car represented a refinement of what had gone before. Why mess around, after all, with a winning combination? For the first time, all Chevrolets featured independent front suspension; and the emphasis was upon comfort, quiet and economy. The trim level, especially of the top-of-the-line Special Deluxe series, was exceptionally luxurious for a low-priced car. Ease of handling was featured, too, including the vacuum-assisted gearshift, carried over from

1939-40. The public obviously liked the combination, for Chevrolet was far and away the best-seller. With 880,346 new car registrations for 1941, the Chevy accounted for 23.6 percent of the total market.

Driving Impressions

Thanks to the enthusiastic cooperation of their owners, we were able to drive and compare three excellent examples of these fine, prewar automobiles. The cars themselves have widely divergent histories, and we found that each has its own particular areas of strength. Let's take a look at each one:

Our comparisonReport *Plymouth* was very nearly a total loss when Doyle Thompson, of Hemet, California, pulled it out of the weeds four years ago and set about to restore it. It's a top-line Special Deluxe business coupe. Except for the upholstery and the plating, Doyle did all the work himself, including a total mechanical overhaul. It's no show car; neither the plaid upholstery nor the metallic green paint is authentic, according to original Plymouth specifications. But it's a neat, attractive little automobile and it runs like a watch.

Acceleration, particularly at the low end, is good. At higher speeds it runs out of breath a little sooner than the other cars, especially the Ford. Steering

is the lightest of the three cars, but i requires substantially more space for U-turn than the others. Shifts are easy however the throws are so long that i high gear the lever touches the driver' knee. This particular car does not hav the "Powermatic" vacuum assist; as fa as we're concerned it doesn't need it.

The "floating power" engine mounts d their job well; there's no vibration fro that department. The ride is comfortabl under most conditions, perhaps a littl harsh over rough terrain. We'd rathe have it that way than to have to endur a wallowing, too-soft ride, howeve Brakes, in the Chrysler tradition, ar excellent. But the Plymouth's best fea ture, to our way of thinking, is its deep cushioned, chair-height seat. We coul sit there in comfort all day long. An oddly enough, the Plymouth, alon among the three rivals, has no runnin boards. Both of the other cars hav them, concealed under a flare at th bottom of the doors.

The one thing we didn't like about th Plymouth was the numerically high sec ond gear. At 1.83:1, the ratio is too slo for optimum performance, particularl in the mountains. We can't help won dering why the company didn't stic with the 1.55:1 ratio of previous years.

The *Ford* was restored nine years ag by owner Doug Watson, of Costa Mesa

California, who started with a decent (though relatively high-mileage) one-owner car. Performing all the work himself, including a lovely paint job in authentic Mayfair Maroon, he has produced a strikingly good-looking automobile. And a dependable one. Doug's car is often seen on tour with his chapter of the Early V-8 Club.

We've had some experience with pre-war Fords, and it came as a surprise to us to find that of the three cars in this comparison test, the V-8 had the smoothest clutch. This one is a Super DeLuxe model, in the rare body style that Ford referred to as the "coupe with auxiliary seats." Two folding jump seats are located behind the full front seat; and while the leg room up forward is ample, passengers in the rear won't be comfortable for long-distance travel.

The V-8 has a familiar, powerful sound and feel. Acceleration seems to be about on a par with the two six-cylinder cars until highway speeds are reached. At that point, partly because of its engine and partly due to the tall gears with which it is fitted, the Ford really begins to stretch its long legs. It corners well, with perhaps a bit less tendency to lean than the other cars. It's easy to override the synchronizers and clash the gears if the driver isn't careful.

Steering isn't quite as light as that of

111

Comparative Specifications
1941's "Big Three" Low-Priced Cars

	Chevrolet	Ford	Plymouth
Prices (at model introduction time, f.o.b. factory):			
4-door sedan, top-line	$859	$820	$840
SIA test car	$808	$807	$760
ENGINE			
Type	OHV in-line "6"	L-head "V-8"	L-head "6"
Bore/stroke (inches)	3½ x 3¾	3.06 x 3.75	3⅛ x 4⅜
Displacement (cu. in.)	216.5	221.0	201.3
Compression ratio	6.50:1	6.15:1	6.70:1
BHP @ RPM	90 @ 3,300	85 @ 3,800*	87 @ 3,800
Torque @ RPM	174 @ 1,200	157 @ 2,200	160 @ 1,200
Induction system	1¼" Carter downdraft	.94" downdraft (own)	1½ Carter downdraft
CLUTCH			
Type	Disc	Disc	Disc
Diameter	9⅛"	9"	9¼"
TRANSMISSION RATIOS			
1st	2.94:1	3.11:1	2.57:1
2nd	1.68:1	1.77:1	1.83:1
3rd	1.00:1	1.00:1	1.00:1
Reverse	2.94:1	4.00:1	3.48:1
DIFFERENTIAL			
Type	Semi-floating	¾ floating	Semi-floating
Ratio	4.11:1	3.78:1	4.10:1
Drive axles	Hypoid	Spiral bevel	Hypoid
STEERING			
Type	Worm & roller	Worm & roller	Worm & roller
Turns, lock-to-lock	4½	4½	4¼
Ratio	17.5:1	18.2:1	18.2:1
Turn circle (curb/curb)	36'4"	38'1"	39'11"
BRAKES			
Type	Hydraulic	Hydraulic	Hydraulic
Drum diameter	11"	12"	10"
Lining area (sq. in.)	158.2	163.0	144.0
SUSPENSION			
Front (springs)	Independent, coil	Transverse, leaf	Independent, coil
Rear (springs)	Longitudinal, leaf	Transverse, leaf	Longitudinal, leaf
Tires	6.00 x 16	6.00 x 16	6.00 x 16
Wheels	16" x 4" steel disc	16" x 4" steel disc	16" x 4" steel disc, safety rims
WEIGHT (4-door sedan)	3,090	3,121	2,889
MEASUREMENTS			
Wheelbase	116"	114"	117"
Overall length	195¾"	194¹¹⁄₃₂"	194¾"
Front tread	57⅝"	55¾"	57"
Rear tread	60"	58¼"	59¹⁵⁄₁₆"
Ground clearance	8⅛"	8⅜"	8⅝"
CAPACITIES			
Crankcase	5½ quarts	5 quarts	5 quarts
Cooling system	14 quarts	23¾ quarts	14 quarts
Fuel tank	16 gallons	17 gallons	17 gallons

*Raised to 90 BHP at mid-year.

Source: *Automotive Industries*, March 1, 1941, and October 15, 1940; turning circles measured during ComparisonReport test.

either of the competing cars, but it's easy enough for all that. Thanks to the rather primitive transverse suspension to which Ford continued to cling through 1948, we'd rank it third in terms of riding comfort; but there really is no complaint in that department, either. And the brakes—Ford had finally adopted hydraulics in 1939, you'll remember—are very effective.

To compare. Dr. Dave Underwood's *Chevrolet* to the others is hardly fair, for this unit is really a brand-new car. The reader will find a complete driveReport on this very same automobile in *Special Interest Autos* #45. It's worth rereading. This '41 Chevy, you see, was the proud possession of the late Mrs. Minnie L. Poessnecker, of Atkinson, Nebraska, and for 30 years it did nothing but carry Mrs. Poessnecker from home to church to market and back. It registered a little over 6,000 miles when Dr. Underwood acquired it, through the good offices of Bob Wingate, in 1971. Today the odometer stands at 8,700 miles!

It's an interesting sensation, driving a brand-new, 41-year-old car. It feels tight, crisp, in a way that a restored car simply cannot duplicate. Nevertheless certain comparisons can be drawn.

Ford dash, top, isn't as readable as Chevy's, far right, or Plymouth's. Ford and Chevy use gobs of woodgrain, while Plymouth dash is painted.

Left: Chevrolet coupe has full-width rear seat, while Plymouth hides spare behind front seat for added trunk room. Ford coupe has two jump seats. **Below:** Three distinct approaches to motive power. Plymouth, left, uses reliable, quiet flathead six developing 87 hp; Ford uses sturdy, peppy flathead V-8; and Chevrolet, of course, uses the immortal overhead-valve "stovebolt six."

For one thing, Chevrolet seems to have done the best job of sound insulation. Even at highway speeds, with the little 216.5-c.i.d. engine churning through a 4.11:1 axle, the car is quiet. Fit and finish are superb—and except for tires, hoses, and belts, this automobile is totally original. No restoration work has ever been done to it.

The Chevy appears to us to have the most comfortable ride of the group, though to some extent this may reflect the outstanding condition of Dr. Underwood's car. It also turns in a tighter circle than either of its rivals. Steering is nearly as light as that of the Plymouth, and just a little bit faster. Chevy's vacuum shift is a breeze to use when it's working right (and a bear when it's not!) This one works just fine, though its action—characteristically-makes fast shifts impossible.

Chevrolet gave its 1941 coupes a longer greenhouse than earlier models, resulting in a reasonably spacious rear seat for the club coupe body style, as

For styling, it's all a matter of taste. Chevrolet wins in the chrome department, Ford's looks are pleasant and restrained, while Plymouth depends more on sculpture than trim for styling accents.

Chevrolet-Ford-Plymouth 1941 Price Chart

Chevrolet

Body style	Special Deluxe		Master Deluxe
Business coupe	$777		$725
Club coupe	$808		756
Town sedan (2-door)	$818		767
Sport sedan (4-door)	$859		808
Cabriolet	$957		----

Ford

Body style	Super Deluxe		Deluxe
Coupe	$740		$695
Coupe with aux. seats	$807		$761
Tudor sedan	$780		$735
Fordor sedan	$820		$775
Sedan coupe	$810		-----
Convertible coupe	$905		-----
Station wagon	n/a		n/a

Plymouth

Body style	Spec. Deluxe	Deluxe	P-11
Coupe, 2-passenger	$760	$729	$685
Coupe, 2-4 pass.	$805	----	----
Sedan, 2-door	$810	$779	$739
Sedan, 4-door	$840	$820	$780
Convertible	$970	----	----
Station wagon	$995	----	----
Sedan, 7-passenger	$1,045	----	----

Notes:
1. Prices shown are those posted at announcement time, October 1940. Increases of between $30
   and $40 were announced before the model year was over.
2. Some time after the introduction of the 1941 models, Ford announced a new series, the "Special." Intended for fleet buyers, it was priced about $40 below the "Deluxe" and was available in business coupe and 2- and 4-door sedan configuration.
3. The six-cylinder Ford was announced in June 1941. Prices were $15 less than those of the eight-cylinder cars.
4. "n/a" indicates that prices were not announced at introduction time.
Source: *Automotive Industries*, October 15, 1940.

comparisonReport

exemplified by our test car. The seating is low by 1941 standards, but the cushions are comfortable and supportive. The Chevy had the only "chattery" clutch in the group, but it isn't bad enough to be bothersome. The car will idle smoothly in high gear at speeds as low as six miles an hour, then pick up momentum smoothly without changing gears. And like the other two cars, the Chevrolet's brakes do their job well.

Someone asked us which of the three cars we would choose, if it were 1941 all over again and we were shopping for a low-priced car. It's a tough question. Forty-one years ago, when these cars were new, we were in our early twenties. Chances are, at that time we'd have picked the Ford V-8 for its high-speed performance edge. Advance the calendar 20 years and our values would have changed; in our forties we'd have given the nod to Chevrolet for its comfortable ride and generally high level of fit and finish. Today, in our sixties and plagued by problems with our lower back, the Plymouth's excellent, chair-height seat would probably tip the balance in that direction.

All of which is really just another way of saying that the motorist of 1941 had a winner on his hands, no matter which

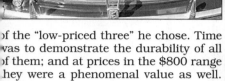

Left and Below: *Plymouth wins hands down in the cargo-carrying department.* **Center:** *All three cars acquit themselves well on the road. The Chevy is very smooth under all conditions; the Ford has the edge in quick highway pickup; Plymouth offers good low-end acceleration.* **Bottom:** *Rear styling of the three cars is quite distinct, a reminder of the times when each US car had its own "look," unlike today's econoboxes with shared body styles.*

of the "low-priced three" he chose. Time was to demonstrate the durability of all of them; and at prices in the $800 range they were a phenomenal value as well.
∂∿

Acknowledgments

Our thanks to John Cavagnaro, Stockton, California; Mike Lamm, Stockton, California; Franca Manocchi, Azusa, California; Walter Kahlenberg, president, WPC Club, North Hollywood, California; special thanks to those who provided the comparisonReport cars: Doyle Thompson, Hemet, California (Plymouth); Doug Watson, Costa Mesa, California (Ford); Dr. Dave Underwood, West Covina, California (Chevrolet), and to Jerry Branton, General Sales Manager, Bob Wingate's Classics, San Dimas, California, who assisted with the arrangements.

Ford Engines 1903-1942

Year	Cylinders	Displacement	Bore x Stroke	Output (Gross HP)
1903	Opposed-2	100.4-cu.in.	4.00 x 4.00 in.	8
1904	O-2	100.4-cu.in.	4.00 x 4.00 in.	8
1904	O-2	120.5-cu.in.	4.25 x 4.25 in.	10
1904	I-4	283.5-cu.in.	4.25 x 5.00 in.	24
1905	O-2	120.5-cu.in.	4.25 x 4.25 in.	10
1904	O-2	127.5-cu.in.	4.25 x 4.00 in.	16
1905	I-4	283.5-cu.in.	4.25 x 5.00 in.	24
1906	O-2	128-cu.in.	4.25 x 4.50 in.	10
1906	I-4	149-cu.in.	3.75 x 3.37 in.	15
1906	I-6	405-cu.in.	4.50 x 4.25 in.	40
1907	I-4	149-cu.in.	3.75 x 3.37 in.	15
1907	I-6	405-cu.in.	4.50 x 4.25 in.	40
1908	I-4	149-cu.in.	3.75 x 3.37 in.	15
1908	I-6	405-cu.in.	4.50 x 4.25 in.	40
1909	I-4	176.7-cu.in.	3.75 x 4.00 in.	22
1910	I-4	176.7-cu.in.	3.75 x 4.00 in.	22
1911	I-4	176.7-cu.in.	3.75 x 4.00 in.	22
1912	I-4	176.7-cu.in.	3.75 x 4.00 in.	22
1913	I-4	176.7-cu.in.	3.75 x 4.00 in.	20
1914	I-4	176.7-cu.in.	3.75 x 4.00 in.	20
1915	I-4	176.7-cu.in.	3.75 x 4.00 in.	20
1915	I-4	176.7-cu.in.	3.75 x 4.00 in.	20
1916	I-4	176.7-cu.in.	3.75 x 4.00 in.	20
1917	I-4	176.7-cu.in.	3.75 x 4.00 in.	20
1918	I-4	176.7-cu.in.	3.75 x 4.00 in.	20
1919	I-4	176.7-cu.in.	3.75 x 4.00 in.	20
1920	I-4	176.7-cu.in.	3.75 x 4.00 in.	20
1921	I-4	176.7-cu.in.	3.75 x 4.00 in.	20

922	I-4	176.7-cu.in.	3.75 x 4.00 in.	20
923	I-4	176.7-cu.in.	3.75 x 4.00 in.	20
924	I-4	176.7-cu.in.	3.75 x 4.00 in.	20
925	I-4	176.7-cu.in.	3.75 x 4.00 in.	20
926	I-4	176.7-cu.in.	3.75 x 4.00 in.	20
927	I-4	176.7-cu.in.	3.75 x 4.00 in.	20
928	I-4	200.5-cu.in.	3.875 x 4.25 in.	40
929	I-4	200.5-cu.in.	3.875 x 4.25 in.	40
930	I-4	200.5-cu.in.	3.875 x 4.25 in.	40
931	I-4	200.5-cu.in.	3.875 x 4.25 in.	40
932	I-4	200.5-cu.in.	3.875 x 4.25 in.	50
932	V-8	221-cu.in.	3.063 x 3.75 in.	65
933	I-4	200.5-cu.in.	3.875 x 4.25 in.	50
933	V-8	221-cu.in.	3.063 x 3.75 in.	75
934	I-4	200.5-cu.in.	3.875 x 4.25 in.	50
934	V-8	221-cu.in.	3.063 x 3.75 in.	85
935	V-8	221-cu.in.	3.063 x 3.75 in.	85
936	V-8	221-cu.in.	3.063 x 3.75 in.	85
937	V-8	136-cu.in.	2.60 x 3.20 in.	60
937	V-8	221-cu.in.	3.063 x 3.75 in.	85
938	V-8	136-cu.in.	2.60 x 3.20 in.	60
938	V-8	221-cu.in.	3.063 x 3.75 in.	85
939	V-8	136-cu.in.	2.60 x 3.20 in.	60
939	V-8	221-cu.in.	3.063 x 3.75 in.	90
940	V-8	136-cu.in.	2.60 x 3.20 in.	60
940	V-8	221-cu.in.	3.063 x 3.75 in.	85
941	I-6	225.8-cu.in.	3.30 x 4.40 in.	90
941	V-8	221-cu.in.	3.063 x 3.75 in.	90
942	I-6	225.8-cu.in.	3.30 x 4.40 in.	90
942	V-8	221-cu.in.	3.063 x 3.75 in.	96

Prewar Ford Clubs & Specialists

For a complete list of all regional Ford clubs and national clubs' chapters, visit **Car Club Central** at **www.hemmings.com.** With nearly 10,000 car clubs listed, it's the largest car club site in the world! Not wired? For the most up-to-date information, consult the latest issue of *Hemmings Motor News* and or *Hemmings' Collector Car Almanac.* Call toll free, 1-800-CAR-HERE, Ext. 550.

PREWAR FORD CLUBS

Early Ford V-8 Club
P.O. Box 2122
San Leandro, CA 94577
925-606-1925
(105 regional chapters, 12 international chapters)

Model A Ford Cabriolet Club
P.O. Box 515
Porter, TX 77365
281-429-2505

Model A Ford Club of America
250 South Cypress Rd.
La Habra, CA 90631
562-697-2712
(302 regional chapters, 35 international chapters)

Model A Restorer's Club
24800 Michigan Ave.
Dearborn, MI 48124-1713
313-278-1455
(150 regional chapters, 8 international chapters)

Model T Ford Club International
P.O. Box 276236
Boca Raton, FL 33427-6236
561-750-7170

(87 regional chapters, 7 international chapters)

Model T Ford Club of America
P.O. Box 743936
Dallas, TX 75374-3936
972-783-7531
(101 regional chapters, 13 international chapters)

Penn-Ohio Model A Ford Club
1542 Gotthard St.
Sugarcreek, OH 44681-9323
330-852-4700
(14 regional chapters)

Other Important Clubs

Antique Automobile Club of America
501 W. Governor Road
Hershey, PA 17033
717-534-1910
(311 regional chapters, 7 international chapters)

Horseless Carriage Club of America
3311 Fairhaven Dr.
Orange, CA 92866-1357
661-326-1023
(91 regional chapters, 7 international chapters)

Veteran Motor Car Club of America
4441 W. Altadena Ave.
Glendale, AZ 85304-3526
800-428-7327
(82 regional chapters)

PREWAR FORD SPECIALISTS

Apple Hydraulics
1610 Middle Rd.
Calverton, NY 11933
800-882-7753
Ford Lever-type shocks

Bob's Antique Auto Parts
P.O. Box 2523
7826 Forest Hills, Rd
Rockford, IL 61132
815-633-7244
Huge inventory of Model T parts

Brass Works
289 Prado Rd.
San Luis Obispo, CA 934501
805-544-8841
Model A and T radiators

Bratton's Antique Auto Parts
9410 Watkins Rd.
Gaithersburg, MD 20882
800-255-1929
New and Reproduction Model A mechanical and trim parts

C&G Early Ford Parts
1941 Commercial St.
Escondido, CA 92029-1233
760-740-2400
Full line of reproduction parts for 1932-1942 Fords

Classtique Upholstery & Top Co.
P.O. Box 278HK
Isanti, MN 55040
763-444-4025
Interior and Top kits for Model T and Model A's

Dennis Carpenter Parts
4140 Concord Pkwy.
South Concord, NC 28027
800-476-9653
*Mechanical, weatherstripping
and rubber products for 1932-
1940 Fords*

Early Ford V-8 Sales
Bldg. 37 Curtis Industrial Park
831 Route 67
Balston Spa, NY 12020
518-884-2825
*Mechanical and body parts for
1932-1942 Fords*

**Engineering & Manufacturing
Services**
P.O. Box 24362
Cleveland, OH 44124
216-541-4585
*Sheet metal and rubber parts for
1935-1942 Fords*

Gaslight Auto parts
P.O. Box 291H
Urbana, OH 43078
937-652-2145
Model T, A and V-8 Parts

Howell's Sheet Metal Co.
P.O. Box 792
Nederland, TX 77627
409-727-1999
1909-1940 Ford sheet metal parts

Kanter Auto Products
76 Monroe St.
Boonton, NJ 07005
800-526-1096
*New mechanical and suspension
parts for all 1932-1942 models*

LeBaron Bonney Co.
P.O. Box 6
6 Chestnut St.
Amesbury, MA 01913
800-221-5408
Upholstery and trim kits

M&S Hydraulics
22275 SW TV Hwy.
Hillsboro, OR 97123
503-642-1122
Model A shock absorbers

Mac's Antique Auto Parts
1051 Lincoln Ave.
Lockport, NY
800-777-0948
Model T, A and early V-8 parts

Mark Auto Co.
Layton, NJ 07851
973-948-4157
*Model A and T mechanical and
electrical parts*

Mike's "A" FORD-able Parts
1930 Patrick Rd.
Dacula, GA 30019
770-945-3671
*Model A engine and mechanical
components*

Old Ford Parts
35 4th Ave. North
Algona, WA 98001
253-833-8494
*Body and mechanical parts for
1932-1942 Fords*

Patrick's Antique Cars & Trucks
P.O. Box 10648
Casa Grande, AZ 85230
520-836-1117
New and reconditioned V-8 parts

PMX Custom Alternators
8420 SE Hinckley Rd.
Portland, OR 97266
800-445-1766
*6 and 12-volt flathead V-8
alternators*

**Smith and Jones Antique Ford
Parts**
1 Biloxi Square
W. Columbia, SC
803-822-8502
New Model T and A parts

Snyder's Antique Auto Parts
12925 Woodworth Rd.
New Springfield, OH 44443
888-262-5712
*New body and mechanical parts
for Model T's and A's*

Steam Bent Bows
122 Ramsey Ave.
Chambersburg, PA 17201
717-264-2602
Oak bows for 1932-1942 Fords

Varco Inc.
8200 S. Anderson Rd.
Oklahoma City, OK 73150
405-732-1637
Trunk repair and parts

Wood for Fords
P.O. Box 278
Superior, AZ 85273
520-689-2734
Wood body framing kits

Ford Model Year Production 1903-1942

Year	Production
1903	1,708
1904	1,695
1905	1,599
1906	8,729
1907	14,887
1908	10,202
1909	17,771
1910	32,053
1911	69,762
1912	170,211
1913	202,667
1914	308,162
1915	501,462
1916	734,811
1917	622,351
1918	435,898
1919	820,445
1920	419,517
1921	903,814
1922	1,173,745
1923	**1,817,891***
1924	1,749,827
1925	1,643,295
1926	1,368,383
1927	356,188
1928	633,594
1929	1,507,132
1930	1,155,162
1931	541,615
1932	287,285
1933	334,969
1934	563,921
1935	942,439
1936	791,812
1937	848,608
1938	410,048
1939	532,152
1940	599,175
1941	600,814
1942	43,407

*Ford's biggest prewar production year